# PERSONALITY AND TI
## POLITICAL

*Personality and the Foundations of Political Behavior* is the first study in more than thirty years to investigate the broad significance of personality traits for mass political behavior. Drawing on the Big Five personality trait framework, Jeffery J. Mondak argues that attention to personality provides a valuable means to integrate biological and environmental influences via rich, nuanced theories and empirical tests of the antecedents of political behavior. Development of such holistic accounts is critical, Mondak contends, if inquiry is to move beyond simple "blank slate" environmental depictions of political engagement. Analyses examining multiple facets of political information, political attitudes, and participation reveal that the Big Five trait dimensions – openness to experience, conscientiousness, extraversion, agreeableness, and emotional stability – produce both direct and indirect effects on a wide range of political phenomena.

Jeffery J. Mondak is James M. Benson Chair in Public Issues and Civic Leadership in the Department of Political Science at the University of Illinois at Urbana-Champaign. He is the author of *Nothing to Read: Newspapers and Elections in a Social Experiment* (1995) and coeditor of *Fault Lines: Why the Republicans Lost Congress* (2009). Professor Mondak's articles appear in outlets including the *American Political Science Review*, the *American Journal of Political Science*, the *British Journal of Political Science*, *Cognitive Brain Research*, the *Journal of Politics*, and *Public Opinion Quarterly*. He has received awards for his research from the American Association for Public Opinion Research, the American Political Science Association, and the Midwest Political Science Association.

# CAMBRIDGE STUDIES IN PUBLIC OPINION AND POLITICAL PSYCHOLOGY

SERIES EDITORS

Dennis Chong, *Northwestern University*
James H. Kuklinksi, *University of Illinois, Urbana-Champaign*

Cambridge Studies in Public Opinion and Political Psychology publishes innovative research from a variety of theoretical and methodological perspectives on the mass public foundations of politics and society. Research in the series focuses on the origins and influence of mass opinion; the dynamics of information and deliberation; and the emotional, normative, and instrumental bases of political choice. In addition to examining psychological processes, the series explores the organization of groups, the association between individual and collective preferences, and the impact of institutions on beliefs and behavior.

Cambridge Studies in Public Opinion and Political Psychology is dedicated to furthering theoretical and empirical research on the relationship between the political system and the attitudes and actions of citizens.

## Books in the Series

*Continued following index*

# PERSONALITY AND THE FOUNDATIONS OF POLITICAL BEHAVIOR

JEFFERY J. MONDAK

*University of Illinois at Urbana-Champaign*

CAMBRIDGE UNIVERSITY PRESS
Cambridge, New York, Melbourne, Madrid, Cape Town,
Singapore, São Paulo, Delhi, Tokyo, Mexico City

Cambridge University Press
32 Avenue of the Americas, New York, NY 10013-2473, USA

www.cambridge.org
Information on this title: www.cambridge.org/9780521140959

© Jeffery J. Mondak 2010

First published 2010
Reprinted 2011

A catalog record for this publication is available from the British Library.

Library of Congress Cataloging in Publication Data
Mondak, Jeffery J., 1962–
    Personality and the foundations of political behavior / Jeffery J. Mondak.
      p.   cm. – (Cambridge studies in public opinion and political psychology)
    Includes bibliographical references and index.
    ISBN 978-0-521-19293-4 (hardback)
    1. Political psychology.   2. Personality.   I. Title.   II. Series.
    JA74.5.M64   2010
    320.01′9–dc22         2010011782

ISBN 978-0-521-19293-4 Hardback
ISBN 978-0-521-14095-9 Paperback

# Contents

# Figures

# Tables

## List of Tables

# Acknowledgments

This book outlines the case for the use of a particular model of personality trait structure, the "Big Five" approach, in research on political behavior. I began thinking about the possible importance of personality for mass politics in 1997, only a few years after psychologists published the first key works on the Big Five. I started gathering data a year later. In the more than a decade since, a great many people have provided numerous forms of assistance. Included are those who have helped in some manner with data acquisition, who have offered feedback on my papers and on this book, and who have joined me as coauthors on related conference papers and journal articles.

Most of the data examined in this study are from original surveys fielded in 1998, 2005, and 2006. The 1998 and 2005 surveys were administered while I was on the faculty at Florida State University. These projects received financial support from the LeRoy Collins Fund and from a Florida State University Developing Scholar Award. Funding for the 2006 survey was provided by the Center on Congress, the Center on American Politics, and the Office of the Vice Provost for Research at Indiana University; the Cline Center for Democracy, directed by Peter Nardulli, at the University of Illinois; the James M. Benson Fund at the University of Illinois; and by the following individuals: Ted Carmines, John Hibbing, Bob Huckfeldt, Gary Jacobson, Walt Stone, and Herb Weisberg. Additional data consulted for this project are from a survey conducted by Mary Anderson as part of her doctoral research at Florida State University, and from a survey directed by Carl McCurley in the state of Washington.

Three individuals who have provided me with a tremendous amount of support, feedback, and encouragement on this project warrant special mention. All are or have been graduate students who have worked with me. One of the genuine joys of this profession is having the opportunity to learn, and to draw energy, from bright and creative students. I have been especially fortunate in this regard. In 2003, Karen Halperin entered graduate school at Florida State like a tornado. For me, the personality project was a low priority at that time, as my focus was mostly on some other studies I had in the works. But Karen forced personality to the fore, where it has remained ever since. Karen coauthored my earliest personality papers, and she offered tremendous insight on countless facets of the study of personality and politics (including, notably, the limits of self-report data for one of the Big Five trait dimensions). Dona-Gene Mitchell always has been my most diligent and discerning sounding board on this project. Dona-Gene, now on the faculty at the University of Nebraska, was a graduate student first at Florida State and then at the University of Illinois. Because of this, she was able to monitor this project from its fledgling state, and she has offered extraordinarily useful comments and critiques. In 2008, Dona-Gene took breaks from work on her award-winning doctoral dissertation to provide detailed feedback on the first drafts of this book's seven chapters. Matt Hibbing entered graduate school at the University of Illinois in 2006, and I have thought of him more as a peer than as a student from day one. Since his arrival at Illinois, Matt and I have coauthored several personality papers, and he has spent countless hours with me devising hypotheses, designing instruments, and analyzing data. I have learned a tremendous amount from him along the way.

It is hard to imagine a more stimulating or collegial environment for the study of political behavior than that at the University of Illinois. In addition to Dona-Gene and Matt, several other graduate students have given me helpful feedback on this project, including Jason Coronel, Matt Hayes, Buddy Peyton, and Sergio Wals. Special thanks are owed to Andy Bloeser, who read one of the final drafts of this book, and who did so with a much-appreciated eye for nuance and detail. Andy also has joined me as a coauthor on some papers on personality that were started as follow-ups to this book. As to my colleagues, I have had countless conversations with many of them on various aspects of this study, and several also have provided feedback on some of this book's chapters and on my other personality papers. For their assistance, and especially for what they contribute to the intellectual environment at Illinois, I thank Scott Althaus, Ira Carmen, Brian Gaines, Jude Hays, Pete Nardulli, and Tom Rudolph. Lastly, Jim Kuklinski is simply the best colleague and friend one could ever wish for, and I could not possibly express or quantify how much I have gained from knowing Jim.

Several people from outside of the University of Illinois also have provided quite helpful feedback on this project. The list includes three anonymous reviewers who read this manuscript for Cambridge University

## Acknowledgments

Press, numerous additional reviewers who have commented on related journal pieces I have coauthored, and Lewis Goldberg, John Hibbing, Bob Huckfeldt, Robert McCrae, Dennis Organ, Paul Quirk, Harald Schoen, Mitch Seligson, and John Zaller. I also greatly appreciate the encouragement and efficiency shown by Eric Crahan and Lew Bateman of Cambridge.

It is important to stay grounded. I am especially fortunate in this regard, in part because my interrelated hobbies surround me with some of the most creative and entertaining people anywhere. My thanks to Sergio Wals, Alex Stangl, and everyone at Songramp; to Dr. Demento and everyone else who has played my songs; to Christine Lavin for writing with me; to Bruce Lansky and his team at Meadowbrook; and to the thousands of elementary school students who have welcomed my performances, and who often have drowned me out with shouts of "and pizza's on the way!"

My family also performs heroic duty in keeping me grounded and, in the case of my sons, in keeping me exhausted. Nothing I have accomplished would have been possible without my parents' support. My wife Damarys does triple duty as wife, colleague, and coauthor. She enriches every facet of my life and, thankfully, forces me to relax each year at the beach. Our sons Ryan and Christopher are incredibly adept at keeping Damarys and me from working (Christopher phoned me twice during this paragraph alone). And good for them for being so, because baseball games, soccer matches, piano lessons, essay competitions, and the rest should be, and are, what life is about. Lastly, although they will not know they've been mentioned here, I've learned vital lessons about the biological bases of personality – and about the virtues of a nice walk – from Pelado and his departed brethren, Pippin and Atticus.

# PERSONALITY AND THE FOUNDATIONS OF POLITICAL BEHAVIOR

# I

## *Personality and Politics*

In a well-known routine from the mid 1970s, the late comedian George
Carlin, an astute observer of language, made light of incongruent phrases
such as "jumbo shrimp" and "military intelligence." As a parallel to
Carlin's list of words that "don't go together"[1] we might add people in
unlikely professions or roles, individuals such as a cautious daredevil, an
unreflective philosopher, a disagreeable yes-man, or an introverted motivational speaker. Or, thinking of social and political actors, we might
contemplate the rude and uncaring volunteer, the timid lobbyist, or the
open-minded ideologue.

These individuals resist imagination because, by their nature, some
types of people seem to be poor fits for certain occupations, avocations,
and roles. The phrase "by their nature" refers to people's enduring tendencies, or traits. Many students of the psychology of individual differences examine the content and significance of basic traits. In simplest
form, such inquiry involves a two-step process: Key differences in traits
are identified, followed by exploration of possible relationships between
these traits and attitudes and behaviors. Intuition and everyday experience underlie many of the patterns we can envision, in some cases to the
point that relationships may seem virtually tautological. For instance,
we expect scientists to be systematic, counselors to be sympathetic, and
entertainers to be outgoing. But these relationships are not tautological. To the contrary, if we study these possible patterns and the resultant
evidence corroborates our expectations, an exercise of this sort would
demonstrate that traits matter. By knowing something about a person's
general psychological tendencies, we potentially would be able to enrich
our understanding of this person's specific behaviors and attitudes.

Traits of the type alluded to here typically fall under the rubric of "personality." Hence, to a substantial extent, the study of the psychology of

---

[1] From the very first episode of *Saturday Night Live*, aired on October 11, 1975.

individual differences involves the study of personality. Personality has had a somewhat curious history in the field of psychology, and also in research on citizens and politics. Although plausible links between personality and political behavior abound, and although few serious scholars of mass politics would doubt that variance in basic traits contributes to differences in political behavior, research in this area has been decidedly sparse. In my judgment, this situation is highly unfortunate. The central thesis advanced in this book holds that personality is consequential for citizens' political attitudes and actions. Through systematic attention to the psychology of individual differences, I contend that we can gain considerable new insight regarding the underpinnings of virtually all aspects of mass political behavior. My goal in this book is to demonstrate this point both analytically and empirically.

Incorporating personality in our accounts of political behavior requires an important change in our views regarding when and how citizens' encounters with the political world gain shape. Some perspectives on political behavior seemingly presuppose that all political judgments are formed in the moment. People receive information regarding a candidate or issue, respond to that information, and come to their own conclusions. Other theories recognize that people's values and political predispositions bring continuity to their views of the political world. Thus, as one example, the long-time Democrat can be expected to vote differently than the loyal Republican. In this book, I argue that the roots of political behavior run even deeper. I contend that any theoretical or empirical account of political behavior necessarily will be incomplete if it fails to contemplate the enduring, and possibly innate, factors that distinguish us. I focus on personality because I believe that people do not encounter the environment as if they were blank slates, political or otherwise. Personality is about who we are as individuals. Moreover, to a substantial extent, our personalities are written in our genetic codes. People are not merely products of their socialization experiences, and behavior is not merely a response to one's environment. We all know people who have exhibited similar patterns of behavior throughout their entire lives, such as friends who always have been punctual, sloppy or shy. These life-long consistencies in behavior reflect in no small part the impact of enduring psychological differences – the impact of personality.

This chapter develops the foundation for attention to personality and politics. First, the concepts of personality and traits are defined and assessed in an effort to clarify the place of traits in contemporary psychological research on personality. Second, past research on personality and politics is reviewed with an eye toward showing that previous work in this area has been insightful, but also that much work remains to be done. Third, I advance the general case for incorporation of a trait approach within multifaceted theories guiding the study of citizens' political attitudes and behaviors. As part of this case, I advocate use of a particular comprehensive, broadscale model of trait structure.

## THE PSYCHOLOGY OF INDIVIDUAL DIFFERENCES

Early in 1991, while finishing my doctoral dissertation, I began my search for employment in academia. Like many students of mass political behavior, my research at that time drew heavily on concepts developed by social psychologists.[2] During one job interview, a faculty member asked, "What's your theory?" I dutifully set out to explain the foundational efforts in cognitive psychology, the adaptations and extensions of the work that had taken place in recent years in social psychology, and the further adaptations and extensions underway among students of mass politics. However, as soon as I uttered the word "psychology," I was cut off and sternly informed that "psychology is about aberrant individual behavior. It has nothing to do with politics." To me, this was a bizarre statement. Yes, I thought, many clinical psychologists do study and treat psychological disorders, but to conceptualize the entire field of psychology exclusively in those terms is, quite obviously, far too limiting.[3] After all, like many of the people then engaged in research on mass politics, I had read and cited countless articles on attitude formation and change, and information processing and decision making, articles that had appeared in outlets such as the *Journal of Personality and Social Psychology*. These works most certainly were not about aberrant individual-level behavior.

In retrospect, my view in 1991 was itself too limited. Although I recognized the political relevance of research on social psychology, the word "personality" in the title *Journal of Personality and Social Psychology* barely caught my attention. If anything, it seemed like an anachronism. In part, my view was a product of the times. Research in the area of trait psychology had experienced a tumultuous, relatively unproductive period that lasted for more than a decade. An era of resurgence had begun by 1991, but this revitalization was in a fledgling state, and news of it had not yet produced much influence on work in political science, where social psychological approaches were the rage. In the ensuing years, the new generation of scholarship on traits grew to healthy maturity. Today, research on personality traits enjoys a stunning vibrancy, cohesiveness,

---

[2] My doctoral research was on the political application of dual-processing models, and, more specifically, on heuristic processing of source cues.

[3] Truth be told, I actually stopped midway through mumbling to myself "this guy is nuts," fearful that by positing such a diagnosis I might be supporting his proposition.

3

and sense of purpose in the field of psychology. Nonetheless, it remains the case that this line of inquiry has had only a minimal impact among students of political behavior. In my judgment, the relative lack of influence to date should not be interpreted to mean that a trait approach is destined to be uninformative. Instead, contemporary trait models offer an exciting opportunity for research on political behavior, but an opportunity that has not yet been seized, or even recognized, by most analysts in the field.

If I am to make the case that attention to variance in personality traits can help us to understand mass politics, the first step entails definition of terms. Psychology is about more than aberrant, individual-level behavior, but it is also about more than models of information processing and attitude change. Traditionally, research on personality has constituted a central pillar of the discipline, and, in turn, trait perspectives have held a pivotal place in research on personality. But what do these concepts mean, and how can we most fruitfully incorporate them in applied research concerning mass political behavior?

In 1973, the noted trait psychologist Raymond Cattell wrote of personality (Cattell 1973, 41), "personality is like love: everyone agrees it exists, but disagrees on what it is." In the ensuing years, this disagreement has not abated. The existence of multiple definitions of personality comes as little surprise in a field populated with such diverse figures as Sigmund Freud, Abraham Maslow, and B. F. Skinner. Searching for an adequate definition of personality, I have reviewed countless journal articles and textbooks. I have encountered some authors who define personality in clear, concrete (but not uncontroversial) terms, others who understand personality as the sum of its parts, still others who view personality in terms of its behavioral consequences, and a last group who cast personality in virtually impenetrable thesaurus-chewing psychological jargon. I am hardly the first student of politics to be frustrated by this state of affairs. To the contrary, many of the most prominent scholars in political psychology have bemoaned this same lack of definitional clarity. For instance, a generation ago Fred Greenstein (1969, 2–3) noted that "psychologists themselves have been chronically unable to arrive at a commonly accepted definition of 'personality.'"

My approach to this situation is three-fold. First, I suggest that we must resign ourselves to the unlikelihood that we will craft a single, definitive, and universally accepted conceptualization of personality and must be satisfied, instead, with construction of a plausible, functional view. Second, development of this perspective should be purposive. Personality can be conceived in multiple ways and toward multiple ends. In this book, I invoke a trait approach in the study of personality, and I do so with the objective of exploring possible links between personality and political behavior. Viewed pragmatically, personality must be considered with ends such as these in mind. Third, I believe that personality is most fruitfully understood via simultaneous attention to form and function. Personality cannot be observed directly, but we can gain a satisfactory sense of the concept of personality through discussion of its component parts and the psychological purposes they serve.

When we contemplate the behaviors of a given individual, one potentially useful categorization scheme involves distinguishing actions that are typical of the person in question from ones that are not. The latter might include, as examples, instances when the person acts unusually in a familiar situation, such as when a generally calm driver bursts into a fit of road rage, and times when the person acts unexpectedly in a novel situation, such as when the easygoing nun breaks out her judo skills to stave off a would-be mugger, or when your quiet friend steals the show on her first time at karaoke night. Although atypical and unexpected behaviors such as these may be interesting, my focus here – and the focus of most trait psychologists – centers primarily on individuals' consistent patterns of behavior. Personality has something to do with these consistent behavior patterns. When we say "it's not like Jerry to fly off the handle like that," what we mean is that Jerry's behavior in this instance sits at odds with Jerry's personality.

My claim that personality "has something to do" with people's patterns of behavior admittedly abounds with ambiguity. To add precision, the first point to emphasize is that several factors combine to define the individual's personality. At question is what elements characterize the person: What makes us who we are? Included may be core beliefs, values, emotions, and so on. Importantly, these elements of personality, for the most part, cannot be observed directly, and, correspondingly, personality itself defies direct observation. Therefore, when we move from the concept of personality to empirical representations of that concept, we necessarily must engage in inference, because a full, direct operationalization of personality is not possible.[4]

Second, personality as conceived of here endures over extended periods of time, bringing continuity to a person's character, and ultimately to his or her behavior. Personality traits exhibit tremendous stability over time, and, in doing so, contribute to persistent tendencies in political behavior. Many students of human behavior examine situation-specific actions, and some work on personality also focuses on situational variance. I in no way reject the value of such perspectives. Clearly, many aspects of human behavior do indeed vary by situation. Nonetheless, my

---

[4] For a related view, see Winter (2003b, 115). The same is true, of course, for most concepts in psychology, including many that have been studied by political scientists.

conception of personality highlights psychological properties that remain stable over time. In other words, they are trans-situational. Introverts sometimes engage in behaviors characteristic of extraverts, and vice versa. But despite this reality, both the introvert and the extravert possess what are, in effect, central psychological tendencies. My interest in this book is in identifying such central tendencies and exploring their possible significance for political behavior. As we will see, in some instances the effects of personality on political behavior emerge in interaction with situational forces. But even in these cases, personality itself remains an enduring source of influence.

Combining these two points, it follows that "personality" as conceptualized in this study refers to a multifaceted and enduring internal, or psychological, structure. It is further assumed that personality is substantially rooted in biology, and that personality influences behavior. From this perspective, there is something intrinsic in each of us, largely present at birth, that defines who and what we are, and that shapes how we behave. We possess traits, values, and goals that combine to give us our individuality and to influence our actions. Sally *is* an extravert, and, as one, she tends to be talkative. James *is* conscientious, and, as a result, he tends to be punctual. Again, my approach is purposive. Personality is construed here in a manner that is rooted in psychological theory, but also in a manner that facilitates empirical inquiry. With this construction in hand, the task I pursue in this book involves development of a means to represent personality in empirical form, followed by exploration of possible consequences of variance in personality for politically significant attitudes and behaviors.

As noted earlier, psychologists who study personality have devised countless definitions of personality, definitions that often bear strikingly little resemblance to one another. Likewise, the view posited here has much in common with some psychologists' interpretations of personality, but very little in common with others. I have defined personality as a biologically influenced and enduring psychological structure that shapes behavior. My approach is most consistent with – and is most informed by – the perspectives of trait psychologists. In my judgment, research on trait psychology, especially research reported in the past two decades, collectively offers a plausible theoretical depiction of personality, a corresponding means to represent personality in empirical form, and a body of empirical research that provides an excellent foundation for the derivation of hypotheses regarding possible links between personality and political behavior.

Although differences can be found concerning the precise meaning of traits, consensus exists at a more general level regarding the nature and significance of traits as they relate to personality. Pervin (2003, 38) notes, for instance, that trait psychologists largely agree on two central points: that "traits represent basic categories of individual differences in functioning" and that "traits are useful as the basic units of personality." Among more specific definitions of traits, several provide insights helpful for our purposes. Kreitler and Kreitler (1990, 4) write that "a trait is essentially a relatively stable tendency or feature characteristic of an individual," and "most of the descriptive terms about people that we have in language are trait names." Allen (1994, 1) defines personality traits as "internally based psychological characteristics that often correspond to adjectival labels." Winter (2003b, 115) views traits as "the public, observable element of personality, the consistencies of style readily noticed by other people." Lastly, McCrae and Costa (2003, 25), leading figures in the revitalization of trait research, initially defined traits[5] as "dimensions of individual differences in tendencies to show consistent patterns of thoughts, feelings, and actions."

Several features of these definitions warrant emphasis.[6] First, traits are presumed to possess an inner locus. As with personality itself, traits typically are seen as psychological structures or properties. Gordon Allport (1937) was one of the first prominent students of traits. Central in his research, and in most subsequent work in the field, was the premise that traits are mental structures. Second, traits are thought to be relatively fixed and enduring. Allen (1994, 427) writes, for example, that "a trait is a permanent entity that does not fade in and out," and Kreitler and Kreitler (1990, 4) suggest that traits are "stable individual characteristics." Most trait psychologists allow for the possibility of some marginal change in traits over time, and especially over the life cycle (e.g., Eysenck 1951), but traits as a whole are depicted as being highly consistent. Indeed, a central claim in Eysenck's research was that there is a biological foundation to traits, and evidence supporting this view will be reviewed in the next chapter. This perspective bolsters the depiction of traits as highly stable internal structures.

A third point to emphasize is that traits influence behavior. Raymond Cattell (1946) summarized matters in a simple, direct form with the contention that personality is what enables us to predict how an individual will behave in a given situation. The relationship between traits and behavior of course is not absolute, but people who possess certain traits will tend to engage in corresponding behaviors. Fourth, traits are susceptible to observation. Traits bring regularities in how we think, feel,

---

[5] McCrae and Costa refined their definition as work on their particular model of trait structure progressed. I discuss these developments in Chapter 2.

[6] For a useful history and discussion of the role of traits in research on personality, see Matthews and Deary (1998, chap. 1.)

and behave, and these give rise to patterns that are observable both to ourselves and to others. People routinely describe one another in terms of the general patterns or tendencies they observe. That we *can* do this is testament to the fact that language has developed in a manner that captures important individual differences. That we *do* engage in such description speaks to the centrality of traits in human behavior and social interaction.

If traits are the basic units of personality, can personality be defined as a sum of an individual's traits? Some psychologists say yes (e.g., Guilford 1959), but the consensus holds that personality constitutes more than just the sum of traits. Consistent with this latter view, I argue that traits represent many important enduring differences across individuals, and, as a result, that a holistic depiction of trait structure captures much of what we mean by personality. Again, this is a functional perspective. Personality includes elements in addition to traits,[7] but attention to traits in this book facilitates exploration of possible links between at least some important aspects of personality and variance in political behavior.

Research that is centered on traits requires an ordering mechanism. Literally thousands of adjectival descriptions exist, corresponding with a large number of distinct traits, creating what John and Robins (1993, 219) described as a "semantic nightmare." This reality constituted one of two noteworthy factors limiting research in trait psychology – and, by implication, applications of a trait approach in the study of political behavior – for many years. The pioneering efforts of Allport, Cattell, and Eysenck were initiated in the 1930s and 1940s. Although numerous scholars in the field subsequently advanced models of trait structure or championed the significance of particular traits, no consensus existed for decades regarding the utility of any single theoretical framework. Scientific progress is difficult in such a context because of the tendency of scholars with differing preferred perspectives to talk past one another. As John and Srivastava (1999, 102) explained, the "systematic accumulation of findings and the communication among researchers has become difficult amidst the Babel of concepts and scales." Today, the situation is much improved. Although disagreements inevitably will persist in such an expansive field, a wealth of research conducted primarily within the past two decades provides strong support for a new generation of holistic

---

[7] Among psychologists, debate persists regarding the precise link between traits and other facets of personality such as beliefs and motives. An interesting perspective on this point is offered by Kreitler and Kreitler (1990, 8–10). Much of the problem in reaching consensus naturally stems from the fact that the elements of personality are not directly observable, and therefore neither are the interactions among those elements.

trait models. These "five-factor" or "Big Five" models have brought a dramatic rejuvenation in research on trait psychology and have led to a vast and rapidly growing body of applied work – a body of work to which the present study contributes. Today, it is possible to represent the central elements of trait structure with parsimonious measures that are focused on five core trait dimensions.

The revitalization of research on personality traits followed a period in which scholars who studied individual psychological differences were shaken, and even embittered, by strong critiques of their efforts. Collectively, these concerns served as a second force that slowed the work on traits. Many years prior to the efforts of Allport, Cattell, and Eysenck, Thorndike (1903) argued against the very existence of personality traits. Scholars in the field mostly disregarded this view once research began to accumulate that demonstrated the existence of replicable trait structures. Starting in the late 1960s, however, a new round of criticism emerged. Goldberg (1995, 34) explained that, as a consequence, "the 1970s witnessed the virtual abandonment of major segments of personality research, including the investigation of personality-trait structure." Walter Mischel (1968) was the most prominent and vociferous skeptic in this period, arguing that purported individual differences measured on trait batteries often bore little relationship to behavior (see also Shweder 1975).[8] Mischel's central argument held that behavior exhibits little consistency across situations, undermining the possible importance of traits.

Taken to its extreme, if we were to assume the absence of trans-situational continuity, this critique would indeed strike a fatal blow against any claimed utility of a trait approach. Kreitler and Kreitler (1990, 16) contend, for instance that

[B]ehavior is not as consistent as the concept of trait would lead us to believe. Indeed, it is not at all consistent, at least as it appears to most researchers. The problem is of paramount importance in the study of personality at large, because without intraindividual consistency, there can hardly be interindividual differences and certainly no basis for upholding a unit such as a trait.

---

[8] Hans Eysenck took on a lead role in defending research on traits against the critique leveled by Mischel. See, for example, Eysenck and Eysenck (1980). This debate clearly seems to have worn on the participants. For instance, the Eysenck and Eysenck piece includes an editorial note that reads, in part, "Professor Mischel has declined an offer of space for a reply, stating that his position is sufficiently well documented to make this unnecessary" (p. 204). Other figures in the field characterize Mischel's influence in disparaging terms. Digman (1990, 420) describes Mischel and other critics as "born-again fundamentalists who excoriated trait theory as akin to scientific sin." Citing Mischel, Goldberg (1993, 26) began one piece with the words "once upon a time, we had no personalities."

In my view, the Kreitlers' position well exceeds the scope of the available evidence. First, Mischel himself did not take such an absolutist stance, contending that trans-situational correlations in individual behavior were low, *not* that these correlations were nonexistent. For example, looking back on the controversy surrounding his work, Mischel wrote that "no one seriously questions that lives have continuity and that we perceive ourselves and others as relatively stable individuals who have substantial identity and stability over time, even when our specific actions change across situations" (1979, 742). Mischel's view of human behavior highlights situation-specific action, but even Mischel reported correlations in the range of 0.30 in patterns of behavior across situations. Such marks clearly fall short of establishing that traits, and especially traits alone, *determine* behavior. However, these findings deny neither the existence of traits nor the suggestion that traits correspond with general tendencies in human behavior. Second, a chief element of Mischel's critique questioned the validity of observer ratings, but later work has responded directly to this point (e.g., Moskowitz and Schwarz 1982). Third, Mischel subsequently (Mischel and Shoda 1995) sought to reconcile his situational perspective with traditional views of traits.[9]

As an outsider to this debate, my view is that the disputants drew unnecessary lines in the sand. Take a moment and think of the calmest, most unflappable person you know, and also the most nervous, easily agitated of your acquaintances. Even the former may emerge a bit frayed following a trans-Atlantic flight seated between a tipsy salesman and a parent with a colicky baby, and even the latter may appear relaxed and content following a weekend at the spa. Thus, the claim that behavior is in part determined by situation rings true. However, the very fact that we can bring these acquaintances to mind speaks to the presence of observable consistency in human behavior. We all have seen our calm friends *be* calm on multiple occasions, including in circumstances that would have driven our nervous friends over the edge. Human behavior is characterized by situational variance around discernible central tendencies. Consequently, identification of intraindividual differences in behavior across situations does not mean that the possible significance of traits should be dismissed.

Researchers in trait psychology concur with this view. Although the Mischel critique marked a setback, scholars in the field rebounded with

---

[9] The general thrust of Mischel's later position is that stable traits can bring conditional effects on behavior if personality is conceived as a mediating process rather than as an enduring general tendency. Some of the tests conducted later in this book are loosely in the spirit of this perspective in that possible interactions between traits and other predictors are examined.

renewed vigor upon the emergence of a new generation of models of trait structure in the late 1980s and early 1990s. But while this debate raged and then receded, most students of mass politics paid little or no attention to the potential influence of traits on political behavior. Although links between personality and political behavior are not difficult to conceive, we will see that relatively little systematic work has been conducted to explore these relationships.

## PERSONALITY AND POLITICAL BEHAVIOR

Research on mass politics seeks to identify the antecedents of citizens' political attitudes and actions. With this focus, a strategy that includes attention to personality holds enormous intuitive appeal. For the most part, neither scholars in the field nor casual observers likely doubt this proposition. A generation ago, Paul Sniderman began his book on personality and politics with the contention that (1975, ix) "it can scarcely be questioned that personality may affect political attitudes or actions; indeed, it has become an article of faith."[10] Likewise, nearly thirty years later, Winter noted (2003b, 110) that "one of the central axioms of political psychology is that political structures and actions are shaped and channeled by people's personalities." But widespread recognition of a probable link between personality and political action has not produced a corresponding flurry of empirical research. Although numerous analysts have made effective use of theories of personality in research on political behavior, such approaches hardly can be characterized as widespread. Instead, the inclusion of personality variables in accounts of mass behavior remains the exception, and use of broadscale models of personality remains extraordinarily rare.

The dearth of attention to personality by students of mass politics is puzzling. Insightful findings have been reported on those occasions when indicators of personality have been included in research on political behavior. Nonetheless, the personality bandwagon abounds with empty seats. Further, among research in the area that does incorporate personality, few inquiries have made use of comprehensive models of trait structure. Instead, when political scientists have introduced measures of traits,

---

[10] Later in this passage, Sniderman comments that the link between personality and politics must be accepted largely on faith due to the lack of "systematic evidence and quantitative analysis" (Sniderman 1975, ix). Although matters have improved since 1975, in part because of Sniderman's research, the level of systematic empirical research on personality and mass political behavior in the past three or more decades can only be characterized as disappointing. Thus, like Sniderman (1975, ix), I propose of the current effort that "this study is an attempt to redress the balance."

they most often have done so with focus on no more than one or two select attributes. This imposes a considerable limitation on the ability to generalize findings and to compare work across studies. My concern echoes one voiced by Sniderman (1975, 16):

(T)he field of personality and politics has acquired a jerry-built appearance. Observation suggests that political scientists inspect the array of psychological hypotheses, personality theories, and experimental findings like single-minded customers at a bargain counter, each bent on obtaining whatever suits his or her immediate purpose. The upshot is a mélange of ideas, borrowed from disparate sources, sometimes tested but more often intuitive and anecdotal in character.

The jerry-built quality Sniderman described is traced to at least three causes. First, as Sniderman himself noted, it was assumed for many years among political scientists that meaningful attention to the whole of an individual's personality was impractical. As anyone who has designed a survey or an experiment is aware, difficult choices must be made regarding which items to include and which to omit. Given this reality, use of an extensive personality battery reasonably might be seen as being out of the question. Addressing this matter, a specific objective I pursue in Chapter 3 involves demonstration that trait batteries included on telephone surveys require relatively few items in order to provide satisfactory representations of trait structure. But, secondly, even if political scientists had desired to depict personality more comprehensively, guidance from the field of psychology was lacking. As previously discussed, it has only been in the past fifteen to twenty years that any noteworthy level of consensus has emerged in trait psychology regarding the utility of particular models of trait structure. There often is a lag time of ten or more years before innovations in other fields affect applied research in political science, and thus it is of little surprise that few students of politics have moved beyond the piecemeal approach bemoaned by Sniderman in 1975.[11] Nonetheless, this situation remains disappointing.

The third and most important cause of inattention to personality in research on political behavior is that we have lacked full-scale theories of personality. "Personality" variables have been included in models of political behavior from time to time, but rarely with any explicit account of how these variables fit within a broader thesis of human behavior. The key theoretical claims I advance are that personality is largely rooted in biology, that traits are the central elements of personality, that traits are stable and endure psychological differences, and that important psychological differences can be represented via a five-factor depiction of trait structure. In contrast, and as Sniderman noted, prior work on personality

---

[11] Greenstein (1992) notes that the field of personality and politics seemingly has had more detractors than practitioners, a situation Greenstein attributes in part to the challenges associated with systematic inquiry in this area.

and politics often has had a much more ad hoc flavor. This quality surely has discouraged greater attention to personality.

If research in political science rarely has made use of broad models of trait structure,[12] then what perspectives on personality have been invoked? Outside of the realm of mass politics, students of elite behavior long have attended to personality. Much of this work has centered on the detailed psychobiographical analyses of individual leaders, especially U.S. presidents. Harold Lasswell (1930) was an early advocate of psychoanalytical applications in the political realm. Perhaps the most prominent inquiry in this tradition is the study of Woodrow Wilson by Alexander and Juliette George (1964).[13] Other works on elite behavior have endeavored to apply consistent frameworks in the study of multiple political leaders. Barber's (1992) research on presidential character is an especially visible effort in this genre. Thoemmes and Conway (2007) offer a more recent example of this type of study in their assessment of the "integrative complexity" of forty-one U.S. presidents. Some research in this area has focused explicitly on traits, bringing at least a loose parallel to the sorts of applications I propose for the study of mass politics. Examples include Etheredge's (1978) investigation of links between presidents' traits and their behaviors concerning foreign policy, and broader studies of presidential performance by Simonton (1986, 1988) and Rubenzer, Faschingbauer and Ones (2000). These latter works, and especially the Rubenzer et al. analysis, model trait structure in a manner reasonably similar to the approach I follow in this book in the study of mass political behavior.

Apart from investigations regarding the personalities of political leaders, a second prominent avenue for research on personality and politics has explored the link between personality and adherence to democratic values. Most of this research, a large portion of which concerns mass politics, has proceeded in three interrelated areas. First, highlighted early on by the work of Adorno et al. (1950), numerous analysts have investigated the authoritarian mindset.[14] The precise status of authoritarianism

---

[12] Since I started work on this book, some broadscale exploratory applications of the Big Five to the study of political behavior have appeared. These include my own co-authored research (e.g., Mondak and Halperin 2008; Mondak et al. 2010; Mondak et al. forthcoming), and recent pieces by Gerber and his colleagues (Gerber et al. 2008; Gerber et al. 2010).

[13] For a review of research on the personalities of political leaders, see Winter (2003a). Recent examples of this research tradition include the assessments of the Clinton administration posited by Renshon and his collaborators (Renshon 1995), and an evaluation of George W. Bush offered by a team of scholars led by Greenstein (Greenstein 2003). For an example of a case study regarding a political leader other than a U.S. president, see Post (1991).

[14] For a critical retrospective on Adorno et al. (1950), see Martin (2001). The most prominent research following that of Adorno et al. has been that of Altemeyer (e.g., 1988, 1996).

with respect to personality has been the subject of a great deal of debate, with arguments having been advanced that an individual's tendency toward authoritarianism is itself a facet of personality, a product of personality, or a broad syndrome that involves both personality and other factors. In a recent statement on this point, Stenner (2005) presents a careful, detailed analysis of authoritarianism, ultimately concluding that "authoritarian predisposition seems to be a relatively innate and enduring trait" (p. 326). As part of her analysis, Stenner identifies a link between authoritarianism and openness to experience, which, as will be discussed in Chapter 2, is a component of contemporary broadscale depictions of trait structure.

Stenner (2005) articulates an important critique of traditional measures of authoritarianism, namely that there is an inherent circularity in how these measures have been used. As Stenner explains, if attitudes are summed to measure authoritarianism, then it is tautological to employ that measure as a predictor of those same, or very closely related, attitudes (for earlier discussion, see Christie and Jahoda 1954; for a contrary view, see Winter 2006). A trait approach, such as the one used in the present study, provides a means to escape this tautology. If the predictor represents an enduring psychological structure rather than the sum of attitudes, then we are on much firmer ground when deriving inferences regarding possible causal relationships.

Although Stenner conceives of authoritarianism as a trait, she also devotes considerable attention to the impact of situational circumstances, and especially those pertaining to threat. Variants of this conditional view of authoritarianism have made several appearances in the past decade (e.g., Feldman 2003; Feldman and Stenner 1997; Lavine, Lodge, and Freitas 2005). This general perspective – that authoritarianism itself constitutes an enduring trait, but that its impact is context specific – represents an application of Mischel's view of the interplay between traits and situational forces.

A second and related line of research has explored possible links between personality and ideology.[15] Among political scientists, McClosky's work (e.g., McClosky 1958, 1964) was the most prominent early on in this area.[16] McClosky's data revealed numerous differences in patterns of traits among liberals and conservatives, with conservatives scoring high in traits such as rigidity. McClosky's initial efforts soon inspired several

[15] Research on ideology has been linked with research on authoritarianism because of the controversial claim of similarity, and even overlap, between authoritarianism and conservatism.

[16] The noted trait psychologist Hans Eysenck (1954) made a controversial foray into this realm early in his career with a two-factor trait model in which radicalism-conservatism received primary emphasis. Also see Eysenck and Wilson (1978).

additional studies on personality and core social and political predispositions (e.g., Basu 1968; Berkowitz and Lutterman 1968; Di Palma and McClosky 1970; Milbrath 1962; St. Angelo and Dyson 1968). More recently, as part of her research on authoritarianism, Stenner (2005) investigated the possible interrelationship between authoritarianism and conservatism using more advanced econometric procedures than those employed a generation earlier (see also Crowson, Thoma, and Hestevold 2005). Stenner's results (see especially pp. 167–72) demonstrate a relationship between conservatism and authoritarianism, but Stenner's full models also identify differences in the antecedents of the two constructs. Other recent work in this area has been conducted by psychologists who have invoked a broad perspective on trait structure similar to the one I employ; these studies reveal links between variance in core trait factors and ideological self-placement (e.g., Riemann et al. 1993; van Hiel, Kossowska, and Mervielde 2000).

Personality also has played a key role in research on a third related topic, political tolerance. In his groundbreaking study, Samuel Stouffer (1992 [1955]) called attention to the significance of several psychological variables such as optimism and rigidity of categorization, ultimately leading to the conclusion that "intolerance may be a systemic factor in personality" (p. 107). Rokeach's (1960) work on dogmatism followed soon after, and Sullivan, Piereson, and Marcus (1982) combined the two perspectives as part of their research on the antecedents of tolerance and intolerance. Sullivan and his colleagues initially operationalized the concept of "psychological security" with indicators relevant to several psychological frameworks, but dogmatism then emerged as the dominant force among these predictors in the authors' full multivariate model (see also McClosky and Brill 1983). Today, psychological security, typically represented by data on dogmatism, is included as a predictor in most research on the determinants of tolerance (for one recent example, see Gibson and Gouws 2003). Sullivan and his coauthors continued to explore the impact of personality on tolerance in their subsequent work (e.g., Marcus et al. 1995, especially chap. 8). In their 1995 study, the possible effects of three broad personality factors on tolerance were examined. Although more abbreviated than the approach I develop in this book, the basic logic advanced by Marcus and his colleagues represents a direct precursor to the analyses conducted here.

Sniderman (1975) also investigated the link between personality and political tolerance, but his central focus was self-esteem rather than dogmatism. Empirical tests revealed links between self-esteem and several variables, including tolerance, support for procedural rights, and levels of political cynicism. In addition to the fact that he cast his net more widely than tolerance alone, two aspects of the Sniderman study warrant emphasis. First, rather than simply demonstrating connections between self-esteem and politics, Sniderman sought to account for why these effects were present, and especially to identify possible situational variance in the impact of personality. Second, cognizant of the limitations associated with focus on a single trait, Sniderman ended his study with a call for broader inquiry. In particular, Sniderman suggested that it likely would be fruitful if future research conceived of personality more comprehensively rather than focusing on a single trait, and if possible interactions between personality and cognitive attributes were considered.

Sniderman's points are well taken. Variables designed to measure personality traits have been included as part of research on authoritarianism, ideology, and tolerance, but the efforts in these areas rarely have employed broad representations of trait structure. To my knowledge, no prior study has anchored research on personality and politics in a full theory that incorporates biology, personality, and a broadscale trait taxonomy. Further, despite strong evidence of personality effects in many prior works, attention to personality has been sparse in research on political behavior outside of the general domain of commitment to democratic values. Most investigations seeking to link personality and other aspects of political behavior have been produced by psychologists rather than political scientists, and have been published outside of mainstream political science outlets.[17]

In recent years, data on two specific personality traits – the need to evaluate and the need for cognition – have been gathered as part of the National Election Studies (NES) surveys.[18] In advocating inclusion of items tapping these traits, Bizer et al. (2000, 34) advance a position similar to my own, contending that incorporating research on personality traits in studies of mass politics would facilitate "understanding how ordinary citizens approach the world of politics using the more general dispositions that they bring from outside that world and that govern all of their thinking and action, political and non-political alike." Although I strongly concur with this general sentiment, I also believe the most progress will be made if we keep Sniderman's (1975) admonitions in mind. A generation has passed since Sniderman offered his assessment of research on personality and politics, yet the field's jerry-built appearance still can be observed. Sniderman's diagnosis of the field remains accurate both in that researchers often continue to pick out a trait or two for attention rather

---

[17] An early example is the Mussen and Wyszynski (1952) research on personality and political participation. More recent examples include studies by Van Kenhove, Vermeir and Verniers (2001), Nail, Bedell and Little (2003), and Vecchione and Caprara (2009).

[18] For examples of research using these items, see Bizer et al. (2004), Kam (2005), and Rudolph and Popp (2007).

than making use of comprehensive models of trait structure, and that personality has been applied in research on mass politics in a seemingly scattershot fashion. Personality has had a regular presence in research on some aspects of mass politics, particularly concerning democratic values, yet personality traits rarely have been incorporated in works examining other political predispositions or political information and political participation. The contribution of Bizer and colleagues (2004) constitutes a noteworthy exception, as these authors employed measures of the need to evaluate as predictors of several fairly diverse aspects of political behavior, but wide-ranging inquiry of this sort remains all too uncommon.

All of the works discussed here serve as examples of successful, insightful efforts to incorporate personality in explanations of political phenomena. In each of these cases, the authors have posited that people possess important, relatively intransient psychological characteristics, and that these characteristics likely influence how individuals interact with the political world. Results of corresponding empirical tests have been highly encouraging. Collectively, these studies constitute a mere handful relative to the vast amount of research produced on mass politics, yet these works unquestionably combine to show that personality does indeed matter for politics. Further advances in the field can be expected and should be welcomed. However, much like Sniderman in 1975, I have strong doubts regarding whether the current trajectory of research on personality and politics best ensures that the potential contributions of attention to personality in this area will be fully realized. In addition to being troubled by the scarcity of work on personality, my concern is that the present path seemingly destines developments to emerge in a piecemeal, idiosyncratic manner. By mapping out a new course, I believe we have the means to promote a much more thorough and fruitful enterprise.

## A NEW AGENDA

The opportunity now exists for the study of personality and mass politics to become more cohesive, more comprehensive, and ultimately more informative. In pursuit of these ends, I advocate a three-part agenda. Each portion of this agenda entails an expanded view of how we conceive of the possible political impact of personality. The research reported in this book represents an initial step toward implementing this strategy.

The first and most important element of a new agenda entails use of a broadscale depiction of trait structure, one anchored in recognition that biological forces account for much of the differences in personality traits. In past research on personality and politics, the most common approach involved the selection of one or two trait indicators. As an alternate, I advocate utilization of more thorough models of personality.

Incorporation of exhaustive representations of trait structure in research on politics remains impractical, but means do now exist to capture the most essential individual differences in an efficient form. In particular, during the past twenty years students of trait psychology have devoted an enormous amount of attention to five-factor personality frameworks. Five-factor approaches emphasize the genetic bases of people's traits, and demonstrate the powerful influence of these traits on virtually all facets of human behavior. This research, which I review in the next chapter, provides a rich foundation for applied efforts in the study of mass politics. Through such efforts, I believe we can produce unprecedented new evidence that people do not begin their political lives as blank slates, but instead that important differences gain shape long before we consciously encounter the political world.

Several rationales underlie my call for use of a broad model of trait structure. First, without adoption of such frameworks, any research on personality and politics necessarily will be incomplete. If no effort is made to represent something approaching the full structure of traits, then results inevitably will speak only to the effects of particular facets of personality, not to personality writ large. At present, I contend that our best and most efficient means to develop thorough tests of links between personality and politics involves implementation of cutting-edge, broad-scale representations of trait structure. Second, use of a comprehensive framework provides context that can help us to interpret the effects of particular trait variables. Whether analysis focuses on predispositions, demographics, or traits, the impact of any single indicator is difficult to interpret if we have no knowledge of how it relates to other variables. For personality, five-factor models offer vital context. Third, use of a comprehensive trait model best promotes integrated, cumulative scientific progress. As John and Srivastava (1999) note, a critical lesson learned by trait psychologists in the past twenty years is that the accumulation of knowledge is thwarted if scholars lack a common language. In the next chapter, I demonstrate that five-factor models have come to bring invaluable continuity and structure in the study of traits. We will see that scholars in multiple fields have employed these models in research on a staggering array of questions, yet use of five-factor approaches in the study of politics remains rare. Political scientists interested in the impact of personality will be best positioned to speak both to one another and to scholars in other disciplines if we incorporate these models in our research.

The second component of the research agenda I advocate involves casting the net widely when exploring the possible political significance of personality. Research on the psychology of individual differences identifies fundamental and enduring patterns in human behavior. Consequently, it is hard to imagine instances in which variables representing these differences would *not* matter for political behavior. Past research on personality and politics has devoted considerable attention to authoritarianism, tolerance, and ideology, but curiously little attention to the great many other topics of interest to students of political behavior. If people differ in basic, fundamental ways, it surely must seem plausible that those differences could influence phenomena such as who is well informed about political affairs, why people join associations or give money to candidates or vote in elections, and which people support health care reform, support efforts to combat global warming, or encourage a return to traditional family values. Numerous specific hypotheses are advanced and tested in the following chapters. The bottom line, though, is that I believe that attention to personality virtually always will contribute to our explanations of political attitudes and behavior.

In this book, I report sweeping tests of the possible political effects of personality. I do so by adopting a five-factor perspective and applying that approach in the study of political information, political attitudes and predispositions, and political participation. An alternate strategy would be to look only in the most obvious places. I do not discount the value of such inquiry. For instance, in my view it was perfectly reasonable to explore the possible link between close-mindedness and intolerance. But I also do not believe that we should limit ourselves only to analysis of this form. Bizer and colleagues (2004, 996) noted that "after a personality measure is developed, subsequent research often shows that the measure has effects on phenomena far beyond the domain initially presented." With this reality in mind, I recommend against closing off research avenues before they have been considered. We should think broadly both in terms of how personality is conceived and in terms of the possible impact of personality traits on political behavior.

The third component of the agenda I advocate concerns the form of potential personality effects. Most of the relationships tested in this study involve possible direct effects of traits on various aspects of political behavior, but full attention to personality ultimately will require that indirect and conditional relationships also be examined[19]. Indeed, it may be that, in the long run, the greatest contributions of research on personality will involve identification of interactive relationships between personality traits and other sorts of predictor variables. Perhaps the impact of ideology on policy judgments is greatest for individuals who are conscientious and emotionally secure. Perhaps the effects of social communication on political preferences are greatest for people who are extraverted and agreeable. Perhaps the influence of exposure to negative

---

[19] For additional discussion of this point, including a conceptual framework regarding personality–environment interactions, see Mondak et al. 2010.

political advertising on voter turnout is positive for individuals with some personality traits and negative for others. Research in psychology has made less progress in identifying these sorts of conditional relationships than in specifying the direct effects of personality, yet a comprehensive assessment of the impact of personality demands that conditional influences be examined. Several examples of plausible interactive effects are described and tested in this book, but these examples admittedly only scratch the surface. Research on personality and politics will be most fruitful when personality is modeled via a broadscale framework, when the possible influence of personality is tested across a wide array of political phenomena, and when both direct and conditional personality effects are considered. To conceive of such effects will require dramatic advances in theory.

What does the agenda proposed here imply for ongoing research on political behavior, research that in most instances does not currently account for personality? My view is not that present efforts are in some manner "wrong," but rather that many of our explanations of political behavior necessarily will remain incomplete if personality continues to be omitted. Put differently, I advocate incorporating personality in our explanations of political behavior, not as an alternate to present approaches, but rather as a complement. That said, serious attention to personality requires more than simply adding a few new variables to our models, or designing a few new interaction terms. To take personality seriously is to recognize both that people differ in fundamental, persistent, and politically consequential ways, and that there is a temporal order to the factors that influence political behavior. Most research on political behavior emphasizes environmental influences – the impact of socialization, exposure to news media, encounters at work and church, and so on. My thesis adds a whole new class of variables, the origins of which predate people's encounters with the environment. Further, I also advocate that our theories of political behavior include a third set of factors, ones capturing interactions between personality and environment.[20]

The key implication of my focus on core psychological differences is that preferences and behaviors may differ even for people whose life circumstances and encounters with the political world are highly similar. Research in political cognition on information effects helps to illustrate this implication. In much of this work (including some of my own), there has been an implicit – and sometimes explicit – assumption that information

---

[20] As noted above, Stenner's (2005) research on the authoritarian dynamic provides an excellent example of how scholars might pursue interactions between enduring predispositions and situational forces – in Stenner's case, between authoritarianism and normative threat.

acts as the great equalizer. If two individuals live in similar contexts and have similar backgrounds, but they differ in how much political information they hold, we assume that raising the information level of the lesser-informed person to equal that of the better-informed person would pull their political attitudes and behaviors into alignment with one another. What such an assumption overlooks is that a chief unmeasured source of variance in this case – personality – still may bring critical differences to political behavior. To name but a few, personality may bring striking disparities in the willingness to embrace sweeping political change, the willingness to think critically of elected officials and the willingness to take part in politically relevant social activities. Likewise, personality may shape both core values and views of specific policies and candidates. Absent consideration of personality, we are tempted to impose a one-size-fits-all view of political preferences. With personality, we recognize that people's fundamental psychological differences may mean that the right choice for one person genuinely is the wrong choice for another.

A second point concerns the temporal order of the antecedents of political behavior. Politics plays out in the now. Policies are debated each day, campaigns are waged each election cycle, and so on. We recognize, however, that how people engage today's politics depends in large part on long-standing predispositions such as partisanship and ideology. More accurately, we recognize that there are complex interactions between long-standing predispositions and elements of the contemporary political world. My belief is that this basic logic needs to be pursued much more thoroughly. Bringing personality into the mix will add further accuracy, yet also further complexity. Personality as defined here encompasses relatively intransient psychological orientations that represent the essence of the person. Research in psychology shows that, to a great extent, the origin of these orientations is biological. Consequently, in advocating attention to personality, I am calling attention to our need for holistic, multifaceted depictions of human behavior. Research in psychology, biology, and many other fields contemplates complex interactions between biological and environmental factors. In contrast, research on political behavior mostly focuses on only the latter, and especially on elements of the immediate, short-term information environment. It would be folly to seek to account for the dynamics of contemporary Middle Eastern or European politics with only a three- or four-month view of history. We are similarly remiss if our accounts of individual-level political behavior begin and end with factors rooted in today's information environment. It follows that serious attention to personality would mark one important step toward a dramatic rethinking of the rich, intricate patterns that underlie political behavior.

The remainder of this book represents a first effort toward implementation of the immediate agenda outlined here. In the next chapter, the properties of five-factor depictions of trait structure are explored. Research on five-factor models has occurred at a frenetic pace in the last two decades, yet this work thus far has had very little influence in studies of politics. Because a five-factor approach constitutes the theoretical and empirical centerpiece of this book, Chapter 2 presents a detailed look at the history of how five-factor models developed, the place of these models in contemporary research on trait psychology, the conventional wisdom regarding the origins of personality traits, and past research on the specific correlates of each of the five major trait dimensions. This discussion provides the foundation necessary for use of five-factor approaches in empirical tests of the impact of personality on political behavior.

In Chapter 3, discussion moves from conceptual to operational. Personality data gathered on three surveys are examined in this book. The properties of these data are assessed in Chapter 3. This walk through the data serves two ends. First, with respect to the immediate task at hand, it is essential that viable indicators be constructed for each of the five core personality traits under consideration. Thus, detailed discussion occurs regarding how and how well the five-factor trait structure is represented with the available data. But although multiple effects of personality are tested in this book, the research conducted here serves only as a first step in application of five-factor models in the study of politics. With this in mind, the second end in Chapter 3 involves attention to the practical matter of issues researchers may face in acquisition of data on personality traits. The topics addressed include the size and length of personality batteries, the relationship between personality items and demographics, and response rates and response times on personality items.

This study's central empirical tests are carried out in the next three chapters. In these chapters, the variables developed in Chapter 3 are introduced as possible explanatory factors in tests involving a wide array of political phenomena. Inquiry in Chapter 4 focuses on political information – on what and how much information about politics citizens acquire, and especially on whether patterns in information acquisition and information use vary as a function of personality. Political attitudes and predispositions are examined in Chapter 5. I revisit the important question of whether personality influences political ideology, but I also explore numerous other variables such as partisanship, political efficacy, policy attitudes, and moral traditionalism. Lastly, the influence of personality on political behavior is assessed in Chapter 6. The impact of personality on voter turnout is considered, but also the possible effects of personality on participation in political campaigns and involvement in local social and political affairs.

The research agenda developed above is revisited in Chapter 7. I have advocated a multifaceted broadening of our approach to the study of personality and politics. The empirical tests conducted in this book offer a first glimpse at the value of such an expanded approach. Hence, in reviewing the lessons learned in these tests, we will be able to develop a new perspective on how best to implement this agenda, and on the likely value of further research on personality and the foundations of political behavior.

# 2

## The Big Five Approach

The previous chapter represents a call to action. The relative neglect of personality in research on mass politics has occurred primarily because, for many years, adequate frameworks for the study of personality were unavailable. But this situation has changed. Developments in trait psychology have led to the construction of taxonomies possessing characteristics ideal for research on mass political attitudes and behavior. These frameworks, which have risen to prominence within the past two decades, are broad, multifaceted, well understood, and relatively easy to employ in empirical research. By utilizing one of these contemporary trait approaches, it should be possible to make substantial progress in exploring the potential political impact of variance in personality.

The particular perspective adopted in this study is the "Big Five" framework. Research on the Big Five holds that five traits collectively provide a highly comprehensive, hierarchical model of trait structure. Following convention, the broad traits, or dimensions, are labeled here as *openness to experience, conscientiousness, extraversion, agreeableness,* and *emotional stability*.[1] In later chapters, empirical indicators of these traits will be developed and the traits will be introduced as possible predictors of a wide array of actions and attitudes familiar in research on mass politics.

As a prelude to those analyses, this chapter offers detailed background on the Big Five for the benefit of those readers who may be unfamiliar with this research tradition and its origins. The discussion addresses three major themes. First, the essential components of the Big Five approach are described. This treatment includes attention to the works of the leading proponents of five-factor models, the history of the emergence of these frameworks, and assessment of the current role of the Big Five relative to

---

[1] It is also common in trait psychology to substitute the term "neuroticism" for its opposite state "emotional stability," thus creating the acronym OCEAN: (O)penness to experience, (C)onscientiousness, (E)xtraversion, (A)greeableness, (N)euroticism.

alternate depictions of trait structure. Second, to place the Big Five and other trait models in a broader scientific context, and to bolster my claim that personality is a source of persistent influence, the possible biological and experiential antecedents of variance in traits are considered. Third, moving from a holistic view to the features of individual traits, the properties of the Big Five trait dimensions are explored. The conceptualization of each trait factor is explained, and research regarding the correlates of the Big Five traits is summarized. The possible politically relevant consequences of the Big Five receive particular attention.

### THE BIG FIVE FRAMEWORK

The sheer quantity of identifiable human traits complicates research in this area. With there being scores of traits and thousands of trait adjectives, scholarly progress dictated that some sort of simplifying organizational scheme be devised. Enter the Big Five. Proponents of five-factor approaches claim neither that only these five traits warrant study, nor that these dimensions fully capture all variance in personality. Instead, the Big Five are seen as broad domains, collectively representing a hierarchy that organizes and summarizes the vast majority of subsidiary traits. For my purposes, which involve the construction of sweeping, first-order tests of possible links between personality and politics, the Big Five approach is ideal. Subsequent research may fruitfully explore particular relationships with greater nuance and depth, but the Big Five offer an excellent starting point and an efficient, workable means to incorporate attention to trait structure in research on political behavior.[2]

In psychology, multiple teams of researchers have advocated five-factor models since the revitalization of work in this area began some

---

[2] Many parallels can be seen elsewhere in research on mass politics. For instance, it often is the case that analysts can capture relevant political predispositions via standard seven-point measures of ideology and partisanship. For some research questions, however, more intricate measures are needed. With respect to personality, research on political behavior rarely includes any measure at all. Hence, putting first things first, the logical initial step involves adding to our models the personality equivalent of standard seven-point partisanship and ideology scales so that we may see when, and in what manner, personality is influential. Measures of the Big Five can serve this role. Once this initial foundation is constructed, measures of the Big Five can be supplemented or refined if more detailed representations of personality are required. A similar view of the Big Five can be seen among its proponents in psychology (e.g., Saucier and Goldberg 1998). Among students of traits, five-factor approaches are viewed as offering broad, comprehensive frameworks, but explicitly *not* as capturing the entirety of personality or, consequently, as constituting the final word on individual differences. Saucier and Goldberg (1998) suggest particular circumstances in which it can be useful to supplement the Big Five.

twenty years ago. From an outsider's perspective, the differences among these frameworks are much less noteworthy than are the similarities. Nonetheless, a brief discussion is warranted regarding the key features of two leading approaches, McCrae and Costa's (2003, 2008) Five-Factor theory and Goldberg's (1990, 1993) lexical interpretation of the Big Five.

## Alternate Perspectives on the Big Five

There are two straightforward, yet also critical, similarities linking the trait research of Goldberg and of McCrae and Costa. First, these scholars concur that five factors are sufficient to provide a reasonably comprehensive and functional representation of personality. Second, they also concur on what the general substantive content of those factors should be. That is, McCrae and Costa are in agreement with Goldberg that the bulk of variance in traits can be captured via attention to five broad factors: openness to experience, conscientiousness, extraversion, agreeableness, and emotional stability.[3]

The key differences between these leading five-factor perspectives center on the breadth of the respective authors' claims regarding the nature and significance of five-factor models, and on the matter of how empirical indicators of the Big Five traits should best be constructed. On the first point, Costa and McCrae have advanced much bolder pronouncements than has Goldberg. Goldberg conceives of the Big Five as being a taxonomy, a useful framework for the representation of individual differences. McCrae and Costa, in contrast, have developed their original "five-factor model" into what they now present as a "five-factor theory," complete with numerous detailed postulates (e.g., McCrae and Costa 1996, 2003, 2008). This distinction between Goldberg and McCrae and Costa brings little influence on the empirical assessments reported in subsequent chapters, where indicators of the Big Five traits are put to work as predictors of political attitudes and behavior. My immediate intent centers on testing a series of specific hypotheses regarding possible political effects of the Big Five. However, because I depict personality as a central pillar in a broader theory of human behavior, I draw heavily on McCrae and Costa's newest works when discussing the biological underpinnings of the five-factor structure.

Goldberg follows a lexical approach in both his conceptualization and measurement of the Big Five (e.g., 1990, 1992, 1993; Saucier and

---

[3] The labels used for the traits differ slightly among these authors, and there also are slight differences in the presumed substantive content of the Big Five traits. On these points, see Goldberg (1993, 30). For additional discussion of similarities and differences in the Goldberg and Costa and McCrae perspectives, see McCrae and John (1992).

Goldberg 1996; see also De Raad 2000). The logic of the lexical hypothesis, which Goldberg attributes to Sir Francis Galton (1884),[4] is that virtually all important differences in human traits are captured in everyday language – typically single adjectival terms. This link to linguistics is not merely coincidence or good fortune. Instead, because language is functional, it is presumed that humans recognize differences in one another, and devise language to represent those differences that are most noteworthy. Goldberg's focus on the central role of language predates his attention to the Big Five. Writing in 1981, for instance, Goldberg argued that:

> Those individual differences that are of most significance in the daily transactions of persons with each other will eventually become encoded into their language. The more important is such a difference, the more people will notice it and wish to talk of it, with the result that eventually they will invent a word for it. (Goldberg 1981, 141–2)[5]

If differences in personality are captured in everyday language, then it follows that appropriate indicators of personality traits can be devised through use of ratings based on simple adjectival markers. This is the approach Goldberg has followed in his research on the Big Five (e.g., Goldberg 1992). The raw materials for Goldberg's Big Five scales are individuals' self-ratings on large sets of adjectives, using univocal and bipolar response formats, and terms such as "talkative," "warm," and "conscientious." To facilitate research on personality, Goldberg has developed a bank of items labeled the "International Personality Item Pool" (see Goldberg et al. 2006).[6] As will be seen in the following chapter, the Big Five traits are measured in the present study using data derived from bipolar, or semantic-differential, markers. Most of these are drawn or adapted from items reported by Goldberg.

McCrae and Costa also emphasize that traits are captured by everyday language (e.g., McCrae and Costa 2003, 34–6). However, rather than measuring traits via univocal or bipolar adjective scales, Costa and

---

[4] Galton, the one-time antagonist of famed African explorer Henry Morton Stanley, also is credited with devising the statistical concept of correlation and with developing the measure of standard deviation.

[5] Between Galton and Goldberg, other influential treatments of the lexical hypothesis include those of Allport and Odbert (1936) and Cattell (1943). A thorough recent discussion of traits and the lexical hypothesis is offered by De Raad (2000, especially chap. 3), and an earlier history is provided by John, Angleitner, and Ostendorf (1988).

[6] Goldberg's efforts regarding development of the International Personality Item Pool reflect his concern with the proprietary nature of many of the leading copyrighted personality batteries. Goldberg's view is that public-domain batteries will best promote both the occurrence of further research on personality traits, and the development of linkages across the research programs of different scholars.

McCrae follow what is known in the field as a "questionnaire" approach. Specifically, Costa and McCrae's (1992) Revised NEO Personality Inventory, or NEO-PI-R, asks respondents to report the extent to which they agree or disagree with statements such as "I really like most people I meet" and "I have a very active imagination."[7] Items have five response options, ranging from "strongly agree" to "strongly disagree." Costa and McCrae's full battery, which they make available as a commercial product, includes 240 such items, and takes approximately 35 to 40 minutes to administer. A shorter version of the instrument includes sixty items.

The research on the Big Five conducted by Goldberg and by Costa and McCrae continues to be highly illuminating. Although a few points differentiate the two perspectives, my own understanding of the Big Five has gained enormously through consideration of the works of both of these research programs. I also have observed that it is common in applied research on the Big Five for analysts to make reference to influential works of both Goldberg and Costa and McCrae. As will be seen below, the two camps conceptualize the Big Five trait dimensions quite similarly. Thus, I follow the lead suggested in most applied studies by devoting attention to the Big Five as a (relatively) cohesive research tradition, rather than by dwelling on those differences that exist between the views of these leading figures.[8]

In the previous chapter, concerns were noted regarding tendencies in both psychology and political science for researchers to cherry-pick individual traits without placing those traits in any broader context. A key reason that five-factor approaches have been so influential stems from the context they offer. The prevailing view among students of trait structure holds that even when research centers on the effects of isolated traits, full understanding of those effects requires that they be seen within the parameters of a broader framework. Five-factor models serve this function. Ozer and Reise (1994, 361) contend, for instance, that "personality psychologists who continue to employ their preferred measure without locating it within the five-factor model can only be likened to geographers who issue reports on new lands but refuse to locate them on a map for others to find."

Before we proceed to embrace the Big Five as a tool for research on political behavior, my claim that this framework has been highly influential in psychology perhaps should be put to the test. Informally, if one were

---

[7] These examples are from McCrae and Costa (2003, 45–6).

[8] In this study, references to five-factor frameworks, perspectives, and approaches and to the Big Five are used nearly interchangeably. Again, my views have been influenced by the works of both Goldberg and Costa and McCrae, and, especially for sweeping first-order empirical tests of the sort reported in subsequent chapters, it is simply not necessary for me to dwell on many of the finer distinctions between these authors' perspectives.

to peruse issues of journals such as the *Journal of Personality and Social Psychology*, the *Journal of Personality*, and *Personality and Individual Differences*, it would quickly become evident that mention of five-factor approaches and references to works by Goldberg and by Costa and McCrae abound, and have done so throughout the past two decades. A bit more formally, by early 2010, an article by Goldberg (1993) had been cited over 800 times,[9] a mark that was not reached by any single article in the first one hundred years of political science's flagship outlet, the *American Political Science Review*. Two other articles by Goldberg (1990, 1992) and one by McCrae and Costa (1987) had garnered over 900 citations each, and a prominent early review piece on the Big Five had recorded nearly 1,400 citations (Digman 1990). Citation patterns differ across disciplines. Still, it is clear that the Big Five has had a profound effect on research on personality, and that the perspectives of Costa and McCrae and of Goldberg have been especially influential. Consistent with this view, references to the dominant role of five-factor approaches are common. Gosling, Rentfrow, and Swann (2003, 506) note, for instance, that the Big Five framework "has become the most widely used and extensively researched model of personality." Similarly, Woods and Hampson (2005, 374) contend that "although there remains some debate in trait theory over how many factors are necessary to provide a complete description of personality, consensus now seems to rest upon a five factor solution consisting of Extraversion, Agreeableness, Conscientiousness, Emotional Stability, and Openness." John, Naumann and Soto's (2008) recent review of research on the Big Five casts the emergence of this perspective as a "paradigm shift" (2008, 114). The authors note that in recent years, published applications of the Big Five have outpaced the *combined* work on two prominent earlier models, those of Catell and Eysenck, at a rate of over ten to one.

How is it that leading treatments of the Big Five came to be so central in contemporary research on personality? To address this question, I first will provide background on the history and development of five-factor approaches, followed by discussion of the relationship between the Big Five and other leading frameworks for the study of individual differences.

### A Brief History of the Big Five

Two questions to consider in assessing the Big Five perspective are why *five* factors, and why *these* five factors? The short response is that these

---

[9] Citation data are from an ISI Web of Knowledge combined search of the Science Citation Index, Social Science Citation Index and Arts and Humanities Citation Index.

conclusions have been derived empirically in multiple studies that have employed factor analytic techniques to explore trait structure. A fuller response requires a brief review of relevant research on traits reported over the past seventy-five years.[10]

The existence of a vast number of traits has long been recognized. In Allport and Odbert's (1936) compilation, for instance, nearly 18,000 trait terms were found in the authors' search of an unabridged dictionary.[11] Factor analysis offers one means to navigate such crowded waters. Although the roots of the five-factor approach arguably can be traced back even further, Thurstone's (1934) pioneering application of factor analysis warrants mention in that Thurstone – who later advocated a larger model (e.g., Thurstone 1953) – reported that five factors were sufficient to account for sixty common descriptive adjectives.

Some of Raymond Cattell's earliest work on personality traits (e.g., 1933) was contemporaneous with Thurstone's, but it is Cattell's research from the 1940s (e.g., Cattell 1943, 1944, 1947) that offers the most direct springboard to development of the Big Five. Cattell began with the exhaustive list of terms compiled by Allport and Odbert (1936), and then narrowed that list down through multiple laborious refinements.[12] Cattell's work led him to advocate personality structures considerably larger than the Big Five, including frameworks with twelve or more factors, and Cattell eventually developed a prominent sixteen-factor model known as the 16PF (Cattell 1956). What is critical is that subsequent researchers who reexamined Cattell's variables consistently found only five factors to be replicable (e.g., Fiske 1949).

The earliest view of trait structure most comparable to today's five-factor approaches appeared in a series of technical reports written by Tupes and Christal for the U.S. Air Force (Tupes 1957; Tupes and Christal 1958, 1961). In research designed to identify correlates of the effectiveness of Air Force officers, research that included reexamination of variables from Cattell's work and from many other previous studies, five factors highly similar in content to today's Big Five were reported. Partly due to the relative obscurity of the Air Force reports, it took the better part of three decades before the lessons learned in the Tupes and Christal studies came to exert significant influence on mainstream research on

---

[10] Thorough reviews of the emergence of the Big Five are provided by Digman (1990, 1996), Goldberg (1993, 1995), John, Naumann and Soto (2008), John and Robins (1993), John and Srivastava (1999), and McCrae and John (1992). The present account draws heavily on these histories.

[11] These were not all personality traits. Also included were moods, evaluative judgments, and physical attributes.

[12] As Pervin (2003) notes, Cattell conducted factor analysis *by hand* in his research in the 1940s.

personality traits,[13] although a few noteworthy works did follow up on the Tupes and Christal findings in the 1960s (Borgatta 1964; Norman 1963; Smith 1967).

Research on trait structure languished for more than a decade following the publication of these studies, partly because of skepticism regarding the trait approach writ large (Mischel 1968). The early 1980s, though, saw renewed attention to the five-factor approaches discussed by Borgatta, Norman, and Smith. Digman and Goldberg were among the first scholars to express enthusiasm for the five-factor perspective in this period. Costa and McCrae's research at this time centered on three of the Big Five factors: openness to experience, extraversion and emotional stability. Digman (1996, 13) credits Goldberg with sharing news of a possible five-factor trait structure with Costa and McCrae in 1983, leading the latter authors to add conscientiousness and agreeableness to their framework. By decade's end, Goldberg and Costa and McCrae had developed active research programs focused on the Big Five, and other scholars soon followed. As we have seen, some of the early works from those programs have achieved remarkable levels of visibility and influence.

In the past two decades, much of the research on the Big Five has sought to explore the framework's validity and scope. With respect to validity, plausible threats leap to mind when we recall that most data on the Big Five are drawn from individuals' ratings of themselves. Viewed most pessimistically, self-ratings conceivably could have no basis at all in reality, instead reflecting nothing more than self-delusion, perhaps coupled with the influence of social desirability. The most obvious means to test the utility of self-ratings, a method employed in numerous studies, involves acquisition and comparison of "self" and "others" ratings. With such data, it can be determined whether others see us as we see ourselves.

McCrae and Costa (1989a) developed such validity tests using five-factor data measured with their NEO-PI. The average correlation between scores provided by main respondents and the ratings of respondents offered by respondents' spouses was 0.56, and the average correlation between data from respondents and from their peers was 0.50. Even ratings of respondents provided entirely by others – peer-peer and spouse-peer ratings of the main respondents – yielded an average correlation of 0.41. Likewise, Costa and McCrae (2003, 43) report that, across several other studies conducted by numerous different research teams, the average correlation between self-ratings and those offered by peers is 0.45 (examples of such studies include Funder, Kolar, and Blackman 1995;

---

[13] Tupes and Christal's 1961 report was republished in a mainstream outlet over three decades later (Tupes and Christal 1992), along with a comment by Christal (1992).

Watson 1989; Watson, Hubbard, and Wiese 2000). Most recently, a meta-analysis by Connolly, Kavanagh, and Viswesvaran (2007) reports mean correlations between self-ratings and observer ratings ranging from 0.46 for agreeableness to 0.62 for extraversion. Self-ratings and observer ratings are not identical, but the consistent finding of a very strong relationship between the two is encouraging. Collectively, these results bring considerable confidence that self-ratings of personality correspond strongly with the outward manifestations of personality perceived by others. In short, self-ratings appear to provide valid indicators of the Big Five traits; these ratings are not merely the products of self-delusion.

A central question regarding the breadth of the five-factor framework concerns whether this same basic trait structure can be identified across languages and cultures. Given that the present inquiry applies the Big Five to the study of political behavior in the U.S. case, this matter is not an immediate cause for concern. Nonetheless, the lexical basis of trait descriptions does raise curiosity about scope. Perhaps a different number of factors, or even different factors entirely, emerge in other nations and with other languages. Addressing this matter, McCrae and Costa (2003, 87–8) write of the "universality" of the five-factor model. Evidence consistent with the five-factor perspective has been derived from personality batteries administered in numerous languages from multiple language families (Church 2000, 2001; McCrae and Costa 1997; Saucier and Goldberg 2001), and much of McCrae's most recent research has involved further cross-cultural analysis (e.g., Allik and McCrae 2004; McCrae and Costa 2006; Schmitt et al. 2007), including exploration of links between the Big Five and Hofstede's (2001) measure of culture (Hofstede and McCrae 2004).

Although impressive evidence has been generated regarding the cross-national applicability of the Big Five, two issues suggest that cross-cultural inquiry should proceed cautiously.[14] First, findings in support of the five-factor perspective in various cultures do not rule out the possibility that *other* factors beyond the Big Five might be present, and might even be more important than the Big Five locally (e.g., Cheung and Leung 1998; Katigbak, Church, and Akamine 1996; Yang and Bond 1990). McCrae and Costa (2003) acknowledge this point. As they explain it, if a given trait is unique to a particular culture, items pertinent to that trait will not be part of the NEO-PI, and thus evidence of that trait's presence will not be obtained. It does not follow that a five-factor approach is inapplicable in areas where additional traits are salient, but it does follow that the Big Five alone may not always be adequate to provide a comprehensive

---

[14] For further discussion of these issues, see John, Naumann, and Soto (2008, 121–4).

representation of trait structure. Second, the fundamental logic of focus on traits can be questioned in cultures that center on the collective more than on the individual (Markus and Kitayama 1998). Ultimately, this should be seen as an empirical question, and thus the continuing efforts of McCrae and others to explore trait structure cross-culturally are to be encouraged.

This brief history offers a sense of how the five-factor perspective developed, of the influence of this perspective in contemporary research on trait psychology, and of the new directions scholars in the field have turned. However, I do not mean to suggest that five-factor approaches have driven out other depictions of trait structure. To the contrary, debate persists regarding the propriety of both larger and smaller taxonomies.[15]

### Alternates to Five-Factor Trait Structures

Given that thousands of trait descriptors have been identified, a near-infinite number of combinations of traits exist. Hence, if trait structure is not to be represented with five factors, then we must ask how many factors there should be, and on what basis those factors should be selected. As we have seen, the ascendance of five-factor approaches has occurred because large numbers of empirical tests have identified close approximations of the same five factors. In other words, the two most important defining features of the framework – how many factors, and which ones – have been determined empirically. Larger and smaller alternates to the Big Five can be found, but the preponderance of evidence favors representation of personality via openness to experience, conscientiousness, extraversion, agreeableness, and emotional stability.

Among larger alternates to the Big Five, Cattell's 16PF (Cattell 1956; Cattell et al. 1970) or its most recent variant (Conn and Rieke 1994) is perhaps the most prominent. Although Cattell himself was a revered figure among students of personality, his original sixteen-factor model was viewed with a degree of skepticism because subsequent researchers consistently failed to identify more than a handful of Cattell's sixteen factors (e.g., Fiske 1949; Howarth 1976; for a discussion, see Goldberg 1981). Cattell's model has undergone continued revision and refinement, but this in itself leads to skepticism of a different variety in that the most recent version of 16PF bears only a rough resemblance to its predecessors

---

[15] For an early critical assessment of the five-factor model, see McAdams (1992). McAdams registers several criticisms about the five-factor approach, ultimately leading to the conclusion that the model offers *a* useful framework, but falls short of representing *the* final integrative model of personality.

(Matthews and Deary 1998, 21), raising the question of whether the continued discussion of exactly sixteen factors is in part motivated by tradition.

Pragmatically, present purposes will be best served if an adequate representation of trait structure requires far fewer than sixteen factors. In the empirical research reported in the following chapters, I have sought to add parsimonious personality batteries to standard political surveys. The goal of parsimony could not be met were it necessary to gather data on sixteen factors. Fortunately, a growing body of research suggests that the primary factors in larger models like Cattell's 16PF can be reduced to a smaller number of global factors. Most critically, several studies have demonstrated that when such an exercise is conducted with the 16PF, what emerges is a secondary structure consistent with the five-factor approach (e.g., Noller, Law, and Comrey 1987; Boyle 1989). Indeed, the technical manual for the most recent rendition of the 16PF (Conn and Rieke 1994) refers to the existence of five global factors, and today the company that markets the 16PF develops explicit parallels between these factors and the five-factor models of both Goldberg and Costa and McCrae (Institute for Personality and Ability Testing 2007).[16] Similar efforts have been made to confirm the relationship between five-factor frameworks and many other leading personality inventories such as Myers-Briggs (McCrae and Costa 1989b) and the Minnesota Multiphasic Personality Inventory (MMPI) (Costa et al. 1986).[17]

Advocates of larger models such as the 16PF hold that personality is most fruitfully captured with primary rather than higher-order traits. Consequently, proponents of these alternates typically do not challenge the existence of broader structures, but rather the utility of such frameworks. Put differently, it generally is *not* the case that advocates of larger typologies believe that the Big Five has left out an important trait or two; instead, they believe that subdividing the five core trait dimensions can be worthwhile. This trade-off between precision and efficiency is not lost on adherents of the five-factor model (e.g., McCrae and John 1992). Although I follow a five-factor approach in the present study, I too recognize that parsimony often comes at a cost. Research involving broad, higher-order factors necessarily captures empirical relationships in somewhat coarse terms. Where links between the Big Five and various aspects of political behavior are identified in later chapters, a logical direction for

---

[16] Simple perusal of the factors in the current version of the 16PF will lead most readers to observe obvious clustering consistent with the Big Five. For example, three of the model's sixteen primary factors are liveliness, social boldness, and privateness; three others are emotional stability, apprehension, and tension.

[17] For discussion of additional tests regarding other personality inventories, see McCrae and Costa (2003, 55).

follow-up research would involve investigation regarding whether these effects trace to specific subsidiary traits. For instance, if extraversion predicts social forms of political participation, subsequent research could refine matters by exploring whether that effect traces more to liveliness or social boldness. This research course – initial identification of general relationships with broad trait domains, followed by subsequent efforts to link those effects to subsidiary traits – is quite common in psychology.

Hans Eysenck, a contemporary of Cattell's and also a highly influential and esteemed figure in the field,[18] developed the strongest case that fundamental representations of personality require fewer than five factors. Eysenck (1947) initially posited that there were two basic personality dimensions, extraversion and neuroticism. As we have seen, these dimensions went on to become incorporated within Big Five frameworks. Eysenck's third dimension, added much later (e.g., Eysenck and Eysenck 1969), is psychoticism. Eysenck presented a strong, direct critique of five-factor approaches (e.g., Eysenck 1991, 1992). Goldberg and Rosolack (1994) demonstrated that psychoticism constitutes a merging of two orthogonal factors, agreeableness and conscientiousness, whereas it was Eysenck's position that agreeableness and conscientiousness are facets of a single, higher-level dimension (and that openness to experience is not a trait in the same sense as the others). Therefore, the case favoring a five-factor trait structure versus Eysenck's three dimensions hinges on whether agreeableness and conscientiousness should be treated separately and whether an adequate case has been made for inclusion of openness to experience. In contemplating these matters, it is again important to note that the Big Five perspective grew from the empirical finding of a consistent and replicable five-factor structure.[19]

Trait structure can be, and has been, depicted with multiple frameworks other than the five-factor approach employed in this study. In opting for the Big Five, I have been persuaded by the model's comprehensiveness,

---

[18] Haggbloom et al. (2002) listed the "100 Most Eminent Psychologists of the 20th Century." Eysenck and Cattell both were in the top seven (along with Freud and Piaget, and just ahead of Skinner) in terms of citations in professional journals, and both were in the top sixteen on the authors' composite index.

[19] Although the Big Five factors typically are defined as higher-order dimensions, Digman (1997) has suggested an even higher-order, two-factor structure formed with the Big Five as its starting point. In Digman's view, openness to experience and extraversion constitute one higher-order factor, and the remaining three Big Five traits a second. Digman's perspective puts the Big Five in a somewhat different context, one that helps suggest possible patterns in correlates of the Big Five. However, when using a trait framework in an effort to account for variance in political behavior, my view is that the two-structure alternate outlined by Digman probably provides too coarse a representation of personality relative to the full five-factor approach.

utility, and rich history in empirical research, and I have been encouraged by the clear parallels between the Big Five factors and the trait structures suggested by both larger and smaller models. Other political scientists also have seen great potential in applied research using the Big Five. Marcus (2000, 227), for instance, views five-factor approaches as offering "a rich opportunity for new research." As will be seen in the following pages, the few extant works in political science involving the Big Five consistently have identified political consequences of variance in traits. Nonetheless, I am not a zealous advocate of this particular perspective. A five-factor structure offers a functional, practical means to conduct a wide array of tests regarding possible links between personality and political behavior, and I use the Big Five toward that end. Numerous relationships between political phenomena and the Big Five traits emerge in the following chapters. In many ways, these effects should be viewed as a starting point. If students of trait psychology come to replace or substantially refine the Big Five, their actions will enable future applied research on personality and politics to build on the initial findings reported in the present study.

STEPPING BACK: EXAMINING THE ORIGINS OF
PERSONALITY

The fundamental thesis pursued in this book is that personality contributes to enduring differences in mass politics. In the chapters that follow, empirical analyses explore the possible links between the Big Five traits and a wide array of familiar concepts from the field of political behavior. Put differently, the trait measures will be employed as independent variables used as predictors of ideology, political participation, and the like. Although such inquiry constitutes the centerpiece of this study, the story would be inherently incomplete without attention to the factors underlying personality. People differ on extraversion, conscientiousness, agreeableness, emotional stability, and openness to experience, but *why* is this case? What are the origins of variance in personality? I have argued that attention to personality pushes our explanations of political behavior from a focus on just the here-and-now interactions between people and the environment toward a recognition that political attitudes and actions may be rooted, at least in part, in forces that are present throughout our entire lives. This case would be bolstered considerably if it could be shown that the origins of personality predate political awareness, and especially if key elements of personality are present from birth.

Given the complexity of personality, and of human behavior more generally, it should be of little surprise that a full answer to these questions does not yet exist.[20] Moreover, comprehensive attention to the possible antecedents of personality is well beyond the scope of the present study. Nonetheless, at least three rationales commend brief discussion of the foundations of personality.

First, on a practical, substantive level, if research on personality and mass politics eventually is to give rise to specific policy prescriptions, then it likely would be useful to also have insight regarding factors that influence personality. Suppose, for example, that it were possible to identify traits that correspond with attitudes and behaviors that can be seen as being part of good citizenship. Perhaps, for instance, extraversion and conscientiousness both exert positive influence on certain forms of political participation. In this scenario, if political participation is valued, then we conceivably could foster participatory behavior through actions that promote extraversion and conscientiousness. If working on group projects in kindergarten – or playing youth sports, working as a newspaper carrier or babysitter, taking music lessons, and so on – increases the likelihood that participants will grow into outgoing, responsible adults, then policy actions today might bring positive effects down the road, even if only on the margins, for citizenship. It certainly can be debated whether policies consciously designed to mold certain types of citizens would be desirable. But discussion will never reach that stage other than in the abstract if we do not first explore both the impact of personality on political behavior and personality's underpinnings.

A second reason to contemplate the sources of variance in traits relates to the nature of the inferences that can be derived from the empirical analyses reported in the following chapters. Ideally, if and when a correspondence is found between personality and political behavior, it will be possible to generate a reasonable inference regarding the causal structure of this relationship. My assumption, of course, is that, typically, this correspondence will exist because variance in personality causes variance in a given political attitude or action. When working with cross-sectional survey data, causal inference of this sort is necessarily inconclusive because the possibilities of reverse causality and spuriousness cannot be definitively ruled out. Nonetheless, some causal accounts will be stronger and more compelling than others. For instance, in the present case, we would have serious grounds for concern if personality were highly fluid, shifting dramatically from day to day or week to week. Under these circumstances, it would be quite easy to conceive of personality as being the consequence of political behavior rather than the other way around. We might suspect,

---

[20] Developments are occurring rapidly in the study of the biological bases of personality, and many new techniques are being applied in this research. For recent examples, see the chapters in Canli (2006).

for example, that being recruited to work on a .petition drive engenders a broader sense of openness to experience, or even that paying especially close attention to politics adversely affects one's emotional stability. It follows that the degree of confidence we can have in inferences regarding the impact of personality on political behavior hinges directly on our knowledge regarding the antecedents of the Big Five traits.

The final and most important reason to consider the foundations of personality is that doing so contributes to a holistic, multifaceted model of political behavior. If identifiable factors exert influence on personality, and personality, in turn, matters for politics, then this suggests an indirect political role for the factors underlying personality. It may be that this role has not previously been detected. Alternatively, it may be that the link to politics has been established but that the mediating role of personality has escaped attention. Either way, efforts to develop a more thorough understanding of the bases of personality promise to add nuance and depth to our theories regarding the antecedents of political behavior.

A considerable body of research has explored the origins of personality. Much of this work has centered on the basic distinction between possible genetic and environmental influences.[21] As is common in research on genetics and human behavior, many of these studies have made use of data on twins. Monozygotic (MZ) twins[22] have identical genes. Consequently, any differences between them, including differences in personality, can be presumed to stem from environmental factors rather than from genetics. Dizygotic (DZ) twins[23] differ genetically, sharing only about 50 percent of their genes. Hence, differences between dizygotic twins may trace to either genetic or environmental sources. It follows that comparison of data from MZ and DZ twins permits researchers to estimate the relative effects of genetic and environmental factors on traits. Environmental effects, in turn, typically are decomposed into those associated with the shared environment experienced by twins and those linked to aspects of the unshared environment. More advanced analyses

[21] Prominent examples include works by Eysenck (1967, 1990; Eaves, Eysenck, and Martin 1989), Loehlin (1992; Loehlin and Nichols 1976), Rushton et al. (1986) and Tellegen et al. (1988). See also Bouchard et al. (1990), Bouchard (1994), Floderus-Myrhed, Pedersen, and Rasmuson (1980), Heath et al. (1992), Jang et al. (1998), Pedersen et al. 1988, and Rose et al. (1988). For a general review of this research, see Matthews and Deary (1998, chap. 5) and Pervin (2003, chap. 5). The discussion in this section draws heavily on Matthews and Deary (1998, chap. 5) and McCrae and Costa (2003). For a general introduction to research using twin data and application of these data in studies involving political behavior, see Medland and Hatemi (2009).

[22] Popularly known as "identical" twins.

[23] "Fraternal" twins.

offer further refinements, considering in particular whether variance in the phenomenon or trait of interest may stem partly from interactions between biological and environmental factors.

Twin studies are useful, but they should not be assumed to be comparable to the fully controlled experiment. One complication, for instance, is that some families attempt to treat MZ twins differently, precisely so that the twins can "develop their own personalities," whereas others treat them as similarly as possible. Likewise, it cannot be assumed that MZ and DZ twins experience identical environments – and thus that genetics alone differentiates them.[24] But, provided that we keep these limitations in mind, review of research based on twin studies can offer us a general sense of what factors contribute to personality, particularly if similar findings are obtained across multiple inquiries. Also, as a complement to twin studies, analysts often examine data from other sources, such as from families with both biological and adopted children.[25]

In endeavoring to account for variance in personality, these works differentiate among several broad classes of variables: genes, shared environment, and nonshared environment. Although not foolproof, research based on twin studies is most adept at distinguishing between the first two possible influences, genes and shared environment. Variance in personality not definitively attributable to these two sources is harder to pin down. Such variance is presumed to result from elements of the nonshared environment; for instance, children in the same family can have different teachers, play on different Little League teams, take up different musical instruments, and so on. However, development of a comprehensive account of such influences quite obviously poses an extreme challenge. In most twin studies, unshared environment is a residual category; it contains the variance that remains after the effects attributable to genetics and to the shared environment have been identified. As a result, although variance not related to genes or shared environment may indeed emerge from aspects of the unshared environment, we typically cannot rule out other factors, such as unmeasured gene-environment interactions or the effects of measurement error.

*Heritability* refers to the impact of genes in a population. Heritability statistics range in value from 0 to 1, with higher scores indicating larger effects of genetics. More specifically, heritability provides an estimate of

---

[24] Twin studies assume that the shared environments of twins raised together are similar. However, if parents treat MZ twins differently than DZ twins, such as by doing more to recognize and foster individuality in DZ twins, then this assumption is questionable, even if only on the margins.

[25] Examples of such research include Loehlin, Willerman, and Horn (1985) and Scarr et al. (1981).

the portion of the observed variance in the concept of interest in a population that corresponds with the variance in genes.[26] Many of the relevant studies predate the development of the Big Five, and thus more research has been conducted regarding the heritability of some traits – especially extraversion – than of others. Nonetheless, across multiple traits and multiple inquiries, a common story emerges. First, genetic effects have been identified in all of the works noted here. For the Big Five, heritability values typically vary between 0.25 and just over 0.50 with self-report trait measures, with slightly higher marks obtained on occasion. Hence, to a substantial degree, the origins of personality are apparently attributable to biology.[27] Second, shared family environment exerts little or no impact on personality. To the extent that environment matters, it apparently is the idiosyncratic experiences of the individual, not the shared experiences of members of a given family, that are consequential.[28]

With heritability marks generally not much higher than 0.50, coupled with evidence of, at best, only weak effects of shared environment, it would appear that much of the variance in personality remains to be explained. McCrae and Costa (2003) challenge this position. Indeed, in one recent depiction of their Five-Factor Theory, McCrae and Costa (2003, 193) emphasize that they do "not admit of any influence of the environment on personality traits."[29] Although McCrae and Costa concede that their

[26] The important point here is that heritability values refer to populations, not individuals. If the heritability level for extraversion is 0.50, this means that genes account for 50 percent of variance in extraversion across individuals, *not* that 50 percent of any given individual's extraversion is genetic in origin.

[27] To put these figures in context, note that many students of genetics argue that nothing is fully heritable, and that heritability levels around 0.80 for attributes such as height (e.g., Xu 2006) mark the approximate high point in terms of heritability.

[28] Evidence that shared environment is of little consequence has been accumulating rapidly for over two decades. An important early work in this tradition is Plomin and Daniels (1987). Although tangential for present purposes, the virtual absence of an effect of shared environment is striking for students of personality. As Eysenck (1990) noted, these findings are rather difficult to reconcile with traditional views in psychology regarding the importance of upbringing.

[29] More recently, McCrae and Costa (2008) have updated their five-factor theory, in part refining their discussion of possible environmental influences on personality. Environmental factors can alter personality, McCrae and Costa now note, provided that those influences alter the biological bases of personality. Examples of such influences include psychiatric medications and the occurrence of traumatic brain injuries. This is a sensible caveat to advance, and one that does not undermine the fundamental claim regarding the biological bases of personality. What McCrae and Costa's theory does not acknowledge is that social processes (i.e., learning) influence personality. A second caveat to note regarding McCrae and Costa's thesis is that their five-factor theory does not yet identify the specific biological mechanisms (e.g., genes, brain structure, etc.) that shape personality.

position is extreme, their rationale warrants consideration. McCrae and Costa posit that measurement error in personality scales may inflate estimates of the impact of the unshared environment, and thus attenuate the observed effects of heritability. From this perspective, an observed heritability value of 0.50 would mark the lower bound, with the true value – unobservable absent perfect measures – potentially considerably higher. With focus on the Five-Factor Model, Riemann, Angleitner, and Strelau (1997) addressed this possibility by examining self-report and peer-report personality data from MZ and DZ twins. Consistent with prior research, heritability values between 0.42 and 0.56 were obtained with self-report data, but these marks rose to between 0.66 and 0.79 when measured more accurately through use of both self-report and peer-report indicators (see also Heath et al. 1992). These are quite high levels, particularly when we recall that attributes such as height have heritability estimates of approximately 0.80.

More recent evidence provides further support for the claim that the genetic contribution to variance in personality exceeds 0.50. First, with focus on the covariance structure underlying the Big Five, McCrae et al. (2001) seek to decompose variance attributed to the unshared environment into two subcomponents, the actual impact of the unshared environment and systematic error attributable to method bias. Following the logic of implicit personality theory (e.g., Borkenau 1992), method bias occurs when people's assumptions regarding trait covariance (e.g., that people who are extraverted also are agreeable) influence personality ratings. Upon conducting a multivariate analysis designed to parse out the impact of method bias, McCrae and colleagues demonstrate that evidence of a five-factor personality structure is not found in the true unshared environment component of their data, but rather only in the error component. Thus, apart from method bias, the only systematic correlate of the five-factor personality structure appears to be genetics. No effect of either shared environment or the true unshared environment is found.[30] Second, Yamagata et al. (2006) examine twins data from North America, Europe, and Asia to test whether there is a commonality of influence of genetics on personality across diverse geographic regions. Results are positive, supporting the conclusion that a universal genetic structure underlies the five-factor personality structure. It follows that personality traits

---

[30] This finding is especially interesting when viewed in conjunction with Turkheimer and Waldron's (2000) review, which highlights the general failure of research on the unshared environment to pinpoint specific environmental components that matter for behavior. If measurement error leads to underestimates of heritability, and if method bias leads to overestimation of the impact of the unshared environment, then it would make sense that actual effects of specific elements of the unshared environment would be rather difficult to identify.

are products of evolved human biology rather than specific acculturation and learning processes (McCrae and Costa 2008).[31]

McCrae and Costa's (2003) claims notwithstanding, I believe that none of this research should be taken to mean that variance in personality traces solely to genetics – or, at the very least, that we should be comfortable at this relatively early point in the history of this research in reaching such a conclusion. However, the evidence of a strong genetic component is vast, whereas the evidence of effects linked to either the shared or unshared environment is considerably thinner. The bottom line is that, across individuals, the bulk of variance in personality apparently is rooted in biology.[32]

If traits are strongly influenced by genes, it logically follows that traits should exhibit a great deal of stability over time.[33] Indeed, as was discussed in Chapter 1, stability of some meaningful degree constitutes a defining feature of traits. There would be little purpose in studying "traits" if the concepts of interest bounced around wildly over short spaces of time. As a general matter, the research finds that personality in adulthood, particularly after age thirty, exhibits little in the way of noteworthy change

---

[31] Gosling and colleagues (Gosling 2001; Gosling and John 1999; Gosling, Kwan, and John 2003) have provided a different take on the genetic bases of personality. In their research, they have demonstrated commonalities in personality across species, including evidence of traits resembling all of the Big Five dimensions except for conscientiousness.

[32] For a cautionary view of this conclusion, see Endler (1989). In my view, the critical point to keep in mind is that heritability values indicate only that there is a correspondence between variance in personality and variance in genes within a population, but not *why* this correspondence exists. Some analysts argue that twin studies support the inference that genes *determine* personality, but I believe a firm conclusion toward that end would outpace the evidence presently available. For discussion of future challenges for researchers in this area, see Bouchard and Loehlin (2001). Efforts to link particular genetic markers with specific traits will constitute an important step forward in this line of research, but not an easy step, as it now appears likely that different biological processes may operate on different personality traits and at different levels of the personality hierarchy (for a discussion, see Krueger and Johnson 2008). For a variety of approaches and perspectives in this area, see the chapters in Canli's edited collection (2006). For examples of alternate neurophysiological measures of correlates of the Big Five, see the Stough et al. (2001) analysis of photic driving and the Wright et al. (2006) investigation of personality traits and the cerebral cortex. For recent research linking physiological response to political attitudes, see Oxley et al. (2008).

[33] For various reasons, *complete* stability should not be expected. As McCrae and Costa (2003) note, genetic effects are inherently dynamic, with effects varying in form over the life cycle. Additionally, McCrae and Costa point out that biological changes experienced by the individual over time (e.g., brain atrophy) can alter personality irrespective of any tendency toward stability associated with genes.

(e.g., Caspi 2000). As Matthews and Deary conclude (1998, 54), "Large-scale reviews and large single sudies, therefore, offer overwhelming evidence for the stability of personality traits over many years."

In research on trait stability, personality measures are obtained from the same individuals at two different points in time, typically several years apart. Of these works, studies conducted by Costa and McCrae speak most directly to longitudinal stability as it pertains to the Big Five. With delays of six years between measures, Costa and McCrae (1988) report a stability level of 0.63 for agreeableness and marks averaging just over 0.80 for the other four Big Five traits (see also Costa et al. 2000). With corrections for reliability, these stability values reach as high as 0.95. Although Costa and McCrae are attentive to characteristic changes in personality over the life cycle,[34] "what is remarkable from a biological point of view is how stable personality traits are" (McCrae and Costa 2003, 200).[35]

Although a great deal of evidence supports the contention that personality traits exhibit noteworthy stability, some recent research has called renewed attention to modest changes in personality over the life cycle (e.g., Roberts, Walton, and Viechtbauer 2006a). This line of research establishes that virtually everyone exhibits a very similar pattern of apparent psychological change. In discussing such findings, Costa and McCrae (2006) note that, at first blush, the findings are consistent with two accounts: that everyone (including diverse peoples from the world's many nations and cultures) are exposed to common environmental stimuli, stimuli that induce changes in personality; or that everyone undergoes a common biologically influenced maturation process. Costa and McCrae

---

[34] As McCrae and Costa (2003) note, if everyone's traits changed at precisely the same rate over time, observed stability values would be 1.0; hence, high retest correlations alone should not be read as demonstrating that personality is set in stone after age 30. In what may be of little surprise to readers who have known teenagers, there is a general tendency for agreeableness and conscientiousness to increase and for neuroticism to decline as individuals move from adolescence to adulthood (Costa and McCrae 1994).

[35] Emphasis on biological foundations distinguishes Costa and McCrae's research from Goldberg's. In Goldberg's take on the Big Five, the lexical model refers to phenotypes, or observable outward characteristics (e.g., Saucier and Goldberg 1996). Although this view does not reject the possibility that genes affect personality, neither is that possibility central to the model's stated purpose of describing individual differences. In contrast, Costa and McCrae put claims of biological foundations of personality front and center in their work. My own view is between those of Goldberg and Costa and McCrae. As trait measures are used in this study's empirical tests, it is adequate to know that the five traits capture the bulk of variance in individual differences. However, the link to biology provides the foundation for the richer theory of political behavior I advocate.

argue that the available evidence is much more consistent with the latter account. They note, for instance that "anyone familiar with puppies and old dogs can understand how the human decline in Excitement Seeking might be biologically based" (Costa and McCrae 2006, 27). At the very least, we can conclude, first, that personality is highly stable, and second, that those changes that do occur do not necessarily reflect an impact of environment on personality, but instead more likely signal the occurrence of biological maturation processes.[36,37]

Collectively, the research reviewed in this section supports two important conclusions regarding the foundations of the Big Five traits. First, biology stands as the greatest source of variance in these traits. Strikingly, genetic differences appear to account for as much as 80 percent of variance in specific traits across individuals, and, conversely, the impact of shared environmental factors is negligible. As to the full five-factor trait structure, the evidence from McCrae et al. (2001) suggests that *only* genetic influences contribute to variance in that structure. Second, in adulthood, traits exhibit a high degree of stability. This point flows logically from the first, but this stability is noteworthy on its own because of what it implies regarding the existence of enduring differences in human behavior.

These conclusions bring important implications for the empirical analyses reported in the following chapters. First, if and when relationships

---

[36] For a rebuttal to this perspective, see Roberts, Walton, and Viechtbauer (2006b).

[37] Importantly, even if it were the case that personality changed to some modest degree in response to environmental influences or personal experiences, this would not pose a threat to the causal claims suggested in the analyses to be reported in later chapters. The Big Five trait dimensions capture fundamental psychological characteristics. Voting in an election or watching a few news stories on television simply are not events that, for most citizens, rise to the magnitude needed for us to even consider it plausible that those events would induce discernible changes in personality. If people's experiences do alter their personalities, those effects almost certainly would emanate from dramatic life-changing events such as surviving a life-threatening disease or seeing combat during military service, and not from occasional interactions with the political world such as posting a yard sign during an election campaign. For example, one empirical finding of a possible impact of environmental factors on personality is acknowledged by McCrae and Costa (2008) as a possible challenge to their postulate regarding the exclusively biological bases of personality. This study by McCrae et al. (1998) found evidence that exposure to an entirely new culture (exposure to Canadian culture by Chinese undergraduates) might bring influence on some aspects of personality, including openness. What is not clear is whether this cultural experience induced changes in actual personality or only changes in respondents' self-concepts. If actual personality changes did occur, it is important to keep in mind that a rather dramatic cultural experience was needed to produce those effects. Signing a petition or adhering a bumper sticker to one's car are not on par with moving from China to Canada in terms of their capacity to alter basic psychological dispositions.

between personality and political behavior are identified, we can be reasonably confident regarding the causal structure of these relationships. If the central underpinnings of personality traits are genetic, and if traits are highly stable in adulthood, then, for the vast majority of survey respondents and for the vast majority of dependent variables to be considered – variables such as presidential approval, participation in political discussion, opinionation, and so on – it would be nonsensical to suggest that cause and effect have been reversed. Although we should not rule out the possibility that people's political experiences can exert marginal influence on their personalities, it most often will be the case that any observed effects reflect the impact of personality on political attitudes and actions.

A second implication relates to recent advances in the study of politics and genetics (e.g., Alford, Funk, and Hibbing 2005; Carmen 2004; Eaves and Hatemi 2008; Fowler and Dawes 2008; Fowler, Baker, and Dawes 2008; Hatemi et al. 2007).[38] These works posit that genetics matters for politics, including for mass political attitudes and behavior. For instance, Alford and colleagues examined data on MZ and DZ twins in an effort to explore the possible impact of genes on political orientations. Strong effects of biology were found. Indeed, results pertinent to ideology resemble those for genes and the Big Five in that heritability levels of approximately 0.50 were identified, coupled with only weak evidence of effects of shared environment.

Research of the sort conducted by Alford and colleagues raises two immediate considerations, one substantive and one pragmatic. Substantively, it is not yet clear how and why genes influence citizens' political orientations. Work in this emerging field has demonstrated a correspondence between genetics and political attitudes, but little is known at this point regarding the processes underlying these connections. At this early point in the research, there remains a "black box" quality to studies of biology and politics because most scholars working in this area have not tested possible mechanisms linking genes to political behavior. Intuitively, it is not easy to imagine a direct path between genetics and many of the phenomena of interest to students of political behavior. To say the least, it would be rather difficult to conceive of there being genetic markers for presidential approval, participation in next Thursday's PTA meeting, or an opinion about same-sex marriage. Pragmatically, research on politics and genetics begs the question of what researchers who study political behavior are to do with knowledge of a relationship between genes and

---

[38] The works cited here are just a few of the studies in this area. These and other authors have numerous other working papers and forthcoming pieces on various issues in the study of politics and genetics.

political orientations. Is this "news we can use"? There are only so many twin studies – and twins, for that matter – available as data sources. If genes exert strong influence on political predispositions, what does this imply with respect to future directions in the field? Are traditional data sources obsolete? Will gains in our understanding of political behavior be limited by the availability of data on MZ and DZ twins? Should we seek DNA samples from future survey respondents?

Evidence regarding the heritability of the Big Five traits potentially provides leverage on these matters. First, in many instances it may be that the link between genetics and politics operates via personality traits, or via interactions between personality traits and environmental factors. Although there may not be a genetic marker for participation in Thursday's PTA meeting, it may be that genes directly influence extraversion, conscientiousness, and agreeableness, along with corresponding connections between these traits and the individual's likelihood of becoming an active participant in local politics. Indeed, researchers working in the area of biology and politics have highlighted the possible significance of personality. Alford, Funk, and Hibbing (2005, 157), for example, write that "the heritability of social attitudes is likely derivative of the heritability of various personality traits." Similarly, Fowler, Baker, and Dawes (2008, 244) emphasize that "an important area of research will study the extent to which the link between genes and participation can be explained by genetic variation in inherent personality traits." In the following chapters, a wide array of evidence will be presented regarding the political significance of the Big Five. It is my contention that, in addition to demonstrating that personality matters, this evidence also will suggest, albeit indirectly, the political importance of genetics.

Second, findings regarding personality do constitute news we can use. As is discussed in greater detail in the next chapter, I have added Big Five batteries to multiple public opinion surveys, including telephone surveys, face-to-face interviews, and paper-and-pencil instruments. In their most efficient form, these batteries are remarkably quick and easy to administer. It is, therefore, possible that personality will offer a highly fruitful means to incorporate lessons on politics and genetics into mainstream research on political behavior. Rather than measuring the survey respondent's genetic code, we can instead measure the respondent's genetically influenced, politically consequential personality traits.[39]

---

[39] The point, of course, is not that attention to biology and politics is unnecessary, because only with such research will we be able to pinpoint the precise effects of biological factors. Instead, the point is that attention to personality provides a means for mainstream research to attend in straightforward form to at least some of the enduring, biologically influenced forces operating on political behavior.

The theory of political behavior advanced here posits that citizens do not engage the political world as blank slates. Instead, politically meaningful differences exist long before political action takes place. Biological forces matter for political behavior, and biological influences also underlie stable psychological differences as represented by the Big Five trait structure. Connecting the dots, I argue that biological effects on politics very likely operate at least partly through personality. Although research on behavioral genetics regarding the impact of biology on human behavior is central to my thesis, I believe that, for political scientists, one of the most fruitful means to study innate, biologically influenced differences may well be via attention to personality.

Thus far, my discussion of the Big Five has considered the framework's central features and the possible biological and experiential bases of variance in these and other traits. However, little attention has been devoted until now toward the attributes of the framework's five core components. Review of both the theoretical foundation and the empirical correlates of each factor will provide necessary context for the exploration of links between the Big Five and mass political attitudes and actions.

## A CLOSER LOOK AT THE BIG FIVE

Past research on the Big Five trait dimensions establishes a solid basis to project relationships between these traits and many aspects of political behavior. To enable fuller appreciation of the characteristics and possible effects of these traits, several features of each trait must be considered. Specifically, for each of the Big Five factors, I will examine its history in research both within and beyond five-factor frameworks, how it has been conceptualized in leading five-factor models, and evidence regarding its impact on attitudes and behavior. In reviewing research regarding the impact of the Big Five, I will report a representative array of general findings for each trait, followed by a discussion of the results of more direct relevance for the study of political behavior.

In the following chapters, exploration of possible links between the Big Five and various facets of mass political behavior occurs in three parts, with one chapter devoted to political information, a second to political attitudes and predispositions, and a third to participation. In each chapter, investigations of two types will be conducted. First, direct links between the Big Five traits and several political variables will be examined. Second, the possible moderating influence of personality will be assessed via tests involving more complex specifications, including interactions between some of the Big Five factors and more familiar variables in research on mass politics. Many of the tests conducted in this study cover new ground, and thus we often have only the general characteristics of the Big Five factors to inform expectations. However, past research does suggest multiple effects of direct relevance to political behavior, and thus these findings warrant particular attention in the present review.

## Openness to Experience

Among the Big Five traits, the greatest disagreement in the literature surrounds openness to experience. Dispute persists on two critical matters: the substantive content of this trait, and whether openness to experience truly constitutes a trait in the conventional sense. Of these, the former issue has arisen largely as a consequence of the differences in the measurement strategies pursued by the leading proponents of five-factor structures, whereas the latter, in my view, reflects misunderstanding of the nature of the construct.

The label "openness to experience" comes from Costa and McCrae. In slight contrast, Goldberg defines this factor as "intellect." This difference in name hints at an underlying disparity in substantive content, and especially breadth. Recall that openness was included in Costa and McCrae's original three-factor model; when Goldberg introduced Costa and McCrae to five-factor frameworks, agreeableness and conscientiousness were the two new dimensions added to the existing three. Costa and McCrae's interpretation of openness to experience, therefore, predates the reemergence of lexicological five-factor models, and draws in part on the work of Milton Rokeach (1960) on dogmatism. McCrae and Costa (2003, 49–50) define openness as a broad, multifaceted dimension that includes not only intellect and perceptiveness, but also aesthetic sensitivity, an intrinsic attraction to new experiences, and so on. Goldberg's (e.g., Goldberg 1992) lexical conceptualization of intellect is somewhat narrower, with focus on traits such as "analytical," "curious," and "imaginative."

McCrae (1990) presents a thoughtful discussion of how this factor came to be conceptualized and operationalized with differing levels of breadth. In McCrae's view, to an extent far greater than with the other Big Five dimensions, accounts of openness to experience must confront the limits of language. Lexical approaches typically employ single-word adjectives, but no such terms exist for some facets of openness to experience. In describing the person low in openness to experience, for example, McCrae (1990, 123) uses phrases such as "insensitive to art and beauty" and "bored by ideas." Because such concepts defy capture by single adjectival markers, McCrae argues that a lexical measure necessarily will lead this dimension to be operationalized more narrowly than will a questionnaire that includes phrases, and even sentences, pertaining to the multiple aspects of openness.[40] Although openness to experience appears to be at least somewhat more expansive than intellect, the magnitude of this difference in breadth is difficult to pin down and its implications are debatable. Saucier (1992) contends that adjectival markers produce adequate representations of both intellect and openness to experience, leading him to caution against overstating the degree of dissimilarity between the two trait dimensions.

The second area of disagreement concerns whether openness to experience should be defined as a trait factor in the same sense as conscientiousness, extraversion, agreeableness, and emotional stability. Here, dispute has emerged largely due to a perceived parallel between "intellect" and "intelligence." Like many analysts, Eysenck (e.g., 1971) differentiated between personality and intelligence. Popular conceptions of personality and intelligence also portray the two as distinct. In my view, proponents of five-factor models retain this distinction. As McCrae and John (1990, 198) note, neither of the two leading approaches to the Big Five equates the trait dimension of openness to experience or intellect with measured intelligence. Tendencies toward creativity and curiosity, and to welcome new experiences, may be weakly correlated with intelligence,[41] but it hardly follows that intelligence and openness to experience are one and the same, or that openness to experience is not a measurable trait factor.

Although five-factor frameworks have received wide discussion, a large portion of the literature examines issues of measurement, replicability, and validity, and only in recent years have applied efforts regarding possible effects of the Big Five become commonplace. Employers often administer personality inventories to prospective employees, and thus a great deal of early research on correlates of the Big Five concerned work activity. Hence, in reviewing research on possible consequences of variance in these trait dimensions, particular attention will be devoted to evidence from the workplace.

---

[40] In my view, McCrae makes a strong case regarding both the relative breadth of openness to experience and the limits of the lexical approach in this case. As will been seen in the next chapter, this study's empirical indicators are derived from bipolar adjective scales. A general limitation of my approach is that the Big Five traits are measured somewhat coarsely because I use data from as few as ten items, versus the hundreds of items often available in full-scale personality inventories. A more specific consequence for openness to experience is that this factor is measured more narrowly than ideally would be the case. When effects of openness to experience are reported in later chapters, the obvious questions that arise – questions deserving of further inquiry – are whether these effects trace to particular facets of openness to experience, and whether stronger or weaker relationships would be observed with richer, more nuanced trait measures.

[41] For a recent empirical study on this point, see Moutafi, Furnham, and Crump (2006).

Openness to experience has been found to be related to a host of work-related phenomena, including creative behavior in the workplace (George and Zhou 2001), decreased loyalty to the organization (Moss et al. 2007), turnover (Timmerman 2006), earnings (Mueller and Plug 2006), and successful adjustment to international work assignments (Huang, Chi, and Lawler 2005). Outside of the work arena, openness to experience has been linked to substance risk-taking, operationalized as drinking alcohol, drinking and driving, and tobacco use (Booth-Kewley and Vickers 1994), but also to a decreased tendency toward risky driving (Dahlen and White 2006), and, leaving no stone unturned, toward greater consumption of fruit and vegetables on the part of Dutch teenagers (de Bruijn et al. 2005). In one of the few direct applications of the Big Five in research of relevance for elite politics, Kowert and Hermann (1997) found a link between openness to experience and risk taking in foreign policy decision making in a test involving 126 undergraduate students (see also Satterfield 1998).

Several studies speak to the potential significance of openness to experience for political information. People high in openness to experience especially crave experiences that will be cognitively engaging. As a result, these individuals willingly seek information of virtually all sorts. As examples, openness to experience predicts both incidental information exposure and the expenditure of effort in information seeking (Heinstrom 2003), exposure to literature (except romance novels), exposure to culture, the viewing of informative television programs (Kraaykamp and van Eijck 2005), and the tendency to search online for health information (Flynn, Smith, and Freese 2006). These findings support the expectation that openness to experience will be related to an array of political information variables such as levels of political knowledge, opinionation, attentiveness to news about politics, and participation in political discussion.[42] Looking to participation more broadly, the inherent willingness of those high in openness to experience to try new activities should correspond with favorable views toward political engagement. Consistent with this, Bekkers' (2005) analysis of data from the Family Survey of the Dutch Population reveals modest positive relationships between openness to

---

[42] The general tendency of individuals high in openness to experience to welcome new information potentially brings an important methodological implication for social scientists, and especially survey researchers. Marcus and Schutz (2005) find that openness to experience corresponds with low levels of nonresponse, suggesting that nonresponse may yield bias in terms of levels of openness to experience – and, by implication, in terms of the many political attitudes and predispositions that may be influenced by this trait. A related matter is that personality as represented by the Big Five has been shown to influence one response tendency on politics surveys, extreme response style (Hibbing et al. 2009).

experience and membership in voluntary associations, and a similar link with respondents' levels of activity within those associations. Likewise, Lounsbury, Loveland, and Gibson (2003) report significant correlations between openness to experience and psychological sense of community. Mak and Tran (2001) note a correlation between openness to experience and social self-efficacy, a finding which may portend effects for internal and external political efficacy.

I also hypothesize strong effects of openness to experience on political attitudes and predispositions. Openness to experience encompasses a willingness to seek new paths, and a corresponding weak attachment to familiar ways. People high in openness do not impose rigid restrictions on their own thoughts or behaviors, or those of others. Given a choice, the person who is open to experience would opt for "anything goes" rather than "my way or the highway."

Although additional effects on political behavior are easily contemplated, two relationships warrant emphasis. First, openness to experience is expected to predict traditional ideological liberalism. The small-c conservative prefers slow, cautious action, and maintains an affinity for the status quo. These inclinations run oppose those of the person high in openness to experience. Several studies have reported evidence consistent with this hypothesis, with individuals scoring low in openness to experience tending to express political conservatism. McCrae (1996, 325), directly addressing the potential value to social scientists, and especially political scientists, of incorporating measures of openness to experience in their research, writes "there are recognizable patterns that endure beneath shifting political fashions, and the most conspicuous of these is the distinction between liberalism and conservatism. The basis of these two perspectives is ultimately not political, sociological or economic, but psychological." Empirical links between openness to experience and political liberalism have been reported by Alford and Hibbing (2007) with data from the United States, Riemann et al. (1993) and Schoen and Schumann (2007) with data from Germany, and van Hiel, Kossowska, and Mervielde (2000) with data from Belgium and Poland.[43] All data in the present study were gathered from U.S. samples. Therefore, it is expected that openness to experience will correspond with self-reported political liberalism and possibly with affinity for the Democratic party.

---

[43] Jost's research on system justification provides indirect corroboration of this effect in that political conservatism is a component of system justification, and low openness corresponds with system justification. See Jost and Hunyady (2005) for a summary. More recently, Jost and colleagues have published several papers discussing ideology, and especially links between ideology and personality. For example, see Carney et al. (2008), Jost et al. (2003), Jost, Nosek, and Gosling (2008), and Jost, Federico, and Napier (2009).

In a recent study that marks a rare direct application of the Big Five to the study of mass politics, Barbaranelli et al. (2007) report evidence consistent with this latter expectation. Data were obtained from over 6,000 respondents on a nonrandom internet survey. Results reveal a strong relationship between openness to experience and support for Democratic nominee John Kerry in the 2004 U.S. presidential election.

Recall from Chapter 1 that measures of authoritarianism have been criticized on the grounds that they lead to analyses that are tautological. Charney (2008a) advances a similar concern about indicators of openness to experience. Specifically, in a recent critique of the Alford, Funk, and Hibbing (2005) research on politics and genetics, Charney pauses to comment on works linking personality and ideology. (For further dialogue on the critique itself, see Alford et al. 2008; Hannagan and Hatemi 2008; and Charney 2008b). Charney is disturbed by reports of a correlation between openness and ideological liberalism. Charney's concern is with the possibility that some measures of openness explicitly include indicators of political liberalism, thereby establishing by construction a correlation between openness and ideology. Specifically, Charney contends that (2008a, 315) "in a wholly circular fashion, openness is correlated with liberalism *by definition*" (emphasis in original). Charney certainly is correct that circularity is introduced when one uses a variant of the dependent variable to measure the independent variable. Whether Charney is right, as an empirical matter, in his assertion that the observed correspondence between openness and liberalism is "wholly circular" is unclear, because Charney presents no evidence to support his claim. One could, for instance, identify a correlation between openness and ideology using an openness scale that includes liberalism as one of its subcomponents, and then reexamine that relationship with a revised version of the openness scale that omits liberalism. If the correlation were to vanish in the second test, that would be evidence consistent with Charney's assertion. Ideally, Charney either would have offered such evidence or would have deferred from making such a definitive pronouncement. This matter will receive further attention in Chapter 5. For now, it is sufficient to note that the measures of openness I develop in the next chapter do not include political indicators, a strategy that renders Charney's complaint moot, at least for the present study.

The second area in which relationships are expected between openness to experience and political attitudes harkens back to the research of Rokeach. Again, openness to experience partly represents the inverse of dogmatism. People high in openness to experience are not rigid in their own views nor in the expectations they hold for others. Consistent with this depiction, negative correlations have been observed between openness to experience and multiple aspects of prejudice and intolerance. In one recent study with data from the United States and Russia, low openness to experience in both nations corresponded with stigmatizing attitudes toward HIV/AIDS (McCrae et al. 2007). Similarly, other research has identified negative relationships between openness to experience and racial prejudice (Duriez and Soenens 2006; Flynn 2005) and white racial identity (Silvestri and Richardson 2001), authoritarianism (Stenner 2005) and right-wing authoritarianism (Butler 2000; Sibley and Duckitt 2008), political intolerance (Marcus et al. 1995), and homophobia (Cullen, Wright, and Alessandri 2002).

### Conscientiousness

Apart from Eysenck (1991), who viewed conscientiousness as being a component of the newest dimension of his three-factor framework, psychoticism, little disagreement has existed regarding the claim that this dimension holds a rightful place among the Big Five. Further, although early works introduced several alternate labels,[44] the term "conscientiousness" now receives near-universal usage among five-factor practitioners. As with openness to experience, one point that has not been fully settled regards the breadth of this trait dimension. Considerable agreement exists that conscientiousness includes a basic dispositional sense of dependability, with adjectival terms such as "organized," "reliable," and "punctual" employed to capture this meaning. Viewed more broadly, most analysts now concur that conscientiousness also includes a volitional component represented by terms such as "hardworking," "industrious," and "persevering." Additionally, conscientiousness can be defined partly in terms of other narrower traits such as self-control. Roberts et al. (2005) conducted a thorough analysis of conscientiousness, and reported a hierarchical structure with six subsidiary factors: industriousness, order, responsibility, self-control, traditionalism, and virtue. In the next chapter, conscientiousness is operationalized primarily in terms of the first three of these subsidiary factors.

Unsurprisingly, strong links exist between conscientiousness and job performance. It would be rather odd, after all, for workers who are not dependable, punctual, and hardworking to be named "Employee of the Month" with any great regularity.[45] In part, the positive impact

---

[44] These alternates include "prudence" (Hogan, Hogan, and Gregory 1992), "control" (Tellegen 1991), "will" (Digman 1989), and "work" (Peabody and Goldberg 1989).

[45] Early reviews on this subject include Barrick and Mount (1991) and Tett, Jackson, and Rothstein (1991). For a more recent work examining the link between job performance and particular facets of conscientiousness, see Dudley et al. (2006).

of conscientiousness on work performance may reflect the impact of honesty and integrity. In an interesting laboratory study, Horn, Nelson, and Brannick (2004) show a strong correspondence between conscientiousness and honest behavior, whereas Ones, Viswesvaran, and Schmidt (1993) find that integrity is linked positively with job performance and negatively with undesirable work behaviors such as absenteeism and employee theft.

Conscientiousness exerts numerous additional effects beyond those identified in the workplace. One finding closely related to evidence regarding job performance is that conscientiousness predicts high levels of academic achievement (Wagerman and Funder 2007). Other research specifies links between conscientiousness and a healthy lifestyle (Booth-Kewley and Vickers 1994), including physical fitness (Hogan 1989) and physical activity (Rhodes and Smith 2006), mammography use (Schwartz et al. 1999), lower levels of alcohol consumption (Hopwood et al. 2007), lower rates of involvement in automobile accidents (Arthur and Graziano 1996), and greater life expectancy (Friedman et al. 1993). These findings suggest that conscientious individuals tend to be risk averse, a conclusion supported in the political arena by Kowert and Hermann's (1997) study of foreign policy decision making, where a correspondence between conscientiousness and risk avoidance was found among the undergraduate participants. Other research relates conscientiousness to positive experiences, such as high-quality friendships in adolescence (Jensen-Campbell and Malcolm 2007), decreased anger (Jensen-Campbell et al. 2007), and marital stability (Tucker et al. 1998).

Few connections between conscientiousness and media consumption were identified in the Kraaykamp and van Eijck (2005) study, except for preference for literature. Individuals with high levels of conscientiousness were found to be relatively unlikely to read literary and suspense novels, tending instead to gravitate toward romance novels. No effects for media variables more directly related to political behavior were identified.

Concerning political attitudes, predictions for conscientiousness are roughly the inverse of those for openness to experience. People high in conscientiousness value personal responsibility, tradition, and virtue. Thus, conscientiousness should be related to ideological conservatism, again in the small-c sense of that term, where conservatism implies a preference for caution in policymaking and a presumption in favor of the status quo. The emphasis on traditionalism also suggests that conscientiousness may be related to attitudes encompassed by social conservatism, such as a pro-life view on abortion and support for moral traditionalism.

For the most part, past research has not explored these hypotheses, although three modest relationships between conscientiousness and political predispositions have been reported. In Riemann et al.'s (1993) German study, conscientiousness corresponded with both general ideological conservatism and two of three specific dimensions considered by the authors, although all of these effects slipped to statistical insignificance in multivariate specifications that included demographics and indicators of all of the Big Five factors. Stenner (2005) also reported a link between conscientiousness and ideological conservatism. Second, Barbaranelli et al.'s (2007) research on voting intentions in the 2004 U.S. presidential election detected a link between conscientiousness and support for Bush over Kerry, but the substantive effect was the weakest among the Big Five traits, and the authors' model included no control variables other than age and sex. Lastly, Schoen (2007) found that German respondents scoring high in conscientiousness tended to express foreign policy attitudes averse to international cooperation and supportive of the use of military force.

Given the strong record of conscientiousness as a predictor of job performance, one intriguing area of present interest concerns how people fare in the "job" of citizenship. It seems conceivable that individuals with high levels of conscientiousness would dutifully vote in elections, participate in local politics, and endeavor to keep themselves well informed about political affairs. However, it is important to emphasize that people who are high in conscientiousness are conscientious in execution of their *duties*, such as in school and at work. It does not necessarily follow that these individuals will be conscientious in all aspects of life. After all, diligence brings an opportunity cost. For instance, the conscientious employee, spouse, or parent might struggle to find the time to be a faithful soap opera aficionado. If people who are high in conscientiousness see political engagement as more akin to an extracurricular activity than a central duty, then conscientiousness would not be positively related to participation.[46] Thus far, I know of very little research on the Big Five examining these possible effects. One exception, Bekkers' (2005) research on civic engagement, yielded modest but consistent *negative* relationships between conscientiousness and membership in nonpolitical and quasipolitical voluntary associations, and levels of involvement in those associations. Lastly, conscientiousness was found to be strongly related to a psychological sense of community in the Lounsbury, Loveland, and Gibson (2003) study.

### Extraversion

Extraversion enjoys the longest and most distinguished scholarly history of the Big Five dimensions. As we have seen, Eysenck (1947) included

[46] My thanks to Jim Kuklinski for suggesting this point.

extraversion as part of his original two-factor model. Extraversion also appears to be the broader trait dimension encompassing several of Cattell's (1956) sixteen factors, and it is labeled as such in current commercial depictions of Cattell's 16PF (Institute for Personality and Ability Testing, 2007). Prior to either of these authors, of course, Carl Jung (1917, 1923) invoked the concepts of introversion and extraversion when he classified people based on whether they direct their psychic energy outward toward the world or inward toward their own internal processes and psyches. Jung's specific views are of only indirect relevance for contemporary research on trait structure, but his basic classification provided a foundation for future attention to extraversion. Today, no meaningful controversy exists regarding whether extraversion deserves a preeminent place in research on the psychology of individual differences.

As with the other traits, mild disagreements have occurred over labeling and content. Not surprisingly, these differences were more commonplace when work on the Big Five was in a fledgling state. For instance, Goldberg (1990) initially advocated use of the label "surgency" rather than "extraversion." Also, McCrae and John (1992, 195) noted that a level of dispute existed regarding the precise dimensional space occupied by this factor. Today, adjectives typically employed to represent extraversion include words such as "energetic," "bold," "talkative," and "outgoing."

Effects of extraversion in the workplace include greater levels of organizational commitment (Erdheim, Wang, and Zickar 2006), being a workaholic (Burke, Matthiesen and Pallesen 2006), and successful adjustment to overseas job assignments (Huang, Chi and Lawler 2005). Conte and Gintoft (2005) report an intuitively satisfying finding in that extraversion brings particular advantages to people employed in sales, with sales staff who score high in extraversion faring well in ratings of customer service and overall job performance. The inherent sociability of extraverted employees also manifests itself in career-advancing networking behaviors (Forret and Dougherty 2001). In addition to these various effects in the workplace, extraversion also corresponds with students' confidence in their academic abilities, bringing an indirect influence on academic success (Pulford and Sohal 2006).

Other effects of extraversion identified in the literature speak to the varied significance of this factor. Associations have been found between extraversion and risk taking among boys (Markey et al. 2006), and smoking outside of the United States and Canada (Malouff, Thorsteinsson, and Schutte 2006), but also to physical activity (Rhodes and Smith 2006) and longevity (Martin, da Rosa, and Siegler 2006; Masui et al. 2006). Extraverted children show an increased likelihood of taking up chess (Bilalic, McLeod Gobet 2007), but despite this, middle-school children with high levels of extraversion fare well in peer acceptance and in the development of friendships (Jensen-Campbell et al. 2002). Clark et al. (2007) link extraversion to effects in the criminal justice system. The Big Five traits were not factors in jury selection in the Clark et al. study, but jurors with high levels of extraversion were more likely to serve as forepersons, and juror extraversion corresponded with verdicts favoring defendants. Research involving applications of the Big Five does, of course, sometimes generate null results. As one example, although optimists may wear rose-colored glasses, extraverts apparently do not – Eperjesi (2007) found no relationship between extraversion and the wearing of eyeglasses with tinted lenses.

Many aspects of political behavior include social components. Working on a petition drive or a political campaign, attending PTA meetings, discussing politics with friends and neighbors, and joining voluntary associations all entail social interaction. Extraversion logically should be a critical determinant of these behaviors, particularly given its positive relationship with a persons's psychological sense of community (Lounsbury, Loveland, and Gibson 2003). Further, the fact that social interaction may include a political component potentially motivates the extravert to be attentive to political information. Unfortunately, with the exception of Bekkers' (2005) study of participation in voluntary associations, these relationships have not been tested. Bekkers found, as expected, that extraverts join and become actively involved in associations at greater rates than do introverts, lending confidence that additional effects would be identified if the extraversion-participation link were explored more fully.

Although relationships between extraversion and political participation seem highly plausible, it is more difficult to hypothesize intuitively satisfying effects of extraversion on political attitudes and predispositions. Democrats and Republicans both can be introverts. Conservatives and liberals both can be extroverts. Likewise, extraversion bears no obvious relationship to most policy attitudes. Consistent with this view, no clear pattern emerged for extraversion in Riemann et al.'s (1993) study of personality and ideology. Most of the coefficients for extraversion were statistically insignificant, and signs on the coefficients were nearly evenly divided between positive and negative. Barbaranelli et al. (2007) reported a moderate relationship between extraversion[47] and support for George Bush in the 2004 presidential election, but little rationale was offered to account for this effect. Marcus et al. (1995) identified a correlation between extraversion and political tolerance, but the effect dissipated in the authors' full multivariate model.

---

[47] The label "energy" was used by the authors.

## Personality and the Foundations of Political Behavior

One direct application of the Big Five to the study of mass politics warrants particular mention for its findings regarding extraversion. Barbaranelli and Caprara (Caprara, Barbaranelli, and Zimbardo 1999, 2002; Caprara et al. 2003, 2006), who, with their coauthors, have been leading figures in introducing five-factor approaches to research on politics, examined data from Big Five measures included on mass and elite surveys in Italy. These data were used to explore the interplay between the personalities of elected officials and public perceptions of those same leaders. Analyses reveal that there is a convergence in the personality attributes of mass and elite adherents to the same political parties. However, the Big Five factors do not contribute equally to mass assessments of political leaders. Instead, perceptions of leaders are dominated by two of the Big Five, extraversion, and the next factor to be reviewed here, agreeableness.

### Agreeableness

Because agreeableness rose to prominence among students of individual differences only with the emergence of five-factor approaches, the empirical record regarding correlates of agreeableness remains somewhat thin. Nonetheless, a review of extant research coupled with a look at this factor's components provide an adequate basis for the formulation of expectations regarding how agreeableness may influence mass political behavior.

Graziano and Tobin (2002) contend that agreeableness may be the least understood dimension of the Big Five. What is clear is that agreeableness involves interpersonal relations, especially the individual's level of desire for positive relations with others. Virtually all scales used to represent agreeableness employ terms such as "warm," "kind," and "sympathetic." Adding breadth, words including "generous" and "altruistic" often are used as well. Collectively, these adjectives define a positive, caring, and compassionate individual. In some depictions of agreeableness, this factor also includes an element of submissiveness or docility,[48] represented by terms such as "trusting," "compliant," and "cooperative." The scales developed in the next chapter operationalize agreeableness primarily in terms of the first of these more specific dimensions, warmth.

Perhaps more so than with the other Big Five traits, data on agreeableness seem likely to be jeopardized by social desirability effects (Paulhus, Bruce, and Trapnell 1995). After all, most people presumably prefer not to think of themselves as being cold, unkind, and uncooperative, and

---

[48] See Digman (1990, 422–4) for a discussion of this aspect of agreeableness, along with an assessment of early disagreement regarding possible labels for this factor.

certainly survey respondents might be reluctant to define themselves in such terms to an interviewer. This matter, which I address more fully in the next chapter, has not escaped the attention of researchers in psychology. From the time of Allport and Odbert (1936), analysts have recognized that social desirability effects potentially complicate the measurement of traits (e.g., Hofstee 1990). Graziano and Tobin (2002) conducted a systematic three-part assessment of the implications of such effects for the measurement of agreeableness. Fortunately, their results demonstrate that there is little cause for concern

Outcomes of these three studies suggest that if Agreeableness is contaminated by self-favoring biases, the contamination is limited in scope [and] relatively small... [T]he overall pattern of evidence suggests that relations with various forms of self-favoring biases do not threaten the interpretation of Agreeableness as a substantive personality dimension related to the motivation to maintain positive relations with others. (Graziano and Tobin 2002, 723)

Research in the workplace reveals that agreeableness produces a limited but interesting array of effects. Not surprisingly, employees with high levels of agreeableness fare well when participating in group activities at work (Barrick and Mount 1991), and Huang, Chi, and Lawler (2005) find that agreeableness also predicts a worker's successful adaptation to an international job assignment. More generally, agreeableness corresponds with career stability (Laursen, Pulkkinen, and Adams 2002). At the top of the corporate ladder, however, disagreeableness reigns; Matthews and Oddy (1993) report that CEOs tend to score quite low on agreeableness.

Among children and adolescents, Jensen-Campbell et al. (2002) contend that agreeableness stands as the most important predictor of avoidance of peer victimization. Students with high levels of agreeableness also tend to be top achievers academically (Chowdhury and Amin 2006; Laursen, Pulkkinen, and Adams 2002), and they are relatively unlikely to engage in risky behaviors (Markey et al. 2006) or to pose behavioral problems (Laursen, Pulkkinen, and Adams 2002). Agreeableness among adults is associated with nonsmoking (Malouff, Thorsteinsson, and Schutte 2006), and lower rates of alcoholism, depression, and arrest (Laursen, Pulkkinen, and Adams 2002).

Because agreeableness primarily concerns interpersonal relationships, some of the most plausible political effects of agreeableness involve social or group aspects of political behavior. For instance, relationships between agreeableness and indicators of interpersonal and political trust can be expected. People high in agreeableness seek to maintain positive relationships with others, a goal that would be compromised if trust were lacking. Influences of agreeableness on social behavior also may be found.

Lounsbury, Loveland, and Gibson (2003) show agreeableness to be related to psychological sense of community. Carlo et al. (2005) report strong correlations between agreeableness and both pro-social behavior and volunteer work, although Bekkers (2005) found no consistent link between agreeableness and involvement in voluntary associations. Agreeableness also appears to matter for individuals' perceptions of others. Duriez and Soenens (2006) report an inverse relationship between agreeableness and racial prejudice. Similarly, Strauss, Connerley, and Ammermann (2003) identify a strong positive influence of agreeableness on attitudes toward diversity, Silvestri and Richardson (2001) establish a strong negative relationship between agreeableness and white racial identity, and McCrae et al. (2007) find negative effects of agreeableness on HIV/AIDS stigmatization in both the United States and Russia.

Beyond attitudes related to prejudice, the possible influence of agreeableness on political attitudes has not been well explored. As noted above, research by Caprara, Barbaranelli, and Zimbardo (2002) highlighted the importance of extraversion and agreeableness for voters' assessments of political candidates. To the extent that agreeableness represents caring and generosity, links between this trait dimension and support for social welfare policies (and parties and candidates advocating those policies) warrant consideration. However, past research paints a mixed picture. Riemann et al.'s (2003) German study found no consistent relationship between agreeableness and political ideology, whereas in the United States the positive effect of agreeableness on support for John Kerry in the 2004 presidential race was the strongest influence of personality identified by Barbaranelli et al. (2007). Research on one specific attitude, opinion regarding capital punishment, finds an inverse relationship between agreeableness and support for the death penalty (Robbers 2006). Schoen (2007) reports that Germans scoring high in agreeableness voice relatively high levels of support for international cooperation.

Past research on agreeableness supports speculation regarding the possibility of two further effects relevant for the study of political behavior. First, agreeableness corresponds with a tendency to provide more positive, or lenient, peer ratings on Big Five measures (Bernardin, Cooke, and Villanova 2000). In other words, people high in agreeableness go easy when providing evaluations of others. This pattern makes good sense, as individuals high in agreeableness may see the offering of positive assessments of others as a means to foster good social relationships. If this tendency carries over to the political arena via a more general positivity bias, then effects such as elevated levels of presidential approval and policy support might be observed. Second, agreeableness shapes how individuals respond to conflict (e.g., Graziano, Jensen-Campbell, and Hair 1996; Park and Antonioni 2007; Suls, Martin, and David 1998). Park and Antonioni (2007) find, for instance, that strategies for addressing interpersonal conflict vary sharply with agreeableness, with individuals scoring high on this trait dimension gravitating toward collaboration and accommodation, and away from competition, in response to conflict. Competition and conflict are integral features of politics. It follows that the distaste many Americans exhibit toward competitive democratic processes (Hibbing and Theiss-Morse 1995, 2002) may be exacerbated by agreeableness. Taken to its logical end, agreeableness may be depoliticizing, and thus agreeableness and overall levels of engagement with public affairs may be inversely related. A related, more specific expectation is that agreeableness will correspond with a tendency toward avoidance of political conflict in social relationships.

### Emotional Stability

Emotional stability, like extraversion, has been the subject of scholarly attention for many decades. In a precursor to Tupes and Christal's research on the effectiveness of Air Force officers, Robert Woodworth (1919) developed his Personal Data Sheet during World War I as a means to identify military recruits who were likely to break down in combat. It asked questions such as "Do you feel like jumping off when you are in high places?" Although hardly a paragon of subtlety, Woodworth's measure proved to be highly predictive, and his research paved the way for a great deal of subsequent inquiry. Subsidiary traits related to emotional stability are included on Cattell's 16PF and, as we have seen, emotional stability and extraversion were the two original factors in the Eysenck framework.

The labels "anxiety" and especially "neuroticism," the word used by Eysenck, appear more often in the literature than does "emotional stability," although the latter terminology is most common in lexical applications of the Big Five. Examples of adjectives used to represent emotional stability in lexical batteries include "calm," "relaxed," and "stable," whereas words such as "tense," "nervous," and "emotional" reflect low levels of emotional stability, or high levels of neuroticism. Some representations of emotional stability include impulse control as a subsidiary component, and thus incorporate data on terms such as "impulsive" in the final trait scale. Overall, though, little disagreement exists regarding either the importance of emotional stability as a component in comprehensive trait taxonomies or in its core substantive content (McCrae and John 1992).

Emotional stability differs from the other Big Five traits in that the bulk of research on its correlates focuses not on job performance, but rather on medical implications, particularly personality disorders. Individuals with low levels of emotional stability feel high levels of tension and stress; they are prone to depression and often worry and complain about various physical ailments (e.g., Bolger and Schilling 1991; Friedman and Booth-Kewley 1987; Schroeder, Wormworth, and Livesley 1992; Wiggins and Pincus 1989; for a review and discussion, see Matthews and Deary 1998, chap. 8).[49] Emotional stability also has more specific health and quality-of-life correlates. For instance, high levels of emotional stability correspond with participation in exercise behavior (Courneya and Hellsten 1998), with satisfaction with close interpersonal relationships and avoidance of marital problems (O'Leary and Smith 1991; White, Hendrick, and Hendrick 2004), and with positive affect and subjective well-being (Costa and McCrae 1980; David et al. 1997; McNiel and Fleeson 2006). On a less positive note, emotional stability predicts an array of risk behaviors, especially in combination with high levels of extraversion and with low levels of conscientiousness and agreeableness (Nicholson 2005).

As with research on the other Big Five trait factors, emotional stability has been employed in efforts to account for an almost curiously wide variety of phenomena. For instance, McCulloch et al. (2005) tested for personality differences between surgeons and other physicians, and found that surgeons exhibit greater emotional stability than do consulting physicians.[50] In addition to becoming surgeons, emotionally stable persons also answer other calls. Compared with the general population, for example, Francis and Kay (1995) found especially high levels of emotional stability among Pentecostal ministry candidates. Lastly, Arias and Spinka (2005) examined Big Five data collected from individuals working on Czech dairy farms. Although workers' attitudes toward cows did not affect farm performance, farms with the greatest proportions of workers scoring low in emotional stability suffered low milk yields and high veterinary costs.[51]

---

[49] As Matthews and Deary (1998) note, it is not entirely clear at first glance whether neuroticism causes medical and personality disorders or is symptomatic of the presence of such disorders. However, Matthews and Deary's review of longitudinal studies (e.g., Ormel and Wohlfarth 1991) leads them to conclude that neuroticism is best viewed as a cause, not merely a symptom, of stress.

[50] Readers who themselves may be high in neuroticism are advised to forget this finding before scheduling their next physical examinations.

[51] If we allow for the possibility that personality varies in response to environmental factors, then reverse causality cannot be ruled out in this instance, as it is possible that a preponderance of underperforming cows leads workers on Czech dairy farms to express agitation and worry. Also, data were not obtained regarding possible variance in the neuroticism of the cows, who surely must be counted among the key actors in any model of dairy productivity. For research on the temperament of dairy cows, see Dickson et al. (1970).

Many of the correlates of emotional stability of most direct relevance to political behavior concern social activity. Past research paints a somewhat mixed picture, but overall, it appears that emotional stability facilitates social and collective action. Lounsbury, Loveland, and Gibson (2003) report a positive relationship between emotional stability and psychological sense of community; Caspi et al. (2006) report a similar relationship with participation in social learning environments; and Thoms, Moore, and Scott (1996) identify a positive effect of emotional stability on self-efficacy in self-managed work groups. However, Parkes and Razavi (2004) find a negative relationship between emotional stability and voluntary union membership, particularly for workers who also have low levels of extraversion.

Few studies have explored possible relationships between emotional stability and political predispositions and attitudes. Riemann et al. (1993) and Barbaranelli et al. (2007) report modest effects of emotional stability on, respectively, ideological conservatism and support for George W. Bush in the 2004 U.S. presidential election. Francis (1997) finds an inverse relationship between emotional stability and dogmatism among English teenagers. Support for the death penalty is highest among individuals with low levels of emotional stability (Robbers 2006).

One intriguing avenue for research on emotional stability concerns the structure rather than the substantive content of political attitudes. By definition, emotionally stable individuals exhibit *stability*. It follows, Robinson and Tamir (2005) suggest, that levels of emotional stability may be associated with variability in basic cognitive operations. Robinson and Tamir test this thesis using response time measures. Emotional stability is not found to be related to mean response time. However, standard deviations in participants' response times varied as a function of emotional stability, with individuals low in emotional stability producing the most disparate response times. Applied to the political arena, it is conceivable that attention to this trait dimension could help generate new insight on prominent topics of interest to students of political behavior, topics such as the causes and significance of variance in ideological constraint and other facets of temporal attitudinal consistency.

Past research on emotional stability and the other Big Five factors has established a multitude of links between personality, attitudes, and behavior. To date, however, relatively little of this research has pursued applications of five-factor approaches in the study of mass politics. This review has sought to demonstrate that this relative dearth of political applications does not mean that the Big Five are irrelevant for students of politics. To the contrary, a great variety of relationships between the Big Five and mass political attitudes and behavior warrant scrutiny. Many such effects are explored in the chapters that follow.

## CONCLUSIONS

Research on personality and mass politics can experience resurgence through application of a viable, multifaceted framework. Toward this end, in this chapter I have outlined the Big Five perspective. Review of research on the Big Five reveals the model's numerous desirable features. The Big Five factors have undergone two decades of exhaustive scrutiny. Much is known regarding effective measurement of the Big Five. Further, the substantive properties of the five factors are well understood, providing a strong basis for the generation of hypotheses regarding the political significance of individual differences. The biological foundation of traits means that research on the Big Five can lead to indirect evidence regarding the importance of genetics for mass politics, with genetics and personality perhaps combining to form a holistic account of innate differences in political behavior. Viewed in total, the story of the Big Five is such that students of political behavior currently sit in an unprecedented position in terms of the capacity to improve our understanding of the psychological underpinnings of mass political attitudes and actions.

Research in psychology on the Big Five clearly has advanced to the point that applied inquiry can be expected to be highly fruitful. That said, it is important to keep in mind that work in psychology continues to produce relevant developments. Although a strong degree of consensus has emerged in support of five-factor approaches, new insights and refinements are reported regularly. Further, it is conceivable that the Big Five will someday fall out of fashion, to be replaced by an alternate framework. These considerations should not be seen as obstacles to applied research on personality and politics. If students of political behavior elect to wait until psychology is "done," possible advancements in our understanding of the influence of traits on politics would be put on indefinite, and probably permanent, hold. The more prudent approach entails that we forge ahead with substantive research, but that we do so while attending to ongoing theoretical developments. My contention is that, first, as a general matter, there is much to be gained through application of a broad trait approach in the study of mass politics, and second, that the Big Five is one such framework, and in my judgment the most useful one presently available. Introduction of the Big Five in the current study constitutes a starting point. Refinements in psychology are to be welcomed, as they will only lead to further substantive advancements down the road. That said, it is hardly the case that I am advocating speculation in a stock with no track record. With two full decades of remarkably productive research behind it, the Big Five approach has been examined quite thoroughly. The accumulated scholarship provides an excellent foundation for applications in the study of political behavior.

Thus far, the Big Five traits have been discussed only on a conceptual level. In subsequent chapters, these traits will be put to work as predictors of political attitudes and behavior. First, however, the empirical properties of the Big Five require attention. Trait measures employed in this study are derived from personality batteries included on several surveys. In the next chapter, these data sources and the resulting trait scales are described.

# 3

## Measuring the Big Five

Application of a five-factor approach to the study of political behavior first requires that data be gathered and scales be constructed. These tasks should not be taken lightly, especially given that the Big Five has only a thin track record in research on political behavior. All measurement procedures in the social sciences bring strengths and weaknesses, and it is important that these characteristics be recognized and their implications understood. Hence, this chapter offers a systematic look at the data sets and trait scales used in subsequent chapters to examine the possible political effects of the Big Five. Several specific matters receive attention in this chapter. First, this study's three surveys are described. Discussion then turns to the features of the Big Five batteries administered on these surveys, including review of coding and scale construction, item content, reliability, and the relationship between Big Five scales and demographics. Lastly, data on response rates and response time are assessed in an effort to glean insight regarding any possible logistical complications involved in use of Big Five batteries.

### THREE SURVEYS

In the period 1998 to 2006, I had the opportunity to include personality batteries on three public opinion surveys that serve as the primary data sources in the present study.[1] One of these surveys was entirely of

[1] I also was able to add a brief Big Five battery to a 2004 telephone survey designed by Mary Anderson as part of her doctoral research at Florida State University. Big Five measures also were included, at my request, on a telephone survey of citizens' attitudes toward jury duty in the field in the state of Washington in 2007, and on face-to-face surveys Mitchell Seligson and his collaborators conducted in Uruguay and Venezuela in 2007 as part of Vanderbilt's Latin American Public Opinion Project. Some findings from the 2004 data are reported in Mondak and Halperin (2008), some results from the Uruguay and Venezuela surveys are reported in Mondak

my design, whereas the other two were collaborative omnibus projects in which I was a participant. The availability of three data sets brings numerous advantages, particularly given the diversity of the surveys: One of the surveys was conducted within a single community and two are national surveys; two were primarily midterm congressional-election surveys and one is not; two of the surveys were conducted by telephone, whereas the third used a self-administered paper-and-pencil instrument; and one of the surveys was conducted during the Clinton administration while the other two were fielded during the presidency of George W. Bush. Collectively, as will be seen in the following chapters, the three surveys included a great wealth of dependent variables, facilitating the construction of numerous tests regarding the possible political significance of the Big Five. Furthermore, many key dependent variables appeared in identical form on two or all three of the surveys, bringing an immediate opportunity for replication. Lastly, although virtually identical procedures for measuring trait structure were employed on the surveys, the number of personality items and the content of those items varied. Consequently, when tests involving particular dependent variables are repeated across multiple surveys, it will be possible to determine if basic patterns of results are robust across alternate operationalizations of the Big Five.

The first survey, referred to here as the 1998 Community Survey, or 1998 CS, was conducted under my supervision in the Tallahassee, Florida, metropolitan area following the 1998 elections. Designed primarily as a postelection survey, the instrument included eighty-two items. Data were acquired in telephone interviews with 404 respondents. Design of this survey took place soon after I became familiar with the Big Five, and trait measures were included for exploratory purposes. For the most part, analyses involving data from this survey examine possible links between trait structure and familiar variables of the sort typically included on postelection questionnaires. This survey's small number of cases – roughly one-third the number available on the other two surveys – is a limiting feature. Conversely, the 1998 CS included the second-largest trait battery among the three surveys. As discussed below, each trait factor was represented with data from a minimum of three items. One unique aspect of the 1998 CS relative to the other surveys was that the data set included several interviewer ratings of the respondents regarding the respondents' levels of political interest, information-holding, and opinionation. Tests involving such interviewer ratings bring

et al. (2010; forthcoming), and data from the 2007 jury project are examined in Bloeser, McCurley, and Mondak (2009). In the present study, I have elected to limit primary analyses to those data sets gathered under my immediate supervision, although occasional reference will be made to corroborating evidence from the other data sources.

an important advantage with respect to the establishment of causal relationships, because it *cannot* be the case that any observed correspondence between traits and interviewer ratings reflects the impact of the latter on the former. For instance, suppose that after the completion of the survey an interviewer rated a given respondent as being highly opinionated. This rating cannot be a cause of the respondent's level of extraversion. Consequently, if extraversion and opinionation are correlated, we can rule out the possibility that the direction of the underlying causal relationship has been specified incorrectly.[2]

The second survey was a paper-and-pencil instrument fielded in the spring of 2005. This was an omnibus project designed and administered under my supervision, but with batteries on numerous subjects developed by seven other individuals.[3] The survey included a core set of questions concerning personality, demographics, and political predispositions. These items were completed by all 1,312 respondents.[4] After these core items, each survey included one of three sets of experiments; hence, some questions were answered by all respondents, but other questions were posed to only one-third of the full sample. Respondents on this survey were individuals who had been called for jury duty, but not yet assigned to juries, in nineteen randomly selected counties from across the United States. Analyses of data from what is labeled the 2005 National Jury Survey, or NJS, established that respondents provided excellent matches

---

[2] This feature of the 1998 CS speaks only to reverse causality. As always with cross-sectional designs, even with interviewer ratings as dependent variables we cannot conclusively rule out the possibility of spuriousness. A third possibility, which I view as unlikely, is that respondents' self-ratings on the personality items influenced interviewers' postinterview assessments on the various political engagement items. It is not difficult to envision that respondents' answers on questions about political interests informed interviewers' appraisals. However, it is seemingly much less likely that interviewers recalled how respondents answered the neat–sloppy or calm–tense scale and then drew on those answers when assessing respondents' levels of political interest, information-holding, and opinionation.

[3] The other project participants were political science graduate students enrolled in a research seminar I taught in the Spring 2005 semester at Florida State University. Dona-Gene Mitchell, now at the University of Nebraska, took the lead role in administration of this survey, serving as project supervisor.

[4] We have partial interviews for an additional twenty-six respondents, but these data are discarded for present purposes. The jury survey was made available to potential jurors, and respondents filled out the instrument while waiting to be assigned to a jury, or to be dismissed. Some respondents, mostly from one county and on one particular day, completed only a handful of items before being dismissed. Too few items were completed for these interviews to be useful, and I view it as the luck of the draw rather than anything intentional on the part of potential respondents that these surveys were not completed. Thus, they are simply excluded from present analyses.

to the populations of their source counties, and also that respondents as a whole matched national census data as well as, or better than, respondents on prominent national political surveys such as the National Election Studies (NES) (Lewis, Mitchell, and Rugeley 2005). One noteworthy limitation of this survey is that, because three different forms were used, some of the tests involving NJS data reported in the following chapters centered on dependent variables asked of only one-third of respondents. On the plus side, data from a national sample provide a useful complement to the community survey. Also, the fact that NJS data were obtained from self-administered, paper-and-pencil instruments brings a level of commonality with much of the research on the Big Five conducted in psychology. Lastly, a critical advantage of trait data from the 2005 NJS is that each of the Big Five factors was measured with data from five items, providing richer trait scales than those constructed with data from the other surveys.

The final survey used here is the 2006 Congressional Elections Study, or 2006 CES.[5] This national survey, with content focused primarily on the 2006 midterm elections, includes several noteworthy design features. First, respondents were drawn from 155 congressional districts, including a mix of districts chosen in a random sample and districts determined before the election to be either open seats or to have competitive contests.[6] Oversampling of competitive districts permitted improved attention to campaign effects; with only a random sample, very few respondents would reside in competitive districts. Second, the study included a panel component. There were 1,023 interviews completed before the November elections, with 766 of these respondents reinterviewed after the election. Third, an additional 400 respondents were not contacted prior to the elections, but answered a modified version of the postelection survey. A brief Big Five trait measure was included on both postelection instruments. Thus, for analyses using the panel data,

[5] This study was administered at Indiana University. In 2002, Ted Carmines, Bob Huckfeldt, and I designed and fielded a survey on Congress and the midterm congressional elections. The 2006 project, again headquartered at Indiana University, built on the 2002 effort. Additional participants on the 2006 project include John Hibbing, Gary Jacobson, Dona-Gene Mitchell, Walt Stone, Mike Wagner, and Herb Weisberg. For further discussion of the properties of the 2006 CES, see Mitchell and Mondak (2009). For analyses of data from this survey, see the various chapters in Mondak and Mitchell (2009).

[6] Specifically, we began with random selection of 100 congressional districts. We then identified seventy-two districts as open or competitive. Seventeen of these seventy-two were included in the initial sample of 100 districts, leaving 155 districts in the full sample. Data are weighted to provide a representative sample of the voting age population of the lower forty-eight states.

the maximum number of cases is 766, whereas up to 1,166 (766 + 400) cases are available for models using only postelection data. Data from the 2006 CES enable exploration of links between personality and voting behavior in these historic elections. Additionally, the CES included a much larger battery of policy items than did the other three surveys, and the alternate postelection instrument included response latency measures for the Big Five items.

### DEVELOPING BIG FIVE SCALES

On this study's three surveys, personality traits were measured using bipolar, or semantic-differential, scales. Although originally designed for the measurement of attitudes, the semantic-differential format focuses on contrasting pairs of adjectives, making the format well suited for lexicological research on personality. Further, semantic-differential items are relatively quick and easy to administer, especially in telephone surveys, and their properties are well understood (for early discussions, see Osgood, Tannenbaum, and Suci 1957 and Heise 1970). Cattell's research developing the 16PF employed bipolar adjective scales, and this format remains popular today among students of trait structure. The most common alternates include questionnaires of the sort advocated by Costa and McCrae, and univocal adjective scales.[7]

In the current research, a brief statement prior to the first Big Five item alerted respondents to the substantive content of the battery, and offered a simple explanation of the response format. On the 2006 CES, for instance, interviewers read this introduction to respondents:

The following section contains pairs of words. On a scale of zero to ten, please tell us which word best describes you. For example, the number zero means "relaxed," the number ten means "tense," and the number five is exactly in the middle – neither relaxed nor tense. On this scale, what number best describes you? You can use any number from zero to ten.

Subsequent trait items were presented quickly. For instance, for the second item on the 2006 survey, the interviewer merely said "next, zero is outgoing, ten is shy." Thus, at least in terms of the presentation of questions to respondents, bipolar adjective scales bring considerable efficiency. After introduction of the battery and the initial pair of adjectives, interviewers can utter as few as seven words to present each additional item, and respondents can offer single-word replies.

---

[7] Goldberg (1992) compares bipolar and univocal adjective scales. He finds that both perform well as means to measure the Big Five, although some evidence points to the superiority of univocal items. Woods and Hampson (2005) argue that bipolar scales are preferable when the Big Five dimensions are measured with brief scales.

## Measuring the Big Five

Review of the adjective pairs and resulting responses from this study's three surveys will reveal some of the strengths and weaknesses of these data. Several specific tasks require attention: discussion of coding and scale construction; a listing of the adjective pairs included for each trait on the surveys; demonstration that responses to the items used to measure a given trait are correlated; and assessment of any relevant signs that some respondents may have been unwilling or unable to complete the personality battery.

### Coding of Trait Data

Turning first to coding and scale construction, recall from the previous chapter that social desirability effects potentially can complicate the measurement of trait structure. On the first item from the 2006 CES survey, for instance, it is conceivable that some respondents perceived "tense" as a pejorative term and therefore preferred to cast themselves as being "relaxed," irrespective of whether they viewed that depiction as accurate. Evidence consistent with this concern would be found if, for instance, extreme skews were observed on items that seem especially susceptible to social desirability effects.

This study's largest trait battery was administered as part of the 2005 NJS. To allow for a larger font on this paper-and-pencil instrument, a nine-point response format was used rather than the eleven-point format employed on the two telephone surveys. Although data on many of the twenty-five items were skewed, extreme imbalances were rare. One of the polar-response options emerged as the modal category on only two items: hardworking–lazy and responsible–irresponsible. On both of these items, a plurality of respondents awarded themselves the maximum score in terms of conscientiousness, and just over 80 percent of respondents gave ratings of 1, 2, or 3, leaving fewer than 20 percent of observations distributed among the remaining six response categories. The skewness statistics for these two items and five others have absolute values greater than 1.00.[8] Six of these seven items are indicators of conscientiousness and agreeableness, with the seventh being an indicator of openness to experience. The item with the most evenly balanced distribution was an indicator of extraversion, talkative–quiet.

With the data at hand, no definitive tests can establish the presence of social desirability effects. It could be, after all, that solid majorities truly

[8] A skewness value of zero indicates that the data are perfectly evenly distributed, whereas negative values indicate that the data are skewed to the left (i.e., a preponderance of observations are packed toward the right side of the scale, with a relative few observations distributed over a long tail to the left) and positive values indicate a rightward skew.

are hardworking and responsible, and that self-favoring biases played no role in these data. But this seems unlikely. On items on which there is little or no social consensus regarding the pole that is more desirable, skew levels are minimal. If the skew observed on markers such as responsible–irresponsible signifies nothing more than an actual imbalance in the distribution of this trait, then similar imbalances should have been expected on at least some other items. Erring on the side of caution, a logarithmic transformation was used in the construction of all final scales to minimize the possible impact of skewed distributions and to maximize comparability across the trait measures. Specifically, each item initially was recoded so that a value of one represents the highest possible value on the trait in question (high openness to experience, high conscientiousness, and so on). These recoded variables then were logged. Final trait scales were constructed by summing the logged indicators for each trait, and then recoding the resulting values to range from zero (lowest observed value) to one (highest observed value).

The tangible consequence of the use of logged variables is to assign more weight to small shifts near the center of each distribution, and to assign correspondingly less weight to shifts in the tail. Substantively, the use of logged variables holds the potential to minimize the impact of social desirability effects. As an example, compare two individuals who, when asked to rate themselves on a scale defined by the terms "hardworking" (one) and "lazy" (nine), offered values of three and six respectively. Both have depicted themselves as falling short of the maximum in work effort (a score of one). It is possible, although by no means certain, that nothing more than a difference in susceptibility to social desirability pressures accounts for the gap in their responses. With the data left in their raw form, the deviation from fully hardworking would appear slight for the first respondent, even though it might be of considerable substantive importance. The use of logged variables better accounts for this possibility. Also, more pragmatically, when data on the underlying items have skewed distributions, scales constructed with logged indicators will be more normally distributed – a desirable property for multivariate analyses – than scales constructed with the original data. Lastly, it is important to keep in mind that recording error is inevitable in survey research, especially on telephone surveys. Scale validity would be undermined if undue weight were given to outliers recorded in error.

To provide a sense of the impact of the scaling procedures I have implemented, Figure 3.1 depicts histograms for the conscientiousness and agreeableness scales, with data drawn from the 2005 NJS. Comparing simple additive scales that range in value from zero to forty with the final measures, it is evident that the logarithmic transformations used in construction of the final scales have, in both cases, noticeably reduced the

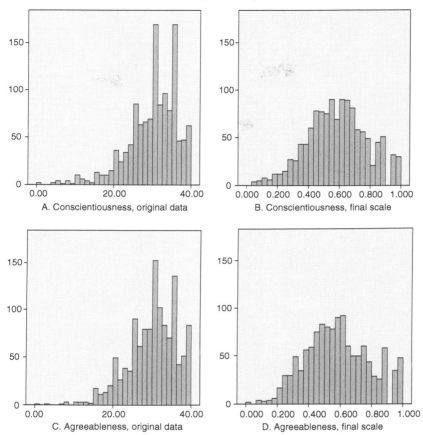

Figure 3.1 Levels of skew in the distributions of trait measures: original and recoded conscientiousness and agreeableness scales.
*Source*: 2005 NJS.

extent to which the distributions are skewed. For both traits, distributions for the final scales appear much closer to normal than do the distributions for scales constructed using the original unlogged data. More concretely, skewness statistics with absolute values greater than 0.70 are obtained for both scales with the raw data, versus marks of less than 0.20 for the final logged scales. The impact of the logarithmic transformation is, of course, much less pronounced for the other three scales because the original data in those cases were less skewed.

Although I believe Big Five scales should be constructed using logged data, the empirical consequences of this decision are minimal, presumably because the actual distributions exhibited notable skews on only a handful of items. Overall, inter-item correlations within each trait dimension were modestly higher using logged rather than unlogged variables, but the same patterns of effects reported in the next three chapters emerged when scales were constructed using data in their raw form.

## The Trait Batteries

Among psychologists, two basic types of research on five-factor approaches have occurred. Many studies, especially works early on in the brief history of the Big Five, have explored properties of the trait data themselves. In these inquiries, researchers have sought to establish the presence of the Big Five factors, to identify the subsidiary traits encompassed by each factor, and to demonstrate the reliability, validity, and cross-cultural applicability of the five-factor perspective. Other efforts, in contrast, take the existence of the Big Five as a starting point, and then put the trait structure to work in applied research that examines possible attitudinal and behavioral consequences of variance in traits. The present study is of this second type. In the next three chapters, the Big Five indicators developed here are introduced as predictors of a wide array of political variables.

Recognition of this distinction between foundational and applied research on the Big Five provides a basis for understanding a key difference in measurement strategies seen in the literature. Research that explores the properties of the Big Five factors often makes use of very large personality batteries. Costa and McCrae's NEO-PI includes 240 items. Goldberg's (1992) investigation of the properties of alternate indicators of the Big Five examined a series of fifty-item batteries. Use of such large batteries proves to be especially valuable in research intended to gauge item performance and to assess nuanced aspects of the Big Five. In these sorts of endeavors, the study of personality is an end in itself, and little data beyond Big Five markers are needed. Research efforts such as these often use undergraduate students as subjects, with personality items administered in writing through either paper-and-pencil or computer-based instruments.

In applied research, resource limitations often preclude administration of such lengthy personality batteries. This is particularly true with telephone surveys. Telephone interviews rarely last as long as thirty-five or forty minutes, yet the full NEO-PI takes this long to complete.[9] Hence, if a survey is to include anything else in addition to personality inventories, then abbreviated personality batteries must be devised, as in the

---

[9] Use of brief personality measures is less of an issue for some applied studies, including many of those cited in Chapter 2, as these works often involve acquisition of data from a captive respondent base (most often university undergraduates) via self-administered instruments. Still, even applied studies involving undergraduates

case of the 2006 CES. In designing personality measures for this study's three surveys, my objective was to construct batteries of sufficient brevity that their use by other researchers in future studies of political behavior would be plausible. After all, there would be little point in identifying links between personality and politics if there were no viable means for future researchers to make use of these findings. Some recent research in psychology also has recognized the pragmatic need for efficient measures of the five-factor trait structure. For instance, Gosling, Rentfrow, and Swann (2003) developed five-item and ten-item measures of the Big Five, labeled FIPI and TIPI, respectively. Likewise, Woods and Hampson (2005) presented a five-item measure of the Big Five, the SIMP, and Rammstedt and John (2007) advanced a ten-item variant of the Big Five Inventory. The careful analyses reported by these authors brings confidence that functional representations of the Big Five can indeed be developed with data on only one or two items per trait factor. Drawing on their findings, ten-item Big Five batteries were included on this study's third survey, the 2006 CES.

Table 3.1 depicts all component items used to construct this study's indicators of the Big Five traits. Following convention in psychology research, data from the 1998 CS were subjected to factor analysis, and items used to represent the Big Five were selected on the basis of factor analysis results. Component items for scales on the two subsequent surveys were predetermined, although reliability analyses were performed in each case. In selecting specific items to include on the surveys, two somewhat competing goals were pursued. First, comparability across the surveys was desired. Consequently, some items were repeated verbatim from one survey to the next. Second, some variance in item content was preferred, however. The ideal content of Big Five markers is not yet set in stone, especially for indicators designed to be asked as part of telephone surveys of public opinion. I was cognizant of this point when designing the various batteries, and I also was interested in determining whether any impact of the Big Five on political behavior was robust across alternate operationalizations of the traits. Thus, I engaged in some mixing and matching of item content across the three surveys.[10]

For the most part, results of reliability analyses reveal little cause for concern. In section A of Table 3.1, the Cronbach's alpha values for trait scales from the 1998 CS all reach reasonable marks, especially

---

frequently measure personality with either the abbreviated sixty-item version of the NEO-PI or forty or fifty items drawn from Goldberg (1992).

[10] Further inquiry along these lines would be beneficial. One logical next step would be research that replicates some of the basic tests reported in the next three chapters, but that does so using Big Five scales constructed using either univocal markers or a questionnaire approach.

Table 3.1 *Indicators of the Big Five Factors*

| A. 1998 Community Survey | | | | |
| --- | --- | --- | --- | --- |
| Trait Factor | Component Items | Scale Mean (s.d.) | Cronbach's Alpha | Number of Cases |
| Openness to experience | Perceptive–shortsighted Efficient–inefficient Self-assured–unself-assured Intelligent–Unintelligent Confident–unconfident Complex–simple | 0.42 (0.22) | 0.72 | 394 |
| Conscientiousness | Neat–sloppy Organized–disorganized Careful–careless Responsible–Irresponsible Cautious–reckless | 0.45 (0.23) | 0.75 | 402 |
| Extraversion | Extraverted–introverted Outgoing–reserved Talkative–quiet | 0.43 (0.23) | 0.70 | 390 |
| Agreeableness | Warm–cold Kind–unkind Agreeable–disagreeable Sympathetic–unsympathetic | 0.49 (0.22) | 0.67 | 397 |
| Emotional stability | Secure–insecure Calm–tense Relaxed–nervous | 0.46 (0.22) | 0.71 | 398 |
| B. 2005 National Jury survey | | | | |
| Trait Factor | Component Items | Scale Mean (s.d.) | Cronbach's Alpha | Number of Cases |
| Openness to experience | Imaginative–unimaginative Analytical–unanalytical Creative–uncreative Curious–uncurious Intellectual–unintellectual | 0.52 (0.20) | 0.75 | 1,224 |

| | | | | |
|---|---|---|---|---|
| Conscientiousness | Systematic–unsystematic<br>Hardworking–lazy<br>Neat–sloppy<br>Careful–careless<br>Responsible–<br>Irresponsible | 0.59<br>(0.19) | 0.76 | 1,254 |
| Extraversion | Extraverted–introverted<br>Talkative–quiet<br>Bold–timid<br>Spontaneous–inhibited<br>Outgoing–shy | 0.40<br>(0.19) | 0.79 | 1,219 |
| Agreeableness | Warm–cold<br>Gentle–harsh<br>Kind–unkind<br>Polite–rude<br>Sympathetic–<br>unsympathetic | 0.58<br>(0.20) | 0.79 | 1,253 |
| Emotional<br>stability | Calm–angry<br>Relaxed–tense<br>At ease–nervous<br>Steady–moody<br>Content–discontented | 0.44<br>(0.20) | 0.79 | 1,258 |

C. 2006 Congressional Elections Study

| Trait Factor | Component Items | Scale<br>Mean<br>(s.d.) | Pearson's R | Number<br>of Cases |
|---|---|---|---|---|
| Openness to<br>experience | Philosophical–<br>unreflective<br>An intellectual–not an<br>intellectual | 0.46<br>(0.22) | 0.28 | 1,098 |
| Conscientiousness | Hardworking–lazy<br>Neat–sloppy | 0.57<br>(0.25) | 0.29 | 1,132 |
| Extraversion | Outgoing–shy<br>Extraverted–introverted | 0.41<br>(0.26) | 0.53 | 1,102 |
| Agreeableness | Sympathetic–unsympathetic<br>Kind–unkind | 0.63<br>(0.25) | 0.47 | 1,128 |
| Emotional<br>stability | Relaxed–tense<br>Calm–nervous | 0.40<br>(0.22) | 0.43 | 1,131 |

*Note*: all scales range in values from 0 (lowest observed score) to 1. High values indicate high levels of the named trait. Many of the adjective pairs were reversed on the actual surveys.

77

for indicators of broad, multifaceted trait dimensions.[11] As should be expected, the alpha levels are larger still in section B for the five-item trait scales on the 2005 NJS. But what of the two-item scale on the 2006 CES? Bivariate correlations for the two items used to form each scale range from 0.28 to 0.53. To put these marks in context, the mean inter-item correlation on the 2005 NJS was 0.41. By this standard, somewhat low correlations are observed on the 2006 CES for openness to experience (0.28) and conscientiousness (0.29).

Although these low correlations are not ideal, neither are they cause for alarm. That conscientiousness and openness produced low marks is not surprising. Openness to experience generally is seen as the most difficult of the Big Five traits to measure. Here, scales for this trait dimension yielded the lowest alpha on the 2005 NJS and, despite use of six items, only a modest alpha on the 1998 CS. As to conscientiousness, I deliberately selected both a dispositional (neat–sloppy) and a volitional (hardworking–lazy) item for inclusion on the 2006 CES. Compared with use of two dispositional items, this strategy better reflects the breadth of this trait dimension, but also inherently limits the correlation between the two indicators. For Gosling, Rentfrow, and Swann's (2003) ten-item scale, the lowest bivariate correlation equals that seen in Table 3.1, that is, a mark of 0.28 for openness to experience. Despite this, Gosling and colleagues demonstrate that their scale performs adequately in a series of tests of validity.[12]

Closer inspection of data from the 2005 NJS may bring further insight regarding the properties of two-item trait measures. Again, on the NJS, the trait scales are constructed using data from five items. For each of the Big Five factors, these items can be used to construct ten subsidiary two-item scales similar in form to the two-item scales available on the 2006 CES (i.e., item #1 paired with item #2, item #1 paired with item #3, and so on). Then, the correlations between these two-item scales and the full five-item scales can be assessed to help gauge the slippage brought by a reduction in scale size. For instance, for openness to experience, we can test the relationship between the full five-item measure and a scale constructed only with data from the items creative–uncreative and curious–uncurious, and this test then can be repeated for the other nine pairs of trait items, and for the other four Big Five factors.

Results from this exercise are summarized in the first section of Table 3.2. For each trait factor, the table reports the average value of the ten

---

[11] As a general rule of thumb, an alpha value of 0.70 or greater signifies the existence of a reliable scale, although the alpha level will vary to some extent depending on whether the concept in question is broad or narrow in form. Nine of the ten alphas in Table 3.1 meet or exceed the 0.70 mark, and the tenth narrowly misses at 0.67.

[12] Similar issues are discussed by Bizer et al. (2004, 1019) with respect to use of "concentrated" measures of need to evaluate.

Table 3.2 *Evidence Regarding the Quality of Two-Item Indicators of the Big Five*

| Trait Factor | A. Correlations between the Full Five-Item Scale and Ten Subsidiary Two-Item Scales | | |
|---|---|---|---|
| | Average Correlation | High Correlation | Low Correlation |
| Openness to Experience | 0.86 | 0.89 | 0.81 |
| Conscientiousness | 0.86 | 0.89 | 0.82 |
| Extraversion | 0.87 | 0.90 | 0.83 |
| Agreeableness | 0.87 | 0.89 | 0.85 |
| Emotional Stability | 0.87 | 0.89 | 0.85 |
| | B. Correlations between the Two-Item Scales and Residual Three-Item Scales | | |
| | Average Correlation | High Correlation | Low Correlation |
| Openness to Experience | 0.60 | 0.69 | 0.45 |
| Conscientiousness | 0.60 | 0.65 | 0.55 |
| Extraversion | 0.65 | 0.69 | 0.59 |
| Agreeableness | 0.64 | 0.69 | 0.58 |
| Emotional Stability | 0.64 | 0.68 | 0.60 |

*Source*: 2005 NJS.

correlations, along with the highest and lowest observed marks. The news is quite positive. An average correlation of 0.87 is observed, and similar results emerge for all five trait factors.[13] These are high levels, suggesting that we suffer only a modest loss when moving from larger trait scales to bare-bones indicators of the sort included on the 2006 CES. On the 2005 NJS, the lowest bivariate correlation was a mere 0.24 for the openness to experience items analytical–unanalytical and creative–uncreative. This mark falls short of the levels of the weakest correlations in Table 3.1, yet even a scale constructed with these two items is correlated with the full five-item scale at a level of over 0.80. Collectively, the initial findings in Table 3.2 bring a great deal of comfort. Although use of such limited indicators unquestionably is not ideal,[14] these results corroborate the claims

---

[13] A similar exercise is conducted by Rammstedt and John (2007). There, the average part–whole correlation comparing two-item and nine-item scales is 0.83.

[14] John, Naumann, and Soto (2008, 137) advise that brief Big Five measures should be avoided "unless a researcher encounters truly exceptional circumstances, such as the need to measure the Big Five as part of a national phone survey." That, of

of Gosling, Rentfrow, and Swann (2003) and Woods and Hampson (2005) that even brief scales can provide adequate representations of the Big Five trait factors.[15]

Part of the reason the two-item scales are well correlated with their five-item counterparts is, of course, because the same two items are included in both scales. Importantly, this fact does not in itself account for the large correlations in section A. As a simple demonstration of this point, we also can consider the correlation between each two-item scale and a scale formed with data from the remaining three items for that trait dimension. These results are reported in the second section of Table 3.2. Even here, large correlations emerge, with an average mark of 0.63. Past research provides an opportunity to place these findings in context. Woods and Hampson (2005) compare both their single-item Big Five measure (SIMP) and the Gosling, Rentfrow, and Swann (2003) two-item measure (TIPI) with various larger measures of the Big Five. The resulting correlations range between 0.41 and 0.80, with a mean of 0.64 for the SIMP and 0.66 for the TIPI. Viewed in this context, the present 0.63 average is quite encouraging.

### The Big Five and Demographics

In the next three chapters, I explore possible links between the Big Five trait dimensions and various aspects of political behavior. The multivariate tests include all of the Big Five variables as predictors, along with controls for four demographic attributes: the respondent's age, education level, sex, and race.[16] This analytical strategy raises the question of whether there are any strong and consistent relationships between the personality variables and the demographic indicators. If demographics capture all or most of the variance in personality, then accounting for personality necessarily would add little to our understanding of political

course, is precisely the situation I faced in designing my instruments. That said, follow-up research that reexamines the findings reported in this study, but that does so with the benefit of richer Big Five scales, is strongly encouraged.

[15] More evidence relevant to this point is presented in the following chapters. Again, for many dependent variables, identical or nearly-identical tests are conducted with data from two or more of the three surveys. With multiple independent tests, assessment of the results as a whole should provide a strong sense whether the core effects of personality can be captured with brief trait measures. For example, it would be a red flag if consistent statistically significant effects are found in a given test using the multi-item trait scales on the 1998 CS and 2005 NJS, but corresponding effects fall short of significance with two-item measures from the 2006 CES.

[16] Age is coded as age in years. Education is a categorical indicator with groupings ranging from less than a high school graduate to postgraduate degree. Sex and race are dummy variables; sex is coded 1 if the respondent is female and 0 if male, whereas race is coded 1 if the respondent is black and 0 if otherwise.

behavior.[17] Past research suggests that demographics and the Big Five are related, but only modestly so. Goldberg et al. (1998) examine variants of the same four demographic indicators under consideration here. The average bivariate correlation between personality and demographic variables in that study was only 0.08. To see whether similar patterns emerge with the present data sets, each of the Big Five variables is regressed on the four demographic indicators. High $R^2$ values and strong and consistent patterns for particular predictors would support concern about the value-added associated with the Big Five.

The results in Table 3.3 reveal only a minimal overlap between personality and the demographic variables. Likewise, the results offer little evidence of consistent relationships between individual demographic indicators and specific personality trait dimensions. With one exception, all of the $R^2$ values in Table 3.3 fall well below 0.10, and they average only 0.05. Hence, to an overwhelming degree, the substantive content of the trait measures is distinct from demographics. Among the demographic variables, sex emerges as the most consequential for personality. Compared with men, women report somewhat higher levels of conscientiousness, extraversion, and especially agreeableness. No other effects operate in a consistent manner across all three surveys, although results suggest that perhaps openness to experience decreases with age and is greatest among the well educated, and that emotional stability increases with age. Race also appears to correspond with personality, with black respondents scoring high on openness to experience, conscientiousness, and emotional stability. Two of these relationships – that women tend to be more agreeable than men, and that emotional stability tends to rise with age – corroborate findings reported by Goldberg et al. (1998). However, current evidence is mixed regarding Goldberg et al.'s two strongest findings, a positive correlation between education and openness to experience, and a similar correspondence between age and conscientiousness. Overall, results in Table 3.3 clearly should be seen as encouraging. Personality apparently is not coterminous with demographics, and thus the Big Five variables will bring something new to the table in the following chapters when they are included as predictors of political behavior.

RESPONSE PATTERNS ON THE BIG FIVE TRAIT MEASURES

When we contemplate adding new items to surveys, one important pragmatic matter to consider involves how respondents will perceive the questions. In most cases, for instance, little would be gained by

---

[17] On a related matter, Gerber et al. (2010) consider whether personality effects on political behavior may be conditional on demographics.

Table 3.3 *Relationships between the Big Five Trait Dimensions and Demographics*

| | 1998 CS | 2005 NJS | 2006 CES |
|---|---|---|---|
| A. Openness to Experience | | | |
| Age | 0.000 | −0.002*** | −0.001** |
| | (0.001) | (0.000) | (0.000) |
| Education | −0.005 | 0.026*** | 0.027** |
| | (0.006) | (0.003) | (0.003) |
| Race | 0.092** | −0.029 | 0.111** |
| | (0.030) | (0.021) | (0.034) |
| Sex | −0.021 | −0.026* | 0.007 |
| | (0.023) | (0.011) | (0.013) |
| $R^2$ | 0.02 | 0.07 | 0.07 |
| B. Conscientiousness | | | |
| Age | 0.002** | 0.002 | 0.000 |
| | (0.001) | (0.000) | (0.000) |
| Education | −0.016** | 0.011** | −0.009* |
| | (0.006) | (0.003) | (0.004) |
| Race | 0.100** | −0.018 | 0.185*** |
| | (0.029) | (0.021) | (0.034) |
| Sex | 0.064** | 0.022* | 0.074*** |
| | (0.022) | (0.011) | (0.015) |
| $R^2$ | 0.08 | 0.01 | 0.05 |
| C. Extraversion | | | |
| Age | 0.000 | −0.001* | 0.000 |
| | (0.001) | (0.000) | (0.001) |
| Education | −0.001 | 0.003 | 0.004 |
| | (0.006) | (0.003) | (0.004) |
| Race | 0.006 | −0.037 | 0.084* |
| | (0.031) | (0.022) | (0.042) |
| Sex | 0.104*** | 0.029** | 0.062*** |
| | (0.024) | (0.011) | (0.016) |
| $R^2$ | 0.04 | 0.01 | 0.02 |
| D. Agreeableness | | | |
| Age | 0.001 | 0.001 | 0.001 |
| | (0.001) | (0.000) | (0.000) |
| Education | −0.012* | 0.006 | −0.011** |
| | (0.006) | (0.003) | (0.004) |

| | | | |
|---|---|---|---|
| Race | 0.037 | 0.008 | 0.197*** |
| | (0.029) | (0.022) | (0.038) |
| Sex | 0.092*** | 0.087*** | 0.165*** |
| | (0.022) | (0.011) | (0.014) |
| $R^2$ | 0.06 | 0.05 | 0.14 |

| E. Emotional Stability | | | |
|---|---|---|---|
| Age | 0.001* | 0.002*** | 0.000 |
| | (0.001) | (0.000) | (0.000) |
| Education | −0.004 | 0.005 | −0.008* |
| | (0.005) | (0.003) | (0.003) |
| Race | 0.135*** | 0.010 | 0.108** |
| | (0.028) | (0.021) | (0.034) |
| Sex | −0.032 | 0.014 | −0.030* |
| | (0.022) | (0.011) | (0.013) |
| $R^2$ | 0.06 | 0.02 | 0.02 |

*** $p < .001$, ** $p < .01$, * $p < .05$

posing questions respondents likely would find to be confusing or disconcerting. With Big Five batteries, the most obvious risks in this regard are that respondents may be unwilling to evaluate themselves on these trait dimensions, or they may be inexperienced, and thus ineffective, at doing so. Because I have adopted a lexicological approach, an additional possibility is that some respondents may be unfamiliar with the adjectival terms included as part of the Big Five markers. In a general sense, the data reviewed thus far allay these concerns. Respondents on all three surveys answered the Big Five items, and the data scaled very much as should be expected based on lessons learned in past research. Still, the matter can be considered more closely. Two types of indicators offer at least circumstantial evidence pertaining to possible logistical difficulties in measuring the Big Five: response rates on the personality items and information regarding how slowly or quickly respondents provided answers.

Several factors potentially contribute to nonresponse on survey questions. For Big Five items, some respondents may be unwilling to discuss with an interviewer what they consider to be private, personal matters. Also, respondents may not know how to evaluate themselves on some items, either because they have never previously thought of themselves in those particular terms or because they are unfamiliar with the vocabulary used in the questions. And, as with any question, respondents may refuse to answer one or more of the Big Five items because of fatigue or boredom with the interview, or, in the spirit of the Big Five, perhaps because they are introverted or disagreeable.

Nonresponse on survey questions leads to missing data, a vexing concern for multivariate analyses. Although imputation techniques (e.g., King et al. 2001) have been developed to address this problem, and now are included with all of the major statistical software packages, we still can learn a great deal about item performance through assessment of nonresponse rates. For example, it surely would mean something different both substantively and logistically if nonresponse on a given question were 10 or 15 percent rather than 2 or 3 percent.

Rates of nonresponse for the Big Five items and for several questions concerning political predispositions, policy attitudes, and demographics are reported in Table 3.4. For the personality batteries, cell entries reveal the average nonresponse rate per item for each of the traits. The level of nonresponse on the personality items differs noticeably across the three surveys, but in no case does nonresponse reach the point of causing alarm. Nonresponse rates are highest on the 2005 NJS. This survey included the longest personality battery, and it also was the only self-administered, paper-and-pencil instrument. But even here, nonresponse barely surpasses 3 percent, a very modest level. Nonresponse is minimal – less than 1 percent overall – on the 1998 CS, and similarly low on the 2006 CES. Nothing in these results arouses concern. At least in terms of the simple act of answering the questions, respondents experienced no apparent difficulty in navigating the Big Five items.

Corroboration of this point emerges with comparison of nonresponse levels for the Big Five data with nonresponse on political and demographic questions. In this context, the personality indicators fare quite well. Nonresponse rates on the personality items exceed those on political and demographic measures on the paper-and-pencil 2005 NJS. In contrast, on the two telephone surveys, nonresponse levels for the Big Five batteries resemble those for items regarding political predispositions and demographics. On average, levels of nonresponse are highest for the political items on the two telephone surveys, but it is unnecessary to split hairs. These data demonstrate the key point that, in terms of response and nonresponse, personality items fall very much in line with the other sorts of measures typically asked as part of surveys on politics and political behavior.

Despite low levels of nonresponse on the trait items, we still might be able to glean a bit more insight into why some respondents declined to provide answers to these questions. In Table 3.4, looking within each survey, nonresponse varies a bit across the Big Five trait factors. Further, this variance appears to be at least partly systematic, as extraversion stands as the trait that yielded the highest nonresponse rates on the 1998

Table 3.4 *Nonresponse Levels on Personality Items and on Measures of Political Attitudes and Demographics*

| | 1998 CS | 2005 NJS | 2006 CES[a] |
|---|---|---|---|
| A. Big Five Measures | | | |
| Openness to experience (average nonresponse per item) | 0.8 | 3.7 | 2.2 |
| Conscientiousness (average nonresponse per item) | 0.0 | 3.2 | 0.5 |
| Extraversion (average nonresponse per item) | 1.3 | 3.8 | 2.0 |
| Agreeableness (average nonresponse per item) | 0.6 | 3.2 | 0.6 |
| Emotional Stability (average nonresponse per item) | 0.7 | 3.1 | 0.4 |
| B. Political Attitudes and Predispositions | | | |
| Partisanship | 2.5 | 0.5 | 0.4 |
| Ideology | 2.7 | 1.5 | 0.9 |
| Presidential approval | 0.7 | 3.0 | 0.5 |
| Average, five-item battery, civil liberties and the criminally accused | N/A | N/A | 3.3 |
| Average, five-item battery, civil liberties and terror suspects | N/A | N/A | 1.8 |
| Average, three-item battery, support for traditional values | N/A | N/A | 2.0 |
| C. Demographics | | | |
| Year of birth | 1.2 | 0.3 | 1.3 |
| Education | 3.0 | 0.5 | 0.3 |
| Marital status | N/A | 0.0 | 0.0 |
| Employment status | N/A | N/A | 0.0 |

[a] For the 2006 CES, nonresponse rates are for respondents who participated in both waves of the panel survey.

*Note*: Nonresponse rates are calculated using the sum of data coded as "don't know" and "refused" on the original surveys, and then reported as percentages. In section B, the civil liberties batteries each were asked of half of respondents.

CS and the 2005 NJS, and the second-highest rate on the 2006 CES. At face value, this result does not support the possibility that nonresponse stems from any reticence on the part of respondents; as noted above, data on extraversion were much less skewed than were data on conscientiousness and openness to experience, suggesting that questions tapping extraversion probably do not spark concerns with social desirability. Closer inspection of the data reveals that higher nonresponse on extraversion most likely results from the relative linguistic complexity of the adjective pair extraverted–introverted. On the 1998 CS, this item generated eleven "don't know" responses (2.7 percent), nearly twice as many as the next-highest question.[18] High "don't know" rates were also recorded for this same adjective pair on the 2005 NJS and the 2006 CES.[19] On the latter survey, the only item to generate a similarly high nonresponse rate was itself a mouthful, philosophical–unreflective.

Collectively, the data reported in Table 3.4 constitute positive news. Nonresponse rates on the Big Five items run low relative to those on questions concerning political attitudes. With careful selection of adjective pairs, average response rates in excess of 99 percent can be expected on most telephone surveys. Logistically, this brings reassurance that inclusion of Big Five batteries on surveys will not be problematic. Substantively, the fact that respondents exhibited no noteworthy lack of willingness or ability to answer the trait items supports the notion, albeit indirectly, that individuals' self-conceptions typically do include the trait dimensions represented by the Big Five.[20]

Data from the 400 respondents who completed the alternate postelection version of the 2006 Congressional Elections Survey afford additional insight regarding the properties of this study's Big Five measures. On this portion of the 2006 survey, passive, or latent, timers were included for every item, along with activated timers for a few key questions. Only latent timers were used for the ten personality items. With latent timers, the clock on a given question starts the moment the text of the item appears on the interviewer's computer screen, and runs until the interviewer inputs the respondent's answer to the item. Response time is measured in hundredths of seconds. An advantageous feature of this

---

[18] Six "don't know" answers were given for shortsighted/perceptive, itself a relatively complex adjective pair when compared with the likes of neat/sloppy and kind/unkind.

[19] Also, on my recommendation, Carl McCurley of the Washington State Center for Court Research included fifteen Big Five items on a survey he administered to help determine citizens' views regarding jury duty. On this survey, fielded in 2007, fifty-six respondents of 1,923 answered "don't know" on extraverted/introverted. The next-highest mark was a mere twenty-one, and some items had no "don't know" responses.

[20] As mentioned above, I was able to place Big Five batteries on national face-to-face surveys fielded in Uruguay and Venezuela in 2007. On these surveys, interviewers reported that respondents clearly enjoyed the personality items more than most of the surveys' political questions, and that, as a result, inclusion of the personality batteries improved the dynamics and rapport of the interviews.

approach is that the measurement of response time occurs unobtrusively, without active involvement by either the interviewer or the respondent (see Mulligan et al. 2003 and Bassili 2000 for discussions). Assessment of the resulting *response latency* data (Fazio 1990) can be suggestive as to the relative salience of the Big Five traits for respondents.[21]

Attention to these data is of both practical and substantive significance. I noted earlier that I added Big Five batteries to these three political surveys, and that response rates on the personality items are high. Hence, any obstacles to inclusion of trait measures on surveys clearly are not insurmountable. Response latency data bring further perspective on this matter. It is a reality of survey research that surveys rarely run as long, or include as many items, as their designers would prefer. Because survey length is limited, there is an opportunity cost associated with the addition of new items to surveys. As discussed above, trait measures on this study's three surveys employed a bipolar, or semantic-differential, format. This format was used in part because of the characteristic speed and efficiency of semantic-differential items (Heise 1970). But efficiency in format would be of little value if the content of the trait items were such that respondents engaged in lengthy struggles to provide answers. Response latency data speak directly to this issue. By comparing latency data for the trait measures with corresponding data for items on political predispositions and demographics, we can gain a sense of whether respondents found the Big Five items to be easy or difficult to answer. Further, latency data for the full ten-item battery will reveal in concrete terms the cost associated with measuring personality as part of a telephone survey.

Substantively, research on latency holds that accessible judgments are accessible precisely because individuals are practiced at, and find value in, their use. As explained by Huckfeldt et al. (1999, 892), "while accessible points of orientation are more useful, their utilization makes them more accessible." Short response times imply that the judgments are highly retrievable, implying in turn heightened levels of cognitive structure and importance to the individual (e.g., Judd et al. 1991; Krosnick 1989). Conversely, long response times would suggest that the survey questions have caused respondents to tread on a less-traveled cognitive path, or even to forge a new path altogether. A simple example comes from my own research (Huckfeldt et al. 2005), where my colleagues and I found that respondents struggled – taking prolonged amounts of time – to

---

[21] For recent examples of research using response latency data in studies involving familiar issues in political behavior, see Huckfeldt et al. (1999) and Mondak and Huckfeldt (2006). The first of these studies examines response latency data from a telephone survey, whereas the second examines latency data from both a telephone survey and a laboratory experiment.

offer assessments of candidates with atypical combinations of attributes, candidates such as a conservative Democrat, a liberal Republican, and a pro-life Democrat. Judgments of liberal Democrats and conservative Republicans were provided much more quickly, indicating that respondents were accustomed to thinking of political candidates in some terms, or combinations of terms, but not others.

For present purposes the importance is that latency data will provide at least suggestive signs regarding the centrality of the Big Five traits to respondents. Proponents of five-factor approaches argue that these trait domains represent important differences across individuals. It would be more difficult to make the case for attention to trait structure, or at least this particular depiction of trait structure, were we to infer from latency data that respondents rarely think of themselves in terms of conscientiousness, agreeableness, and so on.

In Table 3.5, response time data are reported for the Big Five questions, and also, for purposes of comparison, for an array of political and demographic variables.[22] On average, it took less than nine seconds per item to complete the ten-item personality battery, or an average of just under a minute and a half for the full battery.[23] This is fast. Respondents typically worked through the first six or seven personality items in under a minute, whereas a pace of three or four questions per minute is more common in survey research on attitudinal items. Also, respondents picked up the pace as the personality battery proceeded. The three items that took the longest to complete were among the first four to be asked. Conversely, the last three items in the battery were completed more quickly, an average of nearly two seconds per question faster than the first three items. Assuming that respondents and interviewers could maintain this faster pace a bit longer, a fifteen-item Big Five battery apparently can be completed by the average respondent in just over two minutes.

Two demographic items – the respondent's marital status, and the year of the respondent's birth – were completed quite quickly. Apart from these items, however, interviewers and respondents navigated the Big Five battery very rapidly as compared with other political and demographic items.

[22] Latency data for partisanship and ideology are not reported, as these were measured using activated timers rather than latent timers, bringing a lack of comparability with latency data for the Big Five items. In multivariate analyses using data from the 2006 CES, cases are weighted to reconstitute a random sample despite the oversampling in competitive districts. Data in Table 3.5 are not weighted, as I have no reason to expect response times to vary by type of congressional district.

[23] In Table 3.5, the trait items are grouped by trait. On the survey, the items were asked in the following order: relaxed, outgoing, hardworking, philosophical, introverted, nervous, sympathetic, not an intellectual, unkind, sloppy.

Table 3.5 *The Accessibility of Self-Reported Trait Judgments: A Comparison of Response Latencies*

| Item | Response Time (seconds) |
|---|---|
| A. Big Five Measures | |
| Not an intellectual–an intellectual | 9.23 |
| Philosophical–unreflective | 10.04 |
| Sloppy–neat | 7.61 |
| Hardworking–lazy | 8.95 |
| Outgoing–shy | 10.00 |
| Introverted–extraverted | 8.52 |
| Unkind–kind | 7.38 |
| Sympathetic–unsympathetic | 8.20 |
| Relaxed–tense | 10.82 |
| Nervous–calm | 7.73 |
| Average | 8.85 |
| B. Political Attitudes and Predispositions | |
| Presidential approval | 19.89 |
| Average, five-item battery, civil liberties and the criminally accused | 19.01 |
| Average, five-item battery, civil liberties and terror suspects | 17.91 |
| Average, three-item battery, support for traditional values | 17.01 |
| C. Demographics | |
| Year of birth | 5.55 |
| Education | 12.44 |
| Marital status | 3.47 |
| Employment status | 12.91 |

*Note*: Data are obtained from latent response timers, and indicate the total length of time required for interviewers to ask and respondents to answer each question. In section B, the civil liberties batteries each were asked of half of respondents.
*Source*: 2006 CES, Alternate Postelection Survey.

Data in section B of Table 3.5 show that measures of social and political attitudes typically take between seventeen and twenty seconds per item to complete, a pace over double that recorded for the trait measures. Some of this difference in length is a function of item format, not item content. Nonetheless, given that it took less than nine seconds for the average trait item to be asked and answered, it evidently is not the case that respondents were stumped or left speechless by the Big Five battery.

As a practical matter, the evidence is clear that addition of personality measures to opinion surveys brings only a minimal cost and requires relatively little effort. Respondents as a whole apparently found the Big Five battery to be neither off-putting nor confusing, and a viable representation of trait structure can be formed at the cost of under a minute and an half of interview time. Substantively, data in Table 3.5 support the claim that people are accustomed to thinking of themselves, and presumably also defining themselves, in terms of traits such as those represented by the Big Five. The evidence admittedly speaks only indirectly to this point,[24] but nothing in the present account casts doubt on the salience of personality. High response rates and quick response times combine to bolster the case that personality, particularly as represented by the Big Five framework, holds a prominent place in Americans' self-conceptions.

## CONCLUSIONS

The purpose of this chapter has been to transform the five-factor approach from the abstract conceptual framework described in Chapter 2 into a functional state that can be put to work in a series of empirical tests. Along the way, I have sought to demonstrate that no particularly daunting barriers stand in the path of routine inclusion of Big Five indicators on public opinion surveys. Toward these ends, in the present chapter a careful look at this study's data has established that the Big Five perspective offers a practical, efficient means to facilitate attention to personality traits in research on political behavior.

As a prelude to empirical analyses, the treatment of personality has narrowed considerably over the course of this book's first three chapters. Moving from the broad – and arguably unwieldy – concept of personality itself, the focus shifted, sequentially, to trait approaches writ large, then to the specific view of traits depicted in five-factor models, and lastly to

---

[24] I was not able to locate more direct evidence in any research reported by students of trait structure. Numerous books and articles were consulted. In no instance did I find reference to "accessibility," "latency," or "response latency" in conjunction with a discussion of the Big Five, nor did I locate Big Five studies that include citations of Fazio's (1990) pioneering research on latency. A simple, direct test regarding the centrality of personality traits would involve use of a common semantic-differential format, with items focusing on the Big Five, political attributes (e.g., liberal vs. conservative, Democrat vs. Republican) and physical traits (e.g., tall vs. short, heavyset vs. thin). By holding format constant, response latency measures derived from these items would provide a clear indication of the relative salience of personality.

the particular operationalizations of the Big Five detailed in this chapter. Putting matters in full context, this chapter has reviewed how the Big Five factors are measured in this study via a lexicological approach, with data gathered through a series of bipolar, or semantic-differential, items.

Especially when compared with the sorts of inquiries commonly reported in trait psychology, the chief limitation of the present approach concerns the somewhat thin representation of the Big Five factors. Trait scales with data from as few as two items per trait dimension are constructed, as compared with the dozens of items used in the largest personality inventories. Pragmatic demands require this use of limited scales. In my view, it is highly unforeseeable that future surveys on politics will follow the lead of personality researchers and include 240, or even 50 or 60, trait items. Hence, if I am to demonstrate the broad utility of the Big Five, it is imperative that I do so while using scales of limited size. With this in mind, the availability of data from three surveys stands as a central strength of the current study. The Big Five factors are measured similarly, but not identically, across the surveys. Thus, these data collectively provide an excellent opportunity to conduct multiple tests of the possible political effects of the Big Five. With repeated tests from three independent data sets, and with somewhat different constructions of the Big Five variables, we are in a good position to develop a strong baseline sense of the strength and consistency of relationships between trait structure and multiple aspects of political behavior.

The various diagnostic tests conducted in this chapter bring additional confidence. These tests establish that the Big Five scales constructed here provide reliable representations of trait structure. Further, several logistical matters have been addressed satisfactorily. Together, these results show that inclusion of trait items on public surveys appears to be relatively straightforward and uncomplicated. Respondents answered the trait questions in very high rates, the possible effects of social desirability pressures appear to be minimal, and no noteworthy delays in response time were recorded.

Ultimately, this chapter has demonstrated that trait structure *can* be measured on public opinion surveys. What remains to be determined, of course, is whether it *should* be. The analyses thus far have shown that the substantive content represented by the Big Five extends well beyond what is captured by demographic variables, but not that personality is politically consequential. The real value of five-factor approaches for students of political behavior only will be seen in applied tests linking the Big Five to politics. This task occupies the next three chapters.

# 4

---

## *Personality and Political Information*

From the outset, this study has been motivated by the thesis that personality is consequential for mass politics. More specifically, biological factors shape personality, which, in turn, functions as a persistent influence on political behavior. To examine the possible political effects of personality, the indicators constructed in Chapter 3 now must be put to work. In this chapter and the two that follow, a multitude of tests will be conducted to explore the possible political significance of variance in personality. Collectively, these tests offer a sweeping, multifaceted look at potential connections between the Big Five trait dimensions and a wide range of political phenomena. My strategy is to be as comprehensive as possible. Data from all three surveys are examined, and relationships of various forms are considered.

In this chapter, analyses center on political information, broadly defined. Included are tests regarding where citizens receive information about politics, patterns in social communication about politics, and the extent to which people are politically attentive, knowledgeable, and opinionated. In Chapter 5, the focus shifts to political attitudes and predispositions, followed in Chapter 6 by an investigation of the impact of personality on political participation. The dependent variables populating these three chapters constitute a representative array of the factors central in contemporary research on political behavior.

In each of these three chapters, a two-part analytical approach is employed. The first portion of each chapter reports tests regarding possible direct effects of personality on a wide range of dependent variables. Cumulatively, these tests promise to reveal general patterns regarding which Big Five traits are especially prominent as determinants of political behavior, and whether individual trait dimensions tend to have politicizing or depoliticizing influences. The second portion of each chapter then provides a closer look at select variables. Moving beyond direct effects of personality, these analyses consider a variety of more complex linkages between personality and politics. Included are models that contemplate combinational influences of personality traits, nonmonotonic effects, and possible interrelationships between the Big Five and other determinants of political behavior such as demographic attributes and political attitudes and predispositions. Some of these tests demonstrate that personality effects can operate via interactions with environmental forces.

## POLITICAL INFORMATION AND THE BIG FIVE

"Political information" can mean many things. Here, I follow a broad and inclusive course. Under the rubric of political information, I first consider the two most common sources of information about politics, media and interpersonal discussion. Next, I examine personality effects on how well-informed respondents to my surveys actually were (as represented by an objective measure of political knowledge), and how politically engaged they perceived themselves to be (as represented by measures of opinionation and political attentiveness). Lastly, interviewer ratings of respondents in terms of information level, opinionation, and political interest are examined. In all of these exercises, the guiding question concerns whether variance in personality influences patterns in the acquisition of information about politics.

### Media Use

Assessment of the possible relationship between personality and political behavior begins with the topic of media use. Citizens differ widely both in how frequently they follow the news and which news sources they prefer. Personality may contribute to these differences. For media use and for many of the aspects of political behavior that will be examined throughout the next three chapters, the Big Five trait dimensions will not necessarily contribute equally. I expect that all five factors will be important for political behavior, but not that all five will exert effects of similar magnitude for every dependent variable. Therefore, prior to presentation of the various empirical tests, I will outline those personality effects I strongly suspect to be found and those projected effects that are somewhat more speculative or uncertain. I also will note instances in which I have no basis to foresee relationships between particular trait dimensions and the aspects of political behavior under consideration.

In the case of media, my expectations concern openness to experience, conscientiousness, and extraversion. People who are open to experience thirst for information and relish analysis and reflection. Hence, openness to experience should be positively associated with most aspects of information acquisition, including media use. My thesis regarding conscientiousness is more tentative. By definition, people who are conscientious are responsible and dutiful. These characteristics apply in the workplace, education, personal life, and elsewhere, but it is an open question whether they also are important for political behavior. If part of the conscientious personality entails endeavoring to be a good citizen, then the conscientious should strive to be well informed. Lastly, my hypothesis regarding extraversion presupposes that extraverts view media use in somewhat instrumental terms. Extraverts are social beings, and casual political interactions are part of social life. In previous research, I have found that people draw directly on media reports about politics as part of the raw material that fuels political discussion (Mondak 1995b, 1995c; see also Walsh 2004). Hence, irrespective of any explicitly political motivation, I expect that extraverts may follow the news as a means to ensure that they are not left out of conversations. No link to media use is foreseen for the final two Big Five trait dimensions, agreeableness and emotional stability.

To test whether variance in personality underlies variance in political behavior, my strategy here and in the next two chapters will be to regress relevant dependent variables on the indicators of the Big Five described in Chapter 3, along with controls for demographic attributes (specifically, age, sex, race, and education). Two aspects of my approach warrant brief mention. First, indicators of all five trait dimensions are included in the models, even in those instances in which my hypotheses focus on only a subset of the Big Five. One reason I include all of the traits is because many of my analyses are inherently exploratory, and thus I prefer not to preclude by design the discovery of potentially interesting patterns.[1] A more fundamental reason to include all the trait indicators is that they combine to provide a holistic depiction of trait structure. Rather than viewing the indicators as five separate variables, it is more accurate to view them as the subcomponents of a broader taxonomy. Empirical representation of that taxonomy is most accurate if all of the subsidiary dimensions are included.

The second preliminary point meriting discussion concerns my decision to include only a single set of demographic control variables in all models. We saw in Chapter 3 that there are only a few modest relationships

---

[1] In these cases, detection of an interesting pattern obviously does not constitute support for a hypothesis. There is a risk in exploratory work of reading too much into unforeseen effects. In most instances in the current study, similar tests are conducted with data from two of my three surveys, and sometimes all three. This minimizes the risk of embracing seemingly interesting results that, in reality, are merely false positives. If an effect appears to be sensible and it emerges in similar form in more than one test, it typically will at least warrant discussion. Conversely, little notice will be given if an unexpected significant effect turns up with one data set but receives no corroboration in models with data from my other surveys.

between the demographic variables and the personality indicators. By including both sets of variables in my multivariate specifications, the models will capture a wide array of stable differences among people, differences that are both psychological and demographic. Other more transient variables, such as measures of interest in politics or strength of partisanship, are not used. One reason these variables are omitted is to avoid suffocating results in simultaneity. For instance, were I to regress TV viewing on political interest, would a significant coefficient on the latter mean that interest drives media use, or might it be, instead, that TV viewing sparks interest in politics? Disentangling such effects is no easy matter, and, given present purposes, there is simply no reason for me to devise unduly complicated tests. More importantly, factors such as political interest and strength of partisanship may themselves be influenced by personality. Consequently, their inclusion would carry the risk that the full impact of personality on the dependent variables in question would not be identified. This last point brings an important implication for future research. In many cases, it may well be that the effects of personality on particular aspects of political behavior operate in whole or in part via some mediating factor. Apart from one brief exception in Chapter 5, I do not explore such indirect relationships in this study. However, it should be clear that a full understanding of the effects of personality ultimately will require attention to both direct and indirect pathways. I will return to this point in the concluding chapter.[2]

Moving on to the task at hand, the 1998 CS and the 2006 CES both included measures of media use that asked respondents how many days in the past week they read newspapers and watched televised news. These items did not explicitly ask respondents whether they followed political news, but instead targeted media consumption more generally. There were two items of this form on the 1998 CS survey and three on the 2006 CES survey. The latter included three questions, because separate items were posed regarding consumption of local and national TV news. To test whether personality influences media use, data from these

---

[2] A case could be made that the only control variables I should include are biologically determined demographic attributes – that is, sex, age, and race. In other words, if endogeneity is a concern, then perhaps education should be excluded. This is a reasonable position. I have elected to include education here because it is used commonly as a control variable and I hope to be able to establish that the Big Five exert effects over and above those associated with standard demographic control variables. Elsewhere (Mondak et al. 2010), my colleagues and I report results similar to some of those in the current chapter and in Chapter 6, but with education excluded from the models. The chief difference between results in that paper and those reported here concern openness to experience. With education excluded, coefficients for openness typically strengthen.

five items are regressed on the Big Five variables and the four demographic measures.[3]

Table 4.1 depicts coefficient estimates for the media-use models.[4] For the most part, results for openness to experience and for conscientiousness are not consistent with my expectations. Only one statistically significant positive coefficient is obtained, and six of the ten coefficients for these two trait dimensions are negative. The null results for openness to experience are especially surprising. Less unexpectedly, mixed results also are found for agreeableness and emotional stability. Results for extraversion, in contrast, are much as predicted. Four of the five coefficients for extraversion are both positive and statistically significant, providing evidence that extraversion corresponds with a heightened propensity to attend to the news. The four significant extraversion coefficients all are greater than 1.0 in value. Thus, as extraversion rises from its lowest observed value to its highest, respondents are projected to gain more than one full day of newspaper or TV news consumption per week.

This initial foray provides a brief glimpse at the impact of personality on political behavior. For one facet of information acquisition, media use, extraversion proves to be influential. Building on these results, tests regarding other aspects of the information environment are required.

---

[3] In these particular models, estimation is via OLS regression. My general practice in this chapter and the next two is to use binomial logistic regression for dependent variables with two categories, ordered logistic regression for dependent variables with ordinal or interval scales and between three and seven response categories, and OLS regression for dependent variables with ordinal or interval scales and eight or more response categories. Where alternate estimators might have been appropriate (for instance, ordinal logistic regression or a negative binomial count model for the media-use dependent variables), I employed these techniques in models not reported here. There were no instances in which the basic patterns of results changed when an alternate estimation procedure was used. For simple models exploring the direct effects of personality on political behavior, I report only the coefficients for the Big Five variables. For models testing conditional or nonmonotonic effects, I include an appendix reporting full model results, and use figures to display the key patterns.

[4] Recall that the 2006 CES includes a pre-election wave, a postelection wave, and a supplemental stand-alone postelection survey. The Big Five items were included on the two postelection instruments. In models using CES data, the number of cases will be approximately 680 if the dependent variable was asked only on the pre-election wave of the study or on the main postelection wave; this is the case for the three CES models in Table 4.1. The number of cases will be slightly greater than 1,000 if the question for the dependent variable was included both on one of the main waves of the CES and on the alternate postelection instrument.

Table 4.1 *Media Use*

|  | Openness to Experience | Conscientiousness | Extraversion | Agreeableness | Emotional Stability |
|---|---|---|---|---|---|
| Number of Days per Week Respondent Reads a Newspaper (2006 CES) | 0.24 (0.57) | -0.77 (0.48) | -0.35 (0.44) | 0.16 (0.50) | 0.56 (0.53) |
| Number of Days per Week Respondent Reads a Newspaper (1998 CS) | 0.55 (0.80) | -0.76 (0.71) | 1.53* (0.64) | -0.28 (0.70) | 0.32 (0.69) |
| Number of Days per Week Respondent Watches the National News on TV (2006 CES) | -0.62 (0.52) | -0.40 (0.44) | 1.13** (0.40) | 0.81# (0.46) | -0.99* (0.49) |
| Number of Days per Week Respondent Watches the Local TV News (2006 CES) | -1.02# (0.54) | 0.44 (0.45) | 1.12** (0.41) | -0.32 (0.48) | 0.04 (0.51) |
| Number of Days per Week Respondent Watches News on TV (1998 CS) | -0.44 (0.76) | 1.74* (0.68) | 1.41* (0.61) | 0.04 (0.66) | -0.18 (0.66) |

*Notes*: Cell entries are OLS regression coefficients; standard errors are in parentheses. Models include controls for sex, race, age, and education. The dependent variables are coded 0 days per week to 7. Number of cases = 681, 363, 681, 681 and 367.

** $p < .01$, * $p < .05$, # $p < .10$

## Political Discussion

People engage in casual conversations with one another on a multitude of subjects. When politics comes up in these conversations, it may be by design, such as when one of the discussion partners has it in mind to persuade another to support a particular candidate. Alternately, conversations may flit from one topic to another, sometimes touching on political matters and sometimes not (e.g., Walsh 2004). To at least some extent, participation in political discussion is not wholly voluntary. Friends or neighbors may corner us to champion their favorite causes, and we are left either to endure their pontificating or seek our escape. Such involuntary association is especially common in the workplace (e.g., Mutz and Mondak 2006), but the broader point is that patterns in political discussion may be influenced by factors external to the individual. These may include the residual properties of the individual's discussion network (Huckfeldt, Johnson, and Sprague 2004), and even features of the national political context (e.g., Anderson and Paskeviciute 2005; Gibson 2003; Iglic 2003; Mondak and Gearing 2003).

Although some of the forces contributing to patterns in political conversation are external to the person, it does not follow that personality is inconsequential. The inherently social character of political discussion will be attractive to some people and unattractive to others. Certainly extraverts should be expected to engage in political discussion at relatively high rates. Likewise, people who are open to experience should welcome encounters with others, especially exchanges that involve a free-wheeling give-and-take about current affairs, the state of the nation, or candidates for office. Expectations regarding the remaining Big Five traits are less certain, but intuition suggests that they all may be inversely related to participation in political discussion. The reserved character of the highly conscientious may correspond with adherence to the belief that politics is an inappropriate topic for polite conversation. The contentious qualities of politics may encourage the agreeable to steer conversation toward more friendly turf. Lastly, people high in emotional stability are calm and require little in the way of external validation; they are unlikely to be especially chatty, whether about politics or any other subject.

All three of the available surveys include items pertaining to the prevalence of political discussion. The 1998 CS and 2005 NJS surveys asked respondents how often they discuss politics. These items used a days-per-week format identical to that for the media items examined above. On the 2006 CES, respondents on the postelection wave were asked to name up to four people with whom they discuss politics; a plurality of respondents (just over 34 percent) did, in fact, identify four discussion partners, with the remaining respondents distributed relatively evenly among the other categories. For this survey, the dependent variable will be the 0 to 4 count of network size.

Table 4.2 reports estimates of the impact of the Big Five on network size and on the frequency of political discussion. Findings for the first three trait dimensions are highly consistent. First, strong positive effects emerge for openness to experience in all three models. In the model for network size, the average size of a 2006 CES respondent's political discussion network is projected to increase from 1.99 to 2.80 discussion partners as openness rises from its lowest to its highest observed value. The effects are even more impressive for frequency of discussion, where we see that the number of days per week a respondent discusses politics is predicted to increase by 1.72 across openness on the 2005 NJS survey and by a staggering 2.98 days in 1998.[5] In the analyses reported earlier, no relationship between openness to experience and media use was detected. Here, in contrast, we see very strong effects of this trait dimension on patterns in interpersonal political discussion.

As expected, positive coefficients also are obtained for extraversion. The impact of extraversion on network size is quite similar to the effect for openness to experience. For the frequency of discussion, the coefficients in the 2005 NJS and 1998 CS models are virtually identical,[6] indicating that, on average, an extreme extravert will discuss politics one additional day per week relative to the extreme introvert. In contrast with openness and extraversion, negative coefficients are produced in all three models for conscientiousness, although only the effect for frequency of discussion in 1998 CS reaches statistical significance.[7] The conscientiousness coefficients are of modest size. It appears safe to conclude that high values on this trait dimension do not prompt political discussion, and, if anything, that the conscientious may be moderately averse to talking about politics.

### Political Attentiveness, Knowledge, and Opinionation

This chapter's first two sets of tests tackled specific aspects of the information context, news media and political discussion. As a complement

---

[5] The difference between the two years' results no doubt reflects in part that there simply was more to discuss in late 1998 – during and immediately after the midterm congressional elections, and at the height of the Clinton–Lewinsky scandal – than in the spring of 2005. Consistent with this view, the mean level of discussion is higher in 1998 than in 2005.

[6] The extraversion coefficient for the 2005 model achieves a minimal level of statistical significance ($p < .10$), but only narrowly. In 1998, the effect just misses this same threshold ($p = .101$).

[7] The coefficient for network size narrowly misses the .10 mark; specifically, $p = .108$.

Table 4.2 *Political Discussion*

| | Openness to Experience | Conscientiousness | Extraversion | Agreeableness | Emotional Stability |
|---|---|---|---|---|---|
| Number of Discussion Partners in Respondent's Political Discussion Network (2006 CES) | 1.04** (0.39) | -0.52 (0.33) | 1.03** (0.30) | 0.06 (0.34) | -0.85* (0.36) |
| Number of Days per Week Respondent Discusses Politics (2005 NJS) | 1.72** (0.64) | -0.36 (0.66) | 0.99# (0.59) | 0.44 (0.69) | 0.15 (0.65) |
| Number of Days per Week Respondent Discusses Politics (1998 CS) | 2.98*** (0.77) | -1.57* (0.68) | 1.00 (0.61) | -1.38* (0.66) | -0.62 (0.66) |

*Notes:* Cell entries in the first row are ordered logistic regression coefficients, and cell entries in the second and third rows are OLS regression coefficients; standard errors are in parentheses. Models include controls for sex, race, age, and education. The dependent variable in the first model is a 0 to 3 count of the number of discussion partners named by the respondent. The dependent variables in the second and third models are coded 0 days per week to 7. Number of cases = 683, 398, and 364.

*** $p < .001$, ** $p < .01$, * $p < .05$, # $p < .10$

to those analyses, I now offer something of a grab-bag of variables relevant to political information. Three factors will be examined: how much attention people pay to news about politics, levels of political knowledge, and general levels of opinionation.[8] Once again, positive effects are expected for openness to experience, conscientiousness, and extraversion. For extraversion, especially strong effects are projected for opinionation, because having views on a variety of subjects is particularly pertinent for people who wish to share those views with others – something extraverts often do and introverts tend not to do. Attentiveness and knowledge speak to levels of political information, but also to political engagement more broadly. For these variables, it is conceivable that agreeableness will yield negative effects. If politics is perceived to be ridden with conflict and dispute, the highly agreeable may steer clear. This possibility is tested more thoroughly in Chapter 6, which focuses on political participation, but the results presented in this chapter may offer at least a preliminary glimpse into whether agreeableness is depoliticizing. Lastly, because the emotionally stable often have a "mind their own business" ethos, negative effects for this trait are projected in models concerning opinionation.

The impact of personality on these variables is summarized in Table 4.3. Attentiveness is measured with a single item on the 1998 CS. The 2005 NJS and 2006 CES surveys both included knowledge scales,[9] and the 1998 and 2005 surveys asked respondents how opinionated they are. Looking first at results for openness to experience, note that positive and highly significant coefficients are obtained for all five dependent variables. Being open to experience does not matter for patterns in media use, but high values on this trait dimension correspond with a proclivity to engage in political discussion, to pay attention to politics, to be politically well informed, and to hold a large number of opinions. All of the coefficients for openness in Table 4.3 are quite sizeable. The largest substantive effect is for opinionation as measured on the 2005 NJS. Here, the predicted probability that a person will be highly opinionated, the top category on the four-point scale, increases dramatically across openness, from a mark of 0.02 for individuals with the lowest possible scores on openness to 0.54 at the opposite end of the scale. Collectively, the coefficients in Table 4.3 suggest a central role for openness to experience, at least in terms of those aspects of political behavior directly related to information.

---

[8] For the latter, the items asked whether respondents generally have opinions about most topics or only some; that is, the questions were not specific to politics.

[9] The 1998 CS also included a knowledge battery, but a split-ballot format was used in posing the knowledge questions. As a result, fewer than 200 cases would be available for models using one-half of the data or the other, and thus I opted against estimating personality effects with those data.

Table 4.3 *Political Attentiveness, Knowledge, and Opinionation*

| | Openness to Experience | Conscientiousness | Extraversion | Agreeableness | Emotional Stability |
|---|---|---|---|---|---|
| Attentiveness to Politics (1998 CS) | 1.22** | -0.56 | 0.64 | -0.92# | 0.46 |
| | (0.62) | (0.54) | (0.49) | (0.53) | (0.54) |
| Political Knowledge (2006 CES) | 1.04** | -0.71* | 0.24 | -0.52# | -0.14 |
| | (0.33) | (0.28) | (0.26) | (0.30) | (0.30) |
| Political Knowledge (2005 NJS) | 2.03*** | -1.27** | -0.66* | -0.47 | 0.19 |
| | (0.37) | (0.38) | (0.33) | (0.38) | (0.35) |
| Level of Opinionation (2005 NJS) | 4.02*** | 0.51 | 2.00** | -1.28# | -1.61* |
| | (0.70) | (0.70) | (0.61) | (0.70) | (0.63) |
| Level of Opinionation (1998 CS) | 2.31*** | -1.01# | 1.28** | -0.39 | -1.00# |
| | (0.60) | (0.53) | (0.47) | (0.52) | (0.51) |

*Notes:* Cell entries are ordered logistic regression coefficients; standard errors are in parentheses. Models include controls for sex, race, age, and education. The attentiveness and opinionation dependent variables are coded 0 (low attentiveness and opinionation) to 3. The knowledge dependent variables are 0 to 5 counts of the number of correct answers offered on closed-ended factual political knowledge items, with "don't know" responses discouraged. Number of cases = 365, 1,032, 1,134, 396, and 367.

\*\*\*$p < .001$, \*\* $p < .01$, \* $p < .05$, # $p < .10$

Somewhat surprisingly, four of the five coefficients for conscientiousness in Table 4.3 are negative, and three of these reach at least a minimal level of statistical significance. I had thought that being conscientious might correspond with factors typically associated with good citizenship, but present results seeming to imply that, if anything, the conscientious leave politics to others. As noted in Chapter 2, Bekkers (2005) identified a negative relationship between this trait and membership in voluntary associations. To the extent that conscientiousness includes a sense of deference to authority, current results and those from the Bekkers study might not mean that people who are generally conscientious uncharacteristically shirk responsibility when it comes to politics and civic engagement, but rather that they feel the dutiful course is to entrust such matters to experts. Alternately, it may be that people who are conscientious at work and at home simply do not have much time to devote to following politics. At this point, the matter cannot be resolved conclusively. However, several additional tests in this chapter and the two that follow will provide further evidence regarding the levels of politicization of individuals who score high in conscientiousness.

The effects for the remaining three trait dimensions conform to expectations. First, extraversion and emotional stability produce opposite patterns for opinionation; as predicted, extraverts tend to view themselves as opinionated, but people high in emotional stability do not. Second, all five coefficients for agreeableness are negative, and three reach minimal levels of statistical significance. Although the agreeableness effects are less than overwhelming, it does appear that a warm and sympathetic personality may be at least a modest impediment to political engagement. The findings for agreeableness certainly are not so compelling as to suggest that only mean-spirited cynics will gravitate toward politics, but we still should be alert to whether agreeableness effects continue to accumulate as we delve more deeply into the data over the course of the remainder of this chapter and the two that follow.

Stepping back for a moment, results presented in Tables 4.1 through 4.3 suggest that openness to experience and extraversion function as strong positive forces in terms of exposure to, and acquisition of, political information. Neither of these trait dimensions exerts significant influence across the board – openness is apparently unrelated to media use, and extraversion matters more for media use and opinionation than for being well informed. Still, one or both of these traits yielded a significant positive effect in all but one of the twelve models estimated thus far. Results for conscientiousness, agreeableness, and emotional stability contrast in magnitude and direction with those for openness and extraversion. Most of the effects for conscientiousness, agreeableness, and emotional stability are substantively modest, and a solid majority of the coefficients that reached at least minimal levels of statistical significance – twelve of four-teen – are negative. Investigation of links between personality and polit-ical behavior remains in its early stages, but the general theme emerging thus far is that openness to experience and extraversion function as polit-icizing forces, whereas, if anything, the other three trait dimensions seem-ingly discourage political engagement.

The dependent variables examined thus far mostly represent respon-dents' views of themselves.[10] The most plausible interpretation of find-ings for these variables is that people who are open to experience and are extraverted genuinely tend to be politically engaged, especially in terms of information, and that the conscientious, agreeable, and emotionally stable persons exhibit modest tendencies to avoid different facets of the political world. But an alternate possibility is that personality influences how we see ourselves rather than how we really are or how other people see us. Adjudicating between these scenarios is no easy matter. Results for politi-cal knowledge are instructive to a degree, demonstrating that people who are open to experience truly do possess relatively high levels of knowledge, and that the most conscientious individuals truly do tend to score low in knowledge. Data from the 1998 CS may bring additional insight on this matter. In that survey, interviewers were asked to rate survey respondents on several key constructs. Thus, it is possible to determine if personality influences what sorts of citizens others perceive us to be.

### Interviewer Ratings of Information, Opinionation, and Interest

Throughout this study, numerous relationships between personality and political behavior have been, and will be, reported. One lingering issue concerning these effects involves whether we can be confident regarding what causes what. Earlier in this chapter, for example, we saw that there are positive links between extraversion and the frequency of watching TV news, and between openness to experience and political knowledge. It is possible, although certainly improbable, that these effects signify the influence of the would-be dependent variables on self-reports about personality. In other words, my empirical tests may have the causal order backwards. For this to be the case, the respondent's thought process would have to be something such as "Am I an extravert? Well, I watch a lot of TV news, and that's something an extravert would do. So, yes, I guess I'm an extravert," or "No, I don't think I'm very philosophical. After all, my factual knowledge about politics is limited." Or, if the effect operates outside of the respondent's consciousness, it would have to be

---

[10] The one exception is political knowledge, which is measured with objective data rather than subjective self-reports.

the case, as one example, that watching television transforms viewers not into couch potatoes, but instead into extraverts. These examples admittedly are rather strained, and I see this as to the good. For most of the personality effects identified in this study, it is far easier to conceive of personality influencing political behavior than political behavior somehow driving how respondents answered the personality items. Politics is not front and center in most people's lives, and it consequently is unlikely that respondents will assess their own personalities through reflection on their actions in the political arena. Additionally, we have seen that a strong biological foundation underlies personality, again making it unlikely that a person's recent political behavior could influence stable psychological tendencies. But if any concerns about causal order do remain, they can be allayed with tests involving data from interviewer ratings of the survey respondents.

On the 1998 CS, interviewers were asked to answer a few questions about respondents immediately after the interviews had been completed. The items include the interviewer's perception of the respondent's level of information about politics, the respondent's general level of opinionation, and the respondent's interest in politics. Analytically, the chief virtue of tests involving these data is that it cannot be the case that the interviewer rating caused the respondent's answers on the personality items. When the telephone call between the interviewer and the respondent ends, and the interviewer proceeds to identify the respondent as highly opinionated, the interviewer's rating cannot be the cause of the respondent's decision fifteen or twenty minutes earlier to label herself as "talkative" and "outgoing." Thus, for any effects identified in tests involving interviewer ratings, we can be confident that the causal arrow is not inadvertently reversed.

Tests involving interviewer ratings possess a second interesting property. Any relationships between personality and interviewers' ratings *must* be indirect. Direct relationships are not possible. The fact that a respondent has a persistent psychological tendency toward extraversion cannot directly cause an interviewer to rate that respondent as opinionated. Instead, the tendency toward extraversion must influence the respondent's behavior – behavior that is observable during the interview process – with this behavior, in turn, influencing the interviewer's perception of the respondent.[11]

---

[11] One behavior that could influence interviewers' perceptions is how the respondents answered the personality items. For instance, the interviewer's thought process could be "she rated herself as talkative, and talkative people tend to be opinionated, so I suppose she is opinionated." Several factors suggest that such an effect is unlikely. First, the 1998 CS was a long survey, and it is doubtful that interviewers

This matter of indirect effects of personality on interviewer ratings is important because such effects will emerge only if respondents' personality self-ratings are rooted in reality. Figure 4.1 maps out the key logic. Beginning on the left side of the figure, we see the respondent's actual predisposition on some personality trait dimension. In the present example, the respondent is an extravert. This is a latent construct. Within my surveys, I have no measure of whether the respondent is actually extraverted. Instead, my data are provided by respondent's self-ratings. On the top-center of Figure 4.1, we see that the extraverted respondent also has identified herself as being an extravert. There is a correspondence between the latent construct and the empirical indicator. In this example, it follows that the respondent's self-rating provides a valid representation of the underlying trait dimension. Drawing on a vast wealth of research in psychology establishing the validity of self-rating Big Five indicators, I have assumed my scales in the present study to be valid. However, they need not necessarily be. If people lack the willingness or the capacity to evaluate their own psychological tendencies accurately, then my Big Five indicators would not provide valid representations of personality.

In Figure 4.1, we also see that the latent personality construct influenced the respondent's behavior during the survey interview. In short, personality matters for behavior. What sorts of behaviors are relevant? Perhaps the respondent routinely elaborated on her answers to the closed-ended survey questions, explaining in great detail why she disapproved of Bill Clinton's performance as president, and recounting multiple anecdotes when asked whether her personal financial situation has gotten better or worse in the past year. Later, upon recalling these features of the interview, the interviewer rates the respondent as being highly opinionated. Such behavior by the respondent is witnessed by the survey interviewer. For me, however, this behavior during the interview escapes

could have filed away in memory answers to specific personality items for use later. Second, interviewers did have actual behavior to guide their appraisals – during the interviews, some respondents were opinionated, interested and well-informed, and others were not. Having observed these behaviors, it is doubtful that interviewers would allow recollections of how respondents answered the personality items to override their own observations. Third, available evidence suggests that the direct correspondence between respondents' answers and interviewers' assessments is modest. As a test case, respondents were asked to rate themselves on a confident/unconfident scale, and interviewers later were asked to rate respondents' levels of self-confidence. In this instance, with focus on the same construct, the correlation between the two items is only 0.17. This suggests that the content of interviewers' assessments reaches far beyond how respondents answered the personality items. Further, if the correlation is only 0.17 with identical measures, the relationships almost certainly are weaker still when considering more disparate items such as the possible impact of self-rated extraversion on interviewer-perceived opinionation.

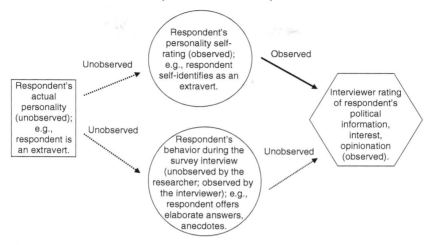

Figure 4.1 Personality, self-ratings, and interviewer assessments of respondents.

direct observation, as I have no record of the respondent's tone of voice, level of chattiness, and so on. Instead, the empirical tests available to me permit me to explore whether respondents' self-ratings on personality correspond with interviewers' assessments of the respondents on opinionation, political information, and interest in politics.

Critically, in Figure 4.1 there is no direct relationship between respondent self-ratings on personality and respondent behavior on the survey; instead, any correlation between the two exists because both trace to the same latent personality dimension. Therefore, the one relationship that I can observe – between respondent self-ratings on personality and the interviewer assessments on the political variables – will exist only if two conditions are met: (1) During the interviews, respondents acted in manners consistent with their latent psychological tendencies (i.e., personality affects how people behave), and (2) respondents' self-ratings on personality accurately represent their underlying psychological tendencies (i.e., personality is measurable).

All of this is a long way of saying that tests involving interviewer ratings not only will matter substantively, but also will provide evidence of the validity of self-ratings of personality. If how we see ourselves is unrelated to how we behave or how others perceive our behavior, then the search for links between my Big Five indicators and interviewer ratings necessarily will produce only null results.[12]

---

[12] Significant results would be evidence both that the relationships tested in the models actually do exist, and, indirectly, that personality self-ratings are valid. Null

Table 4.4 depicts the relevant statistical estimates. Significant positive relationships are identified between openness to experience and all three test variables, along with a positive link between extraversion and perceived opinionation. Conscientiousness produces negative coefficients in all three models, with two of the effects reaching statistical significance and the third narrowly missing. Five of six coefficients for agreeableness and emotional stability are negative, but only one obtains even a minimal level of statistical significance.

Taking the results for openness as an example, what process could generate these findings? First, it must be the case that, during the course of a survey interview, people who have rated themselves as being high in openness to experience behave in some manner that is similar to one another and different from the actions of people low in openness. Second, something about their behavior must cue interviewers that these respondents are interested in politics and are opinionated and politically well informed. Examples of such behaviors might include offering quick, confident answers to the questions, answering the knowledge items correctly, justifying attitudinal positions by mentioning facts or events beyond the immediate scope of the interview, and so on. The effects in Table 4.4 signify that respondents who are high in openness to experience perceptibly exhibit political engagement. From the discussion above, we can infer from these effects that 1) personality influences how people behave, and 2) respondent's personality self-ratings provide valid representations of personality.

The results for extraversion are especially interesting. Extraverts clearly struck interviewers as being quite opinionated. However, interviewers differentiated between opinionation on the one hand and being interested in politics and being politically well informed on the other. Extraverts talk (and talk) the talk, but they do not necessarily walk the walk. Interviewers picked up on this. Consistent with this view, results earlier in this chapter showed links between extraversion and media exposure, discussion, and opinionation, but not between extraversion and either attentiveness or political knowledge.

Lastly, respondents with high levels of conscientiousness score low in the eyes of interviewers. These negative relationships correspond with those in Table 4.3, meaning that the conscientious may be genuinely and perceptibly politically unengaged. I did not expect an inverse relationship between conscientiousness and politicization, yet evidence of such a relationship is accumulating rapidly. For now, I will reserve judgment on

results, in contrast, would not necessarily challenge validity because null findings could instead mean that there simply was no relationship to be detected – that is, that personality is unrelated to perceived opinionation, political interest, etc.

Table 4.4 *Interviewer Ratings of Respondents on Political Information*

| | Openness to Experience | Conscientiousness | Extraversion | Agreeableness | Emotional Stability |
|---|---|---|---|---|---|
| Respondent's Level of Information about Politics and Public Affairs | 1.57** (0.59) | -1.88*** (0.53) | -0.15 (0.47) | -0.15 (0.47) | -0.88# (0.51) |
| Respondent's General Level of Opinionation | 1.50* (0.60) | -0.80 (0.53) | 1.45** (0.48) | 0.13 (0.52) | -0.67 (0.52) |
| Respondent's Level of Interest in Politics | 1.98** (0.60) | -1.46** (0.53) | 0.17 (0.47) | -0.62 (0.52) | -0.28 (0.51) |

*Notes:* Cell entries are ordered logistic regression coefficients; standard errors are in parentheses. All data are from the 1998 CS. Models include controls for sex, race, age, and education. All dependent variables range from 0 (very low) to 4. Number of cases in all models = 367.

*** p < .001, ** p < .01, * p < .05, # p < .10

these findings until we see whether additional corroboration emerges in the remainder of this chapter and in the two that follow.

BEYOND DIRECT EFFECTS

The empirical tests reported thus far in this chapter examine possible direct effects of personality on several variables relevant in the study of political information. Similarly, the analyses to be conducted in the first portions of the next two chapters consider whether personality exerts direct influence on political attitudes and political participation. Collectively, these exercises provide for a sweeping look at the impact of personality on a great many of the phenomena of interest in contemporary research on political behavior. My strategy in presenting these tests is to be as inclusive as possible, so that the cumulative body of results will offer a thorough sense of the extent to which personality is consequential.

My empirical strategy includes a second key component. In this chapter and the next two, the search for direct effects of personality will be complemented with tests examining a variety of more complex relationships. My belief is that applications of this latter form hold the greatest promise of generating dramatic breakthroughs in our understanding of the foundations of political behavior. The opportunities in this area are seemingly limitless, and the tests I will report admittedly merely hint at this potential. In contemplating more complex effects of personality, future research must consider situations in which two or more personality traits may operate in combination, situations in which the impact of a personality trait may be nonmonotonic, and situations in which personality variables may operate in concert with other factors such as demographic attributes, political attitudes and predispositions, or features of the political environment. Examples illustrating each of these types of relationships will be outlined and tested. I begin here with two such endeavors. In the first, I revisit the relationship between personality and political knowledge, this time entertaining the possibility that two personality traits, openness and conscientiousness, exert combinational influence on knowledge levels. In the second, an important variable in research on political discussion is considered, exposure to disagreement in one's discussion network. Past research has shown that network size, one of the dependent variables assessed above, influences the likelihood of exposure to different points of view. I examine whether this effect, in turn, hinges on personality.

## *Openness, Conscientiousness, and Political Knowledge*

In the analyses reported in the preceding discussion, the effects of openness to experience and conscientiousness were found to run in opposite

of conscientiousness. On the left side of the panel, where openness is low, there is a sizable gap in political knowledge between individuals with low and high values of conscientiousness. This gap closes on the right side of the figure, meaning that rising levels of openness to experience negate the effects of conscientiousness. In this scenario, with one exception, respondents with different combinations of openness and conscientiousness all have relatively high knowledge levels; knowledge dips only among respondents with a single array of traits – low openness to experience coupled with high conscientiousness. Another way of summarizing this effect is that neither high openness nor low conscientiousness is necessary to produce a high level of political knowledge, but both traits are sufficient to attain this end.

In panel C, the outlier category includes those individuals who are high in openness and low in conscientiousness. Only for this combination of personality traits are knowledge levels projected to be high. In other words, neither high openness nor low conscientiousness is sufficient to produce a high level of political knowledge, but both of these traits are necessary. Conscientiousness overrides openness in this scenario, because the tendency of openness to foster the acquisition of political knowledge evaporates if conscientiousness is high. As a result, a wide gap between the two lines is evident on the right side of the panel; some people who are open to experience will be politically knowledgeable, but others – those high in conscientiousness – will not.

Using the scenarios in Figure 4.2 as a guide, we can assess the actual patterns that emerge when openness to experience x conscientiousness interaction terms are added to the equations for political knowledge. The inclusion of an interaction term provides a means to capture within the statistical model possible effects such as those described in Figure 4.2. Rather than assuming that all predictor variables exert direct, independent effects, the interaction term allows for the possibility that the impact of one variable is contingent on the effect of another variable. In the present case, the relevant test focuses on openness to experience and conscientiousness, but additional relationships of this form are considered in the next two chapters. Results of the present exercise are summarized in Figure 4.3 (full statistical results are reported in this chapter's appendix, section A).[14] Two features of the results are immediately evident.[15] First,

[14] Variables other than openness and conscientiousness are held constant at mean or modal values in Figure 4.3.

[15] At first glance, the knowledge levels displayed in Figure 4.3 may seem high. Recall, though, that knowledge is measured with data from closed-ended items, with "don't know" responses discouraged. Respondents with no actual knowledge would answer an average of 2.0 questions correctly by guessing on the 2006 survey, and 1.83 in 2005.

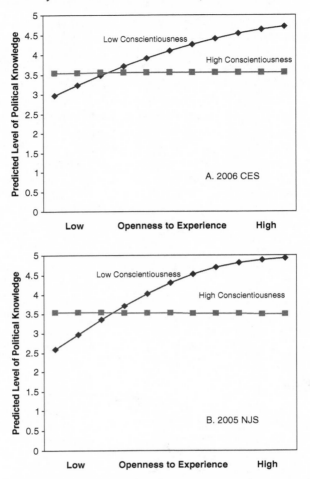

Figure 4.3 The combinational influence of openness to experience and conscientiousness as determinants of political knowledge.

the patterns are extraordinarily similar in the two panels. With the same pattern emerging in independent tests with data from two different surveys, we can have considerable confidence in our conclusions regarding the combinational effects of openness and conscientiousness. Second, the results clearly match the third scenario described previously, that is, as depicted in panel C of Figure 4.2. The lines in Figure 4.3 are not parallel, and the interaction terms giving rise to these estimates (see the appendix) are statistically significant. Thus, we can rule out the first scenario, that is, that openness and conscientiousness exert independent effects. In both panels, the estimated level of political knowledge is utterly flat across openness for individuals high in conscientiousness, but knowledge is predicted to rise sharply – just under two full points with the 2006 CES data, and just over two full points with the 2005 NJS data – where conscientiousness is low. For peak knowledge levels to be obtained, respondents must possess a very particular combination of personality traits: high levels of openness to experience coupled with low levels of conscientiousness.

These results provide an initial glimpse at the promise of moving beyond simple direct specifications of personality effects. In the present example, we see that two of the Big Five trait dimensions combine in their influence on political knowledge. In the next two chapters, several additional demonstrations of this sort will be reported, including examples of mediated effects, conditional relationships, and nonmonotonic effects. Before leaving this chapter, however, one additional test will be reported, this time with focus on properties of individuals' political discussion networks.

## *Personality and Exposure to Disagreement*

Previously in this chapter, links between personality and two aspects of political discussion – the frequency of discussion and the size of discussion networks – were examined. Although these are important variables, in recent years research on political discussion has highlighted the significance of an additional phenomenon, exposure to disagreement. A central benefit of political discussion is its capacity to expose people to new information and differing points of view. Conversations with like-minded others may offer reassurance and support, but such conversations do nothing to broaden the person's perspectives. In contrast, when discussion crosses lines of difference, it brings the potential to foster effects such as political tolerance and awareness of the rationales underlying opposing viewpoints (e.g., Mutz 2006; Mutz and Mondak 2006).

A great deal of research on political discussion in recent years has studied communication that brings exposure to disagreement (e.g., Huckfeldt, Johnson, and Sprague 2004; McClurg 2006; Mutz 2006). These works have excelled at identifying the effects, mostly positive, of cross-cutting political discourse, and they also have revealed many of the social and contextual factors that give rise to such conversations. As one example, we know that weak relationships and discussants who met via contexts such as the workplace are more likely to expose a person to different points of view than are strong relationships and discussants drawn from contexts such as church or a voluntary association (Mutz 2006). Likewise, it has been shown that there is an interdependence linking the members

of a given individual's network such that the presence of like-minded discussants facilitates the retention of non-like-minded discussion partners
within the network (Huckfeldt, Johnson, and Sprague 2004).

One point of dispute in this literature concerns the impact of network
size. As networks grow, the likelihood that they will include at least one
person with a differing point of view rises (Huckfeldt, Johnson, and
Sprague 2004), but it also appears that aggregate homogeneity increases
as networks expand (Mutz 2006). I suspect that personality may be of
relevance here. Specifically, the impact of network size on a person's exposure to disagreement may be conditional on personality. The key point
is this: As network size increases, any tendency toward homogeneity or
heterogeneity should not be assumed to be constant for all individuals.
Instead, persistent psychological tendencies may predispose the person to
prefer homogeneity within the network, or to accept heterogeneity.

In the 2006 CES, respondents were asked to indicate which way they
believed their discussion partners had voted in the local U.S. House of
Representatives race. I operationalize exposure to disagreement within
the network with a dummy variable coded 1 if at least one of the respondent's discussion partners cast a House vote at odds with the respondent's
partisan affiliation, and 0 if otherwise.[16] With the analysis limited to the
nearly 800 postelection respondents who named at least one discussant,
a score of 1 was recorded in just under 40 percent of cases. The chief
independent variable is network size, the dependent variable from the
2006 CES examined in Table 4.2. Four of the Big Five variables stand as
strong candidates to moderate the impact of network size on exposure to
disagreement. First, the rigidity of thought associated with conscientiousness suggests that individuals scoring high on this trait will strive to maintain homogeneity irrespective of network size. Second, the free-wheeling
sociability of the extravert supports the hypothesis that extraverts will
be relatively undiscriminating in their political conversations, in which

[16] Exposure to disagreement occurs under this operationalization if a respondent
who is a Democrat (or leans toward the Democrats) has at least one discussion
partner who voted Republican in a 2006 House race, or if a respondent who is a
Republican (or leans toward the Republicans) has at least one discussion partner
who voted Democratic in a 2006 House race. For discussants, I only have vote data
for the House vote, not partisanship. I opted to use partisanship rather than the
House vote as the indicator for the respondents to avoid two shortcomings associated with use of the vote. First, many respondents did not vote. I lose twenty-one
cases because respondents who are pure independents are omitted from the model,
but more would have been lost had I excluded nonvoters. Second, by focusing on
partisanship rather than vote choice among the respondents, I avoid uncertainty
regarding whether respondents and discussants live in the same congressional districts – a point for which data are unavailable.

case larger networks should magnify the odds of exposure to disagreement. Third, because people high in agreeableness tend to avoid conflict, I predict that the agreeable will surround themselves with like-minded discussion partners. Conversely, exposure to disagreement should be less disconcerting for individuals who are themselves disagreeable. Lastly, owing to their minimal need for social acceptance, I expect that individuals with high levels of emotional stability will tend to have heterogeneous discussion networks.

Network size is not purely an environmental factor because individuals exert at least some control over the size and composition of their discussion networks. Indeed, as noted above, personality matters for network size. Nonetheless, network size is at least partly determined by factors beyond the individual's control, and thus the interactions suggested here represent instances in which personality effects may emerge in combination with environmental – or at least environmentally influenced – forces.

To test these hypotheses, I regressed exposure to disagreement on personality, network size, and interactions between the personality and network size variables. Full results are reported in this chapter's appendix, section B. In two of the tests, results for personality interactions are consistent with expectations. No interaction between network size and either conscientiousness or emotional stability was detected, but the effects for extraversion and agreeableness attained statistical significance.

Figure 4.4 depicts predicted probabilities derived from the extraversion and agreeableness interactions. The patterns in the two panels are quite similar. In both, we first see that some respondents have only a modest likelihood of encountering disagreement in their discussion networks regardless of network size – respondents who are low in extraversion or high in agreeableness. Second, for individuals with the opposite personality traits, however, network size exerts a dramatic effect on the likelihood of exposure to disagreement. Indeed, in each panel we see that a respondent is predicted to have greater than 0.60 likelihood of encountering cross-cutting views only when (a) the network includes four discussion partners, and (b) the individual's personality is amenable to exposure to different points of view. These results establish that the link between network size and exposure to disagreement represents more than the occurrence of a simple stochastic process. By their nature, some people are accepting of exposure to differing political views, whereas other people seek to surround themselves with like-minded conversation partners. Consequently, the extent to which an expansion in the size of a person's political discussion network translates into a higher probability of exposure to disagreement depends to a substantial extent on the individual's

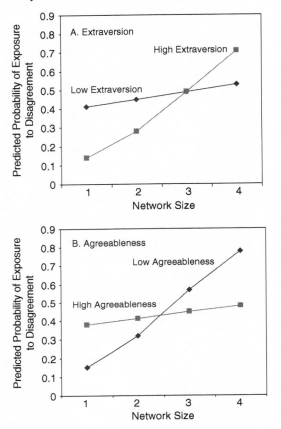

Figure 4.4 Personality and the conditional impact of network size on exposure to disagreement.

personality. This point brings particular significance for extraversion, because, as seen in Table 4.2, extraversion is strongly positively related to network size. Thus, the people whose personalities incline them to have large networks also are the people for whom large networks are most apt to produce exposure to disagreement.[17]

## CONCLUSIONS

This chapter constitutes the first in a three-part look at the potential relationships between personality and political behavior. Collectively, the

---

[17] My thanks to Bob Huckfeldt for calling my attention to this point.

findings reported above make for a highly promising start. Numerous relationships between the Big Five and multiple facets of political information have been identified, including both direct and conditional effects. Further, the emerging pattern suggests that the different Big Five trait dimensions may bring fundamentally different sorts of influences on how people engage the political world.

All of the Big Five traits produced noteworthy effects in the analyses presented in this chapter, although the nature of those effects differed widely. For openness to experience and extraversion, relationships to political information are widespread and uniformly positive. People with high levels of openness participate in political discussion, pay attention to politics, and are politically knowledgeable and opinionated. For extraverts, encounters with political information seemingly facilitate sociability. Extraverts and introverts do not differ in levels of political knowledge, but extraverts tune in to the news, they are opinionated, and they engage in political discussion. In contrast with these relationships, the effects for the remaining Big Five traits were relatively sparse and were consistently negative. Individuals scoring high in conscientiousness tend to defer from participating in political discussion, and they exhibit low levels of political knowledge. The agreeable score low in knowledge, attentiveness, and opinionation. People with high levels of emotional stability tend not to be opinionated. Collectively, these findings suggest that openness and extraversion generally function as politicizing influences, whereas conscientiousness, agreeableness and emotional stability perhaps are modestly depoliticizing.

The final analyses conducted in this chapter explored combinational, or conditional, effects. Noteworthy findings emerged for four of the Big Five traits. Research on political behavior abounds with reports of general relationships between variables, but it is far less common for researchers to consider whether these effects differ in magnitude across subgroups of individuals. Personality certainly stands as a likely candidate for generating such differences. Current results provide a straightforward example. Yes, the likelihood of exposure to disagreement will increase as one's political discussion network grows larger, but no, this effect is not constant for all individuals. People who are introverted and agreeable resist exposure to different points of view; consequently, for these groups, larger networks only tend to bring more of the same. These findings exemplify what I see as one of the most promising avenues for future research on personality and politics, as attention to personality may add tremendous nuance and precision to our understanding of the foundations of political behavior.

Again, the present chapter is only the first in a three-part exercise. Moreover, although these three chapters combine to test a great number of possible relationships, any single study necessarily will leave a tremendous amount of ground uncovered. As a first step, we have seen that personality is indeed linked to many facets of political information, as well as the first hints of what may be a general pattern, with some traits bringing mostly positive effects and others negative. We will gain much more context on the significance of these findings once additional classes of variables have been considered. Toward that end, the next task is to examine the potential impact of the Big Five on political attitudes and predispositions.

Appendix 4.A *Ordered Logistic Regression Models, Openness, Conscientiousness, and Political Knowledge*

|  | Model A. 2006 CES | Model B. 2005 NJS |
|---|---|---|
| Age | 0.03*** | 0.04*** |
|  | (0.00) | (0.01) |
| Sex | −0.79*** | −0.49*** |
|  | (0.14) | (0.12) |
| Education | 0.40*** | 0.40*** |
|  | (0.04) | (0.04) |
| Race | −0.89** | −1.42*** |
|  | (0.31) | (0.23) |
| Openness | 2.92*** | 5.38*** |
|  | (0.80) | (0.93) |
| Conscientiousness | 0.66 | 1.36# |
|  | (0.59) | (0.76) |
| Extraversion | 0.24 | −0.62# |
|  | (0.26) | (0.33) |
| Agreeableness | −0.60* | −0.63# |
|  | (0.30) | (0.38) |
| Emotional Stability | −0.09 | 0.42 |
|  | (0.30) | (0.36) |
| Openness to Experience × Conscientiousness | −2.90** | −5.45*** |
|  | (1.12) | (1.37) |
| Model $\chi^2$ | 295.73 | 348.38 |
| Number of Cases | 1,032 | 1,134 |

*Notes*: Results from these models were used to calculate the predicted probabilities reported in Figure 4.3. Cell entries are logistic regression coefficients with standard errors in parentheses. Models also include five threshold estimates.

\*\*\* $p < .001$, \*\* $p < .01$, \* $p < .05$, # $p < .10$

Appendix 4.B *Binomial Logistic Regression Models, Network Size, and Exposure to Disagreement*

| | |
|---|---|
| Age | 0.00 |
| | (0.01) |
| Sex | −0.51** |
| | (0.17) |
| Education | 0.02 |
| | (0.04) |
| Race | −1.61* |
| | (0.67) |
| Network Size | 0.83** |
| | (0.25) |
| Openness | 0.26 |
| | (1.02) |
| Conscientiousness | −0.11 |
| | (0.95) |
| Extraversion | −2.23* |
| | (1.03) |
| Agreeableness | 2.13* |
| | (0.98) |
| Emotional Stability | 0.02 |
| | (0.96) |
| Network Size × Openness to Experience | −0.40 |
| | (0.33) |
| Network Size × Conscientiousness | 0.06 |
| | (0.30) |
| Network Size × Extraversion | 0.74* |
| | (0.31) |
| Network Size × Agreeableness | −0.87** |
| | (0.31) |
| Network Size × Emotional Stability | 0.05 |
| | (0.32) |
| Constant | −1.96** |
| | (0.84) |
| Model $\chi^2$ | 83.01 |
| Number of Cases | 784 |

*Notes*: Data are from the 2006 CES. Results from these models were used to calculate the predicted probabilities reported in Figure 4.4. Cell entries are binomial regression coefficients with standard errors in parentheses.
** $p < .01$, * $p < .05$

# 5

## *Personality, Attitudes, and Political Predispositions*

The central lesson of the previous chapter is that psychological differences – differences in personality – bring substantial variance to patterns in the acquisition of political information. This point gains significance to the extent that citizens draw on that information when forming opinions about policies, political candidates, elected officials, and political institutions and procedures. In its simplest form, political behavior involves citizen exposure to information about politics and government, the use of that information to provide structure to political attitudes and predispositions, and then introduction of those attitudes and predispositions for tangible acts such as voting in elections, writing letters to the editor of one's local newspaper, or attending PTA meetings. In Chapter 4, multiple relationships between personality and political information have been observed. In Chapter 6, I consider the impact of personality on political participation. To link these two lines of inquiry, my task in this chapter involves exploration of possible connections between the Big Five and what people think and believe regarding various facets of the political world.

Once again, a two-part analytical strategy will be employed to organize and guide attention to personality. In the first section of this chapter, possible direct personality effects are examined broadly. My objective is to identify a representative array of the attitudes and predispositions of interest to students of political behavior, and to assess whether variance in these attitudes and predispositions traces to fundamental psychological differences. Following this, I then offer a more in-depth examination of personality as it relates to attitudes in one specific area, those concerning political processes. This second portion of the chapter seeks to demonstrate the potential value of conditional and nonmonotonic specifications of personality effects.

# Personality, Attitudes, and Political Predispositions

The term "political attitudes" encompasses tremendous ground. Included are broad orientations such as partisanship and political ideology; views of fundamental aspects of a nation's political system such as how the legislature is structured and what rights of citizenship are protected constitutionally; core moral, social and political values; perspectives regarding the citizen's own role in the political arena; and opinions about the salient policies and prominent political leaders of the day. If I am to make a persuasive case that personality warrants serious consideration in research on political attitudes, it is important that the tests I devise collectively provide a reasonable representation of this breadth.

Several groups of dependent variables are examined in this section. I begin by assessing the possible link between indicators of the Big Five and perceptions of internal and external political efficacy. Next, the personality variables are employed in models of the two cornerstone predispositions in research on political behavior, partisanship, and ideology. I then consider whether personality matters for two politically relevant indicators of social values, moral traditionalism and moral judgment. Lastly, I test for whether personality brings effects on opinions about specific contemporary policies; here, the tests probe both whether there are direct influences of personality and whether personality exerts indirect influence via partisanship or ideology or both.

The thesis I have advanced regarding the likely significance of the Big Five holds, first, that personality should matter for virtually all aspects of political behavior, and, second, that all of the Big Five trait dimensions should be politically consequential. It follows that the evidence reported below should be seen as relatively unconvincing if personality brings only a smattering of significant effects or if effects are dominated by one or two of the Big Five dimensions. Conversely, the evidence will be most supportive of my thesis if personality influences a wide range of political attitudes, and especially if most or all of the Big Five traits are found to underlie citizens' judgments about politics.

## Efficacy

Political efficacy involves the extent to which citizens feel that they can be meaningful participants in a nation's political system. The norm in research on political behavior is to differentiate between internal political efficacy (the individual's sense of personal competence and aptitude for political involvement), and external political efficacy (the individual's belief that public officials care about, and will be responsive to, the person's political views).[1] Most research involving political efficacy has examined how the concept should be measured and the impact of efficacy on other aspects of political behavior, such as participation and voter turnout. Early research on the antecedents of efficacy posited that efficacy emerged as a consequence of childhood socialization experiences (e.g., Easton and Dennis 1967). Subsequent investigations of the sources of efficacy have continued to explore the possible impact of socialization (e.g., Pasek et al. 2008).

Prior research on the sources of efficacy typically has not contemplated a role for personality.[2] Past research on the Big Five likewise provides only minimal guidance on the question of whether personality might matter for efficacy. Drawing on Mak and Tran (2001), the one clear expectation I have is that individuals with high levels of openness to experience should exhibit correspondingly high levels of internal efficacy. Openness encompasses perceptiveness and deliberation, along with a feeling of self-confidence. Consequently, it is easily imagined that individuals with high levels of openness to experience will be relatively comfortable and secure regarding their own levels of political aptitude. With the exception of this one probable relationship, however, the search for links between personality and efficacy is necessarily exploratory.

As in Chapter 4, multivariate tests in the present chapter will involve regressing dependent variables of interest on the indicators of the Big Five, along with controls for sex, race, age, and education. All three of the available surveys include a standard measure of internal efficacy, a categorical indicator of whether the respondent finds politics to be too complicated to understand. The two national surveys, the 2005 NJS and the 2006 CES, also include a categorical item regarding whether respondents believe that public officials care what people think; this question taps external efficacy.

Estimates of the impact of the Big Five on internal and external political efficacy are reported in Table 5.1.[3] As expected, very strong and consistent results emerge for openness to experience in the internal efficacy models. Hence, it appears that efficacy constitutes something more than a product of socialization experiences. Apart from the openness–internal efficacy link, however, results in Table 5.1 stand as something of a mishmash, offering no clear evidence of additional relationships between personality and efficacy.

---

[1] For a discussion of this distinction in the literature, see Niemi, Craig, and Mattei 1991.

[2] An exception is Sniderman (1975), who links self-esteem and efficacy.

[3] Efficacy items were asked of only one-third of respondents on the 2005 NJS. Also, efficacy items on the 2006 CES were asked on the pre-election wave, meaning that only respondents who completed both waves of the panel study are included in the models reported in Table 5.1.

Table 5.1 *Personality and Political Efficacy*

|  | Openness to Experience | Conscientiousness | Extraversion | Agreeableness | Emotional Stability |
|---|---|---|---|---|---|
| | | Internal Efficacy | | | |
| 1998 CS | 2.13*** | -2.12*** | 0.13 | 0.11 | 0.53 |
| | (0.60) | (0.54) | (0.47) | (0.52) | (0.52) |
| 2005 NJS | 2.54*** | 0.49 | 0.26 | -2.43*** | 0.79 |
| | (0.65) | (0.66) | (0.56) | (0.67) | (0.60) |
| 2006 CES | 1.38*** | -0.60# | 0.37 | -0.40 | -0.30 |
| | (0.39) | (0.33) | (0.30) | (0.34) | (0.36) |
| | | External Efficacy | | | |
| 2005 NJS | -0.27 | 1.46* | -0.50 | -1.29# | 1.11 |
| | (0.67) | (0.70) | (0.59) | (0.70) | (0.63) |
| 2006 CES | 0.13 | -0.90** | 0.05 | 0.13 | -0.10 |
| | (0.39) | (0.33) | (0.30) | (0.35) | (0.37) |

*Notes:* Cell entries are ordered logistic regression coefficients, with separate models estimated for each row of results; standard errors are in parentheses. Models include controls for sex, race, age, and education. Internal efficacy is measured with data from the item "Sometimes politics and government seem so complicated that a person like you can't really understand what's going on." External efficacy is measured with data from the item "Public officials don't care much about what people like you think." Efficacy scales range from 0 (low efficacy) to 4 on the 1998 CS and the 2006 CES, and from 0 to 3 on the 2005 NJS (this survey did not include a middle, or neutral, response category). Personality variables range from 0 to 1. Number of cases = (internal efficacy) 365 (1998 CS), 379 (2005 NJS), 676 (2006 CES); (external efficacy) 374 (2005 NJS), 677 (2006 CES).

*** $p < .001$, ** $p < .01$, * $p < .05$, # $p < .10$

The most curious results in Table 5.1 are those for conscientiousness. The models from the 1998 CS and the 2006 CES yield statistically significant negative effects, suggesting that individuals high in conscientiousness hold low levels of both internal and external political efficacy. These results contrast starkly with those from the 2005 NJS. The NJS models both produce positive coefficients for conscientiousness, and the coefficient in the model of external efficacy is statistically significant and substantively quite large. Although additional data would be needed for me to provide a definitive account of this difference, my strong hunch is that it relates to elements of the political context. The 1998 CS and 2006 CES surveys primarily concerned voting and elections, and both were conducted in the context of midterm congressional elections. When viewing themselves as one among millions of voters in a national election, individuals scoring high in conscientiousness apparently felt a sense of political powerlessness. But the 2005 NJS was a survey of citizens who have been called in for jury duty, and who completed the survey while waiting to be assigned to a jury. This seemingly provided an ideal context for citizens to perceive that public officials care what people think. Consistent with this view, a mere 24 percent of respondents on the 2006 CES expressed feelings of external efficacy (this mark rises to 31 percent when respondents choosing the neutral category are included), versus 61 percent on the jury survey. It appears that perceptions of external efficacy vary sharply as a function of features of the political context, and, most importantly for present purposes, that individuals high in conscientiousness are especially responsive to this contextual effect.

## Ideology and Partisanship

In research on American political behavior, ideology has stood as one of the central concepts for decades. Philip Converse's (1964) landmark critique triggered a vibrant discussion of the role of ideology in Americans' conceptualizations of politics, and countless scholars have subsequently conducted research exploring the extent to which ideology provides guidance and structure to policy judgments and to evaluations of political candidates. But what are the sources of ideology? Are some people destined by birth to be conservatives and others liberals? Is ideology the product of early socialization and learning? Does ideology constitute a summary of one's core values? Is ideology perhaps merely inferred from the policy judgments and candidate evaluations it is used to predict? And, most centrally for present purposes, do elements of personality – and especially the Big Five trait dimensions – matter for ideology?

Multiple factors undoubtedly contribute to ideology, and a full account of those factors is well beyond the scope of the present study. What I can do, however, is test whether any consistent links exist between the Big Five traits and ideology. As a prelude to such inquiry, two points highlighted in Chapter 2 warrant reiteration: that our personalities change only minimally over time, and that much of the variance in personality across populations originates in biology. It follows that evidence of a relationship between personality and political ideology would imply that the roots of ideology develop long before the age of political awareness. Such a finding would be consistent with recent research on genetics and politics, and especially with the efforts of Alford and colleagues (2005), in which analysis of data from twin studies reveals a biological foundation to political ideology. Importantly, although Alford, Funk, and Hibbing (2005) report clear evidence that genetic factors influence ideology, the authors provide no test of a mechanism leading to this relationship. I believe the impact of biology on ideology may operate in large part through personality.

Numerous prior investigations have explored the possible impact of personality on ideology, with research on this subject spanning more than half a century. Outside of the realm of the Big Five, relevant works range from McClosky's (1958) groundbreaking study on personality and ideological conservatism, to a recent investigation by Block and Block (2006) on connections between personality as observed in preschool and political ideology in young adulthood two decades later. As noted in Chapter 2, several studies conducted in the United States and elsewhere have employed indicators of the Big Five as predictors of political ideology. In these works, the most common findings have been that openness to experience corresponds with a liberal political perspective (e.g., Alford and Hibbing 2007; Riemann et al. 1993; Schoen and Schumann 2007; van Hiel, Kossowska, and Mervielde 2000), and that conscientiousness corresponds with ideological conservatism (e.g., Riemann et al. 1993; Stenner 2005). Also, the studies conducted by Riemann et al. (1993) and Barbaranelli et al. (2007) identified effects of emotional stability on ideological conservatism and support for conservative political candidates.[4] Recall from Chapter 2 that the openness and conscientiousness hypotheses are best understood in terms of traditional views in which liberalism corresponds with a willingness to see government tackle new and varied problems, while conservatism implies a more cautious approach in which presumption favors the status quo.

---

[4] Jost and colleagues recently have produced several papers discussing the psychological bases of ideology, including links between personality and ideology. As part of these analyses, the authors have noted effects of the Big Five – and especially openness and conscientiousness – on ideology. See Carney et al. (2008); Jost, Nosek, and Gosling (2008); and Jost, Federico, and Napier (2009).

My data sets facilitate a three-part reexamination of the personality-ideology relationship. Ideology was measured in nearly identical form on the 1998 CS, the 2005 NJS, and the 2006 CES, with a standard seven-point indicator used in each case. Data from these indicators have been recoded to range from 0 (the respondent is strongly liberal) to 6 (the respondent is strongly conservative). To assess the possible impact of the Big Five trait dimensions on ideology, ideological self ratings are regressed on the Big Five measures; once again, all models include controls for age, sex, race, and education.

Results presented in Table 5.2 reveal several very strong and substantively large relationships between personality and ideology, with effects squarely in line with those identified in past research. All six of the coefficients for openness to experience and conscientiousness have signs in the expected directions, with greater openness corresponding with ideological liberalism and conscientiousness with conservatism; five of these coefficients reach high levels of statistical significance.[5] The ideology scales range from 0 to 6 in value, and their standard deviations vary from 1.45 (1998 CS) to 1.99 (2006 CES). In this context, the five statistically significant coefficients for the first two Big Five traits are especially impressive, as ideology is predicted to shift by between 1.31 and 1.66 points across the observed values of openness to experience and conscientiousness. At their largest, these effects span more than a quarter of the range of the ideology scales.

Apart from openness to experience and conscientiousness, results in Table 5.2 are less definitive. Still, the findings are suggestive. First, the coefficients for extraversion provide no evidence whatsoever that this trait matters for ideology. Mixed signs emerge across the three tests, and all of the coefficients fall well short of statistical significance. This array of null effects replicates Riemann et al.'s (1993) findings from Germany. Therefore, it seems safe to conclude that extraversion brings no consistent or noteworthy impact on political ideology. Second, present findings also offer no compelling basis to conclude that agreeableness predicts ideology. At most, there exists a modest, inconsistent correspondence

---

[5] I do not have a definitive account for why openness to experience produces an insignificant and substantively small effect on the 1998 CS. Because this survey was conducted in a single Southern community, variance on ideology is less on the 1998 CS than on the two national surveys. However, this characteristic did not prevent the emergence of a strong effect for conscientiousness. In any case, we should not be too troubled by the absence of an openness effect in this one instance. The coefficients on the two national surveys both are sizeable, both reach the highest level of statistical significance, and these effects corroborate those found previously by several other teams of researchers. Hence, the preponderance of available evidence supports the conclusion that openness to experience predicts liberalism.

Table 5.2 *Personality and Political Ideology*

| | Openness to Experience | Conscientiousness | Extraversion | Agreeableness | Emotional Stability |
|---|---|---|---|---|---|
| 1998 CS | −0.28 | 1.31** | 0.30 | −0.64 | 0.32 |
| | (0.47) | (0.42) | (0.38) | (0.41) | (0.40) |
| 2005 NJS | −1.66*** | 1.40*** | −0.02 | −0.41 | 1.00*** |
| | (0.29) | (0.30) | (0.26) | (0.30) | (0.27) |
| 2006 CES | −1.42*** | 1.33*** | 0.28 | −1.00** | 0.67* |
| | (0.32) | (0.27) | (0.26) | (0.29) | (0.30) |

*Notes:* Cell entries are OLS regression coefficients, with separate models estimated for each row of results; standard errors are in parentheses. Models include controls for sex, race, age, and education. The dependent variable, ideology, is coded 0 (strongly liberal) to 6 (strongly conservative). Personality variables range from 0 to 1. Number of cases = 358 (1998 CS), 1,133 (2005 NJS), 1,028 (2006 CES).

*** $p < .001$, ** $p < .01$, * $p < .05$

between agreeableness and liberalism. Third, as in the studies by Riemann et al. (1993) and Barbaranelli et al. (2007), results from the two national surveys reveal moderate connections between emotional stability and conservatism. These effects fall short of those for openness and conscientiousness in terms of magnitude, yet they still provide insight on the relationship between psychological and political differences.

The emerging personality profile of the conservative is an individual who is conscientious, level-headed, and fixed in his or her ways. These patterns bring considerable intuitive satisfaction, particularly when we think of the traditional "small c" conservative, the person who is reluctant to entertain dramatic political change, and who endorses limited, fiscally responsible government. Conversely, results in Table 5.2 indicate that the liberal exhibits less psychological reliability and stability than the conservative, but has a greater tendency to embrace new ideas, and perhaps a slight proclivity to be relatively warm and agreeable. Such a profile seems consistent with the traditional view of liberals with respect to ambitious government programs, and especially support for social welfare policies.[6]

It is important to keep in mind that present results denote general tendencies, not ironclad rules of political behavior. In other words, liberals

---

[6] Recall from Chapter 2 that Charney (2008a) has criticized past work regarding a link between openness and liberalism on the grounds that it is circular. As noted in Chapter 2, Charney offered no evidence in support of his position. Unfortunately, my own data do not allow for such a test, as it never occurred to me to include ideological liberalism as an indicator of openness [nor, from what I can determine, did it occur to Goldberg (1992), whose Big Five indicators informed those used in my work]. However, given that my measures of openness include only terms such as "philosophical," "curious," "analytical," and "imaginative," present results presumably should allay Charney's concerns. The findings reported here show that openness to experience as measured on the 2005 NJS and the 2006 CES strongly predicts ideological liberalism – and does so using measures constructed with data from what I believe to be apolitical adjective pairs.

A final note on this point is that my empirical task in this study is to identify relationships, not to issue judgments on ideal personality types. I certainly can see that conservative readers, especially those who presume openness to experience to be an inherently and unequivocally good thing, might be made uncomfortable by the finding that openness is linked with liberalism (and, similarly, liberal readers might be troubled upon finding that low levels of conscientiousness and emotional stability predict liberalism). As a social scientist, I care very much about designing and reporting appropriate tests, but I frankly could not care less if liberal or conservative ideologues are vexed by the patterns those tests reveal. My personal sense, especially as a parent, is that some openness to experience is useful ("Try the peas, you may like them"), but that too much can be perilous ("Do *not* put your finger in there!"). Likewise, readers will recall from Chapter 2 that research in psychology has identified various apparent consequences of openness to experience, some that most people probably would view as positive and others that most people presumably would view as negative.

can be close-minded and conservatives can be irresponsible. But these findings also highlight the fact that young adults are not ideological blank slates when they first encounter the political world, and that ideological leanings constitute something more than a summary judgment about contemporary political affairs. Different points of view survive, and even thrive, in the American political arena, in no small part because people are not all the same. Liberals and conservatives both might believe that, given the opportunity, they could persuade all of their fellow citizens of the wisdom and virtue of their respective ways of thinking. But this is not so. The reason people are not all on the same political page is not that some have seen the light and others have not, but instead because people exhibit fundamental and persistent psychological differences, differences that are largely rooted in biology. These differences are not *about* politics, yet they matter *for* politics. By their nature, some people are psychologically predisposed to be liberals and others to be conservatives.[7]

Moving from ideology to partisanship, the basis for predictions of personality-based effects becomes much less certain. Classic research on the origins of partisanship anchors partisan affiliation largely in family socialization, not personality (e.g., Campbell et al. 1960).[8] Further, partisanship has been shown to shift over time in response to changes in political issues and events (e.g., Franklin and Jackson 1983; Franklin 1984), a dynamic quality that perhaps should be unexpected if partisanship

---

[7] In an odd but fun case of worlds colliding, in late 2009, as I was putting the finishing touches on this study, I collaborated on a song regarding the impact of genetics and personality on political ideology. The song is entitled "Hardwired," and is performed by the incredibly talented folk singer Christine Lavin. Christine and I know one another because we both have written songs about Pluto, and she very kindly helped to get the lyrics to mine included in Neal Tyson's book *The Pluto Files* (2009). Christine did most of the writing on "Hardwired," but the song does include a couple of verses I contributed, along with input from political scientists John Alford and John Hibbing, and Pulitzer Prize–winning author and columnist Gene Weingarten. "Hardwired" can be heard at http://www.songramp.com/mod/mps/viewtrack.php?trackid=75248. Another fun "personality song" is "The Introvert Song," written by Deirdre Flint, and included on the 2009 CD *Diva Nation*.

[8] In *The American Voter* (1960), Chapter 18 focuses on personality, but, for the most part, the discussion bears little resemblance to a contemporary trait approach. Campbell his colleagues first invoke work on the authoritarian personality, and then consider a concept they label as "sense of personal effectiveness." As to partisanship, the authors concede little room for personality: "We would expect little articulation between personality and partisanship for individuals whose voting reflects an established family pattern or one undertaken by the individual early in life" (1960, 508). In hindsight, of course, we might ask whether an established family pattern reflects only the occurrence of a socialization process or perhaps also the impact of highly heritable, politically relevant personality traits.

is influenced by relatively intransient traits such as the Big Five. Lastly, the Alford, Funk, and Hibbing (2005) research on politics and genetics detected a biological foundation for ideology, but no corresponding link between biology and party affiliation.

None of these points necessarily precludes an impact of personality on partisan affiliation, and thus the question warrants empirical study. If we are to speculate about possible connections between the Big Five and partisanship, the relationships identified in Table 5.2 offer reasonable starting points. Partisanship and ideology may not be one and the same, but they walk hand-in-hand often enough to suggest that what predicts one may predict the other. Hence, as a baseline, we might surmise that self-identified Republicans will be high in conscientiousness and emotional stability and low in openness to experience, with Democrats exhibiting the opposite profile.

The regression estimates in Table 5.3 include a mix of foreseeable results and mild surprises. As to the former, openness and conscientiousness operate as expected on the 2005 NJS and the 2006 CES, and, as in the ideology models, extraversion again turns in a poor showing. The surprises emerge in the final two columns. First, the consistent effects of emotional stability on ideology are not replicated for partisanship. But second, agreeableness apparently matters for partisan preference. On all three surveys, high scores on this trait dimension correspond with a tendency toward affiliation with the Democrats, and the effects reach at least minimal levels of statistical significance in each case.[9]

The findings for agreeableness are intriguing. One obvious question – a question not answerable with current data – involves whether Democrats generally tend to be more agreeable than Republicans, or whether present findings speak only to politics in the years 1998 to 2006. Interviews for the 1998 CS were conducted following the 1998 midterm elections, a period that coincided with the Clinton impeachment. If individuals scoring high in agreeableness found the impeachment proceedings to be conflictive and off-putting, a momentary step away from the Republican Party may well have occurred. Likewise, the Bush presidency was quite embattled by the time of the 2005 and 2006 surveys, and the latter survey was fielded following a midterm election cycle in which numerous Republican congressional incumbents had been implicated in a wide array of distasteful scandals (see Hendry, Jackson, and Mondak 2009). Given these features of the 1998–2006 era, I cannot rule out the possibility that the identified effects of agreeableness on partisanship are time

---

[9] Agreeableness also produced a statistically significant negative effect on partisanship in a model estimated using data from Mary Anderson's 2004 Tallahassee survey. This finding is noted in Mondak and Halperin (2008, 352).

Table 5.3 *Personality and Partisanship*

| | Openness to Experience | Conscientiousness | Extraversion | Agreeableness | Emotional Stability |
|---|---|---|---|---|---|
| 1998 CS | 0.14 | 0.43 | 0.68 | -1.48* | -0.21 |
| | (0.68) | (0.61) | (0.55) | (0.58) | (0.61) |
| 2005 NJS | -1.11** | 1.86*** | -0.11 | -0.73# | 0.95* |
| | (0.42) | (0.44) | (0.38) | (0.44) | (0.40) |
| 2006 CES | -1.76*** | 1.29*** | 0.56# | -1.21*** | 0.42 |
| | (0.35) | (0.30) | (0.28) | (0.32) | (0.33) |

*Notes:* Cell entries are OLS regression coefficients, with separate models estimated for each row of results; standard errors are in parentheses. Models include controls for sex, race, age, and education. The dependent variable, partisanship, is coded 0 (strong Democrat) to 6 (strong Republican). Personality variables range from 0 to 1. Number of cases = 338 (1998 CS), 1,136 (2005 NJS), 1,030 (2006 CES).

*** $p < .001$, ** $p < .01$, * $p < .05$, # $p < .10$

bound. It is clearly conceivable that agreeableness matters for which citizens exhibit short-term fluctuations in their partisan attachments, and in what circumstances. At this point, though, a full unpacking of the agreeableness–partisanship connection is not possible. A more definitive statement regarding why this relationship exists must await analysis of additional data from different historical contexts.

## Moral Traditionalism and Moral Judgment

Ideology and partisanship cast politics in broad form. Policy appraisals, which I examine below, capture narrower aspects of the political world. Before turning to evaluations of specific policies, a brief consideration of broad social judgments may provide a fruitful complement to the assessment of personality as it relates to partisanship and ideology. Herbert Weisberg (2005, 648) differentiates between moral traditionalism and moral judgment. Weisberg explains that the former "refers to people's underlying predispositions on traditional family and social organization," whereas the latter "refers to views as to the condemnation of other people's lifestyle choices in such areas as cohabitation and homosexuality." Thanks to Weisberg's initiative, the 2006 CES includes an item measuring moral traditionalism and two items tapping moral judgment.[10] Weisberg (2005) has modeled these phenomena on demographics and religiosity. At question, of course, is whether personality also plays a role in shaping people's views on these items.

As with partisanship and ideology, the most easily envisioned effects of personality on moral traditionalism and moral judgment center on our first two traits, openness to experience and conscientiousness. Openness to experience has scholarly roots tracing to Rokeach's (1960) work on dogmatism. Seen in this light, openness sits at odds with traditionalism, and especially with the tendency to be morally judgmental. Conversely, positive relationships should be expected between conscientiousness and moral traditionalism and judgment. Although conscientiousness on the 2006 CES is operationalized via indicators of order and responsibility, broader depictions of this trait dimension include traditionalism and virtue as subsidiary components (e.g., Roberts et al. 2005). Concrete expectations pertaining to the other Big Five traits are less obvious. Given

[10] The former asked respondents the extent to which they agreed or disagreed with the proposition that "This country would have fewer problems if there were more emphasis on traditional family values"; data are coded 0 (strongly disagree) to 4 (strongly agree). The latter two items used the same format, and the questions are summed to form a 0 to 8 scale. The first moral judgment question is "It is always wrong if a man and a woman have sexual relations before marriage," and the second is "It is always wrong if two adults of the same sex have sexual relations." These items are correlated at a level of 0.61.

that agreeableness has been shown to predict positive views of diversity (Strauss, Connerley, and Ammermann 2003) and resistance to HIV/AIDS stigmatization (McCrae et al. 2007), this trait may exhibit patterns similar to those hypothesized for openness to experience.

Ordered logistic regression results reported in Table 5.4 match well to expectations. For both moral traditionalism and moral judgment, sizeable effects emerge for openness to experience and conscientiousness, with openness corresponding with low values on the dependent variables, and conscientiousness producing the opposite pattern. The openness and conscientiousness trait dimensions have functioned as trailblazers throughout the current chapter, consistently exhibiting strong relationships to an increasingly wide array of social and political judgments. What is especially noteworthy about these traits is that their effects almost always run in opposite directions. It follows that the political and social predispositions of individuals who are high in openness to experience and low in conscientiousness will differ markedly from those of individuals with the reverse personality profile. Table 5.4 also reveals evidence that agreeableness may matter on the margins for moral traditionalism and moral judgment. In both models, the expected negative effects emerge, although neither reaches conventional levels of statistical significance ($p < .16$ and $p < .07$, respectively).

## Policy Attitudes

To a large extent, Americans' policy preferences fall along partisan and ideological lines. We have seen that most of the Big Five traits (openness to experience, conscientiousness, emotional stability, and perhaps agreeableness) influence ideology, and that three traits also affect partisanship (openness, conscientiousness, and agreeableness). Consequently, any impact of partisanship and ideology on policy attitudes would signal an indirect effect of personality. But the existence of such an indirect relationship does not preclude the possibility that personality also brings influence to policy judgments over and above that associated with partisanship and ideology. Such additional effects presumably would be most likely for important, highly visible issues, ones for which citizens' judgments have gained nuance that exceeds the bounds of ideological and partisan predispositions.[11]

---

[11] That personality effects are not entirely mediated by partisanship and ideology would not rule out the possibility that they are mediated by other factors (e.g., core values) not tested here. Indeed, a reasonable case could be made that personality should *not* be expected to exert direct, unmediated effects on specific policy judgments, operating instead through an array of intermediary judgments and predispositions. Much more work is required before the precise causal chain can be specified, a chain that may start with biological forces and end with specific policy judgments, and, along the way, include personality and broad political predispositions.

Table 5.4 *Personality, Moral Traditionalism, and Moral Judgment*

| | Openness to Experience | Conscientiousness | Extraversion | Agreeableness | Emotional Stability |
|---|---|---|---|---|---|
| Moral | -1.54*** | 1.69*** | -0.10 | -0.42 | 0.43 |
| Traditionalism | (0.32) | (0.28) | (0.26) | (0.30) | (0.31) |
| Moral Judgment | -1.29*** | 0.92*** | 0.14 | -0.50# | 0.41 |
| | (0.30) | (0.25) | (0.24) | (0.27) | (0.28) |

*Notes:* Data are from the 2006 CES. Cell entries are ordered logistic regression coefficients, with separate models estimated for each row of results; standard errors are in parentheses. Models include controls for sex, race, age, and education. The dependent variable in the first model is constructed from a five-point categorical item, with data coded 0 (low moral traditionalism) to 4. The second dependent variable is formed by summing data from two five-point items, with data coded 0 (low moral judgment) to 8. Personality variables range from 0 to 1. Number of cases = 1,027 and 1,002.

*** $p < .001$, # $p < .10$

## Personality, Attitudes, and Political Predispositions

Data from the 2006 CES offer an excellent opportunity to test whether personality brings both direct and indirect effects on policy attitudes. The pre-election wave of the CES included a battery of seven policy items. On each, respondents were asked to use a five-point scale to indicate how favorable (maximum favorability = 5) or unfavorable (1) they felt toward the policy. The questions concerned the Patriot Act, the war in Iraq, oil drilling in the Arctic, legalized abortion, legalized gay marriage, federal income tax cuts, and tighter controls over immigration.[12] In statistical models including only demographics, ideology, and partisanship as predictors, ideology and partisanship both produced statistically significant effects in all seven instances. Because personality matters for both partisanship and ideology, these results establish that personality influences policy attitudes indirectly. To test whether there also are direct effects of personality over and above those operating via political predispositions, models must be estimated including partisanship, ideology, and the indicators of the Big Five.

In a separate battery on the CES, respondents were asked their views regarding the importance of the seven issues. In the aggregate, respondents found the war in Iraq and tighter controls over illegal immigration to be the most important issues, and legalized gay marriage and oil drilling in the Arctic to be the least important. Thus, if issue importance provides the opportunity for effects beyond those associated with core political predispositions, we should be most likely to see such effects for the questions concerning the war in Iraq and illegal immigration.

Ordered logistic regression results for five of the policy attitudes are depicted in Table 5.5; the table omits the models for oil drilling in the Arctic and legalized gay marriage – the two issues viewed as least important by CES respondents – because no personality variable produced a statistically significant effect in those instances. Results in Table 5.5 reveal that all four of the personality variables that influence partisanship and ideology also bring at least some direct influence on policy judgments. Openness to experience corresponds with opposition to the war in Iraq and to federal income tax cuts, and to support for legalized abortion. Conscientiousness produces opposition to legalized abortion, along with support for control over illegal immigration. Agreeableness is related to opposition to the Patriot Act, legalized abortion, and control over illegal immigration. Emotional stability shows two modest effects, on support for the Patriot Act and opposition to control of illegal immigration. Lastly, extraversion – the one trait dimension unrelated to both partisanship and ideology – produces significant effects in the income tax and immigration equations.

[12] The wording used here is the same as was posed to the survey respondents.

Table 5.5 *Direct and Indirect Effects of Personality on Policy Attitudes*

| | The Patriot Act | The War in Iraq | Legalized Abortion | Federal Income Tax Cuts | Tighter Controls Over Illegal Immigration |
|---|---|---|---|---|---|
| Age | −0.00 | −0.01 | 0.01 | −0.02** | 0.01 |
| | (0.00) | (0.01) | (0.01) | (0.01) | (0.01) |
| Sex | 0.12 | 0.18 | 0.26 | 0.21 | 0.24 |
| | (0.16) | (0.18) | (0.16) | (0.15) | (0.16) |
| Education | −0.13** | 0.04 | 0.05 | −0.01 | −0.04 |
| | (0.04) | (0.04) | (0.04) | (0.04) | (0.04) |
| Race | 0.24 | −1.49* | −0.40 | 0.70# | −1.15** |
| | (0.38) | (0.64) | (0.38) | (0.37) | (0.37) |
| Ideology | 0.25*** | 0.34*** | −0.43*** | 0.27*** | 0.24*** |
| | (0.05) | (0.06) | (0.05) | (0.05) | (0.05) |
| Partisanship | 0.32*** | 0.45*** | −0.09* | 0.19*** | 0.16*** |
| | (0.05) | (0.05) | (0.04) | (0.04) | (0.05) |
| Openness | −0.22 | −1.05* | 1.56*** | −0.84* | 0.28 |
| | (0.41) | (0.47) | (0.42) | (0.40) | (0.42) |
| Conscientiousness | 0.48 | 0.48 | −0.58# | 0.52 | 0.91** |
| | (0.35) | (0.38) | (0.35) | (0.34) | (0.35) |
| Extraversion | 0.40 | 0.33 | −0.39 | 0.52# | 1.33*** |
| | (0.31) | (0.34) | (0.31) | (0.30) | (0.32) |
| Agreeableness | −0.64# | −0.38 | −1.25** | −0.49 | −0.76* |
| | (0.36) | (0.39) | (0.36) | (0.35) | (0.36) |
| Emotional Stability | 0.68# | 0.17 | −0.13 | 0.05 | −0.71# |
| | (0.38) | (0.41) | (0.38) | (0.37) | (0.38) |
| Model $\chi^2$ | 240.73 | 372.18 | 229.61 | 174.68 | 153.10 |
| Number of Cases | 627 | 673 | 668 | 673 | 673 |

*Notes:* Data are from the 2006 CES. Cell entries are ordered logistic regression coefficients, with separate models estimated for each column; standard errors are in parentheses. Each model also includes four threshold estimates. The dependent variables are constructed from five-point categorical items, with data coded 1 (most unfavorable view of the policy) to 5. *** $p < .001$, ** $p < .01$, * $p < .05$, # $p < .10$

To provide a visual example of the direct and indirect influence of personality, Figure 5.1 displays the significant path effects for support for legalized abortion. Looking first to the top of the figure, we see that openness to experience yields a direct positive effect on support for legalized abortion. Openness also produces two indirect positive effects because

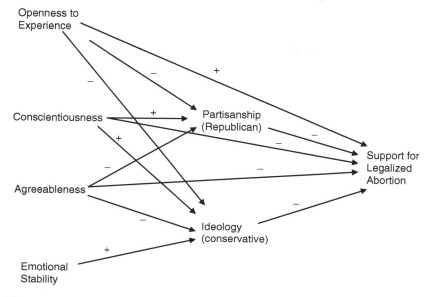

Figure 5.1 Direct and indirect effects of personality on attitudes toward abortion.

this trait is negatively associated with a Republican partisan identification and a conservative ideological stance, both of which, in turn, are negatively linked to support for legalized abortion. Conscientiousness is the mirror opposite of openness, with three negative effects on abortion attitudes, one direct and two indirect. The one unexpected pattern in Figure 5.1 is that concerning agreeableness. The relationships between agreeableness and partisanship and ideology are negative, meaning that persons scoring high on this trait dimension tend to venture away from Republican partisanship and ideological conservatism. It follows that the indirect impact of agreeableness on support for legalized abortion is positive. However, the direct impact of agreeableness on abortion attitudes is negative, meaning that the direct and indirect influences of agreeableness conflict with one another.[13]

Thus far, the examination of possible links between personality and political attitudes and predispositions has been highly fruitful. Personality

[13] When abortion attitudes are regressed on personality and demographics in a model that omits partisanship and ideology, agreeableness produces a statistically marginal ($p < .10$) negative coefficient that is roughly half the magnitude of the coefficient reported in Table 5.5.

effects have been observed at every turn, for internal and external political efficacy, partisanship and ideology, moral traditionalism and moral judgment, and now for several specific policy attitudes. Moreover, as we have just seen, the impact of personality on policy assessments does not operate exclusively through political predispositions. Among the Big Five traits, the effects of conscientiousness and, especially, openness to experience have been of particular note both for their abundance and their substantive magnitude. However, all five trait dimensions have generated multiple significant effects, in this chapter, providing additional support for the value of employing a broadscale model of trait structure.

## PERSONALITY AND ATTITUDES TOWARD POLITICAL PROCESSES

The effects of personality examined thus far in this chapter mostly have involved direct, monotonic relationships. Indicators of the Big Five have been added to a variety of models of Americans' political predispositions and attitudes, and numerous noteworthy relationships have been identified. However, as I have suggested throughout this study, much of the impact of personality on political behavior may come in more complex form. Once again, as in Chapter 4, I will present some clear-cut examples in an effort to demonstrate the potential value of contemplating conditional and nonmonotonic personality effects. As research proceeds, and especially as our theories become more refined, my expectation is that many more relationships of this sort will be identified. Again, it is my view that applications of the Big Five in the study of politics promise to bring the greatest insight once we move beyond the realm of simple, linear specifications.

The present examples center on two items from the 2006 CES, questions concerning citizens' attitudes regarding political processes. In their provocative book *Stealth Democracy* (2002), John Hibbing and Elizabeth Theiss-Morse report a great deal of very persuasive evidence showing that many Americans are troubled by intrinsic features of the democratic process. Americans hold especially critical views of debate and deliberation, and the forging of political compromise. Because they see little legitimate basis for disagreement on many questions of policy, citizens often refuse to acknowledge any need for politicians to consider compromise or to participate in lengthy discussion. As a result, these elements of politics are viewed with suspicion, and many citizens are left wondering why elected officials do not simply quit talking, stick to their principles, and get to work. The original Hibbing and Theiss-Morse data are from 1998, but John Hibbing's initiative led to the inclusion of several items related to their thesis on the 2006 CES. It follows, of course, that we now can explore whether personality matters for Americans' process attitudes.

In 2009 Hibbing and Theiss-Morse, joined by Eric Whitaker, examined the process items asked on the 2006 CES. As part of their analyses, the authors included indicators of the Big Five in their multivariate models. Several direct effects of personality were reported. My interest is with two of the process questions, and, more specifically, with some particular null results obtained when the personality indicators were introduced as predictors of respondents' answers to these items. The first question is "If you could change Congress, would you prefer that members take action without engaging in such lengthy discussions about the issues, or discuss issues more thoroughly before taking action?" Unlike in *Stealth Democracy*, respondents in 2006 voiced a strong collective preference for discussion,[14] choosing discussion over quick action by a margin of four to one. In contrast, respondents were nearly evenly divided on the second item, which asked "Would you prefer that members of Congress stand up for their principles come what may, or compromise with their opponents in order to get something done?" On this question, just over 52 percent of respondents indicated that they preferred that members of Congress stand up for their principles rather than consider compromise.

On the first of these items, that is, concerning action versus discussion, Hibbing and colleagues (2009) detected significant direct effects of openness to experience and emotional stability, with high values on both trait dimensions corresponding with greater support for thorough discussion. Those results are quite logical; people high in openness to experience value information and reflection, and people low in emotional stability are prone to rash action. Moving beyond such direct effects, my curiosity then centered on another of the Big Five traits, extraversion. What interested me was that both of the response options presented on the 2006 CES might appeal to the extravert. After all, extraverts can be both action-oriented and talkative. This presents something of a puzzle. How does extraversion factor into the decision calculus if both of the choice options likely seem attractive to extraverts, and, by implication, unappealing to introverts? For introverts, I suspect that the choices effectively neutralize the possible effects of this aspect of personality. With personality off the table, introverts should default back to alternate criteria. Thus, given that over 80 percent of respondents overall opted for thorough discussion over quick action, my expectation is that most introverts will prefer discussion.

---

[14] Hibbing, Theiss-Morse, and Whitaker (2009) note that question wording differs on the 1998 and 2006 surveys, which may account for part of the difference in aggregate response.

As to extraverts, I foresee personality interacting with demographic attributes. It is common in research on personality traits for scholars to consider whether personality effects vary by age, sex, and so on (e.g., Gomez et al. 1999). In the present case, the question we might ask ourselves is what sort of extravert would be inclined to take fast action, and what sort would be more apt to talk things over first. In contemplating this question, the attributes that appear to be especially good candidates to help clarify the impact of extraversion are age and sex. That is, among extraverts, my expectation is that men, and especially younger men, will be inclined to prefer that members of Congress seek immediate action rather than talk things over first. Conversely, for older respondents and for women, extraversion will manifest itself in a preference for social interaction, and especially conversation.[15] What this implies is that we should observe different response patterns on the Hibbing and Theiss-Morse discussion–action item for male and female extraverts, and for old and young extraverts.

To test this thesis, a binomial logistic regression model was estimated (full results are reported in this chapter's appendix, model A). The key results produced by this model are displayed in Figure 5.2.[16] Panel A reports effects for extraversion and gender. On the left side of the panel, we see that there is no difference between the predicted response selections of introverted men and women, with both preferring discussion at a rate of roughly 80 to 85 percent. On the right side of the panel, however, a stark difference is observed. For moderately extraverted individuals (those with extraversion scores one standard deviation above the mean), women have a 90 percent predicted probability of preferring discussion, versus a figure of only 66 percent for men. At the very highest level of extraversion, the corresponding predicted probabilities are 94 percent for women and a mere 44 percent for men.

A very similar pattern is observed in the second panel of Figure 5.2, this time with estimates differentiated by age. Among male respondents who are age 75, moving from 0 to 1 on extraversion yields only a very modest increase in the predicted probability of preferring a Congress characterized by action rather than discussion. In stark contrast, a dramatic swing

---

[15] For men and women, evidence of this distinction is provided in how they define themselves in terms of extraversion. My best opportunity to test this point is on the 2005 NJS, where I have five adjective pairs for each of the Big Five trait dimensions. On that survey, one of the adjective pairs used to represent extraversion is timid–bold, and another is talkative–quiet. Relative to women, men were significantly more likely to define themselves as bold rather than timid, but significantly less likely to label themselves as talkative rather than quiet.

[16] As in Chapter 4, the predicted probabilities reported in Figure 5.2 and Figure 5.3 are calculated with other variables held at their mean or modal values as appropriate.

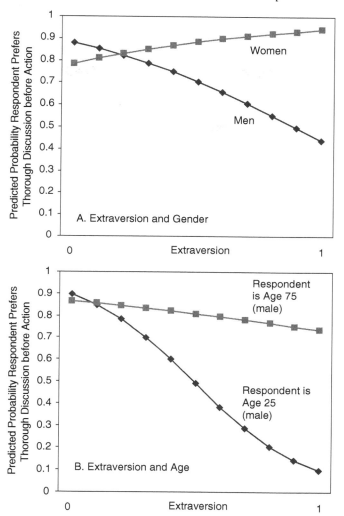

Figure 5.2 The conditional impact of extraversion on discussion versus action in Congress.

occurs across extraversion for men who are age 25, with predicted values of preference for discussion plummeting from 90 percent to 10 percent.

As John Hibbing and colleagues have noted (2009), respondents on the 2006 CES overwhelmingly preferred that members of Congress conduct thorough discussions of the issues rather than racing to act. But this response pattern naturally begs the question of who are the 20 percent or so of Americans who would forego careful discussion in Congress in favor of quick action? Present results demonstrate that we can make considerable headway on this question by contemplating the possible interplay between personality and demographics. By themselves, extraversion, age, and sex all offer incomplete answers because it is simply not the case that all extraverts, all young respondents, or all men have a tendency to prefer action to discussion. Instead, we must consider personality and demographics in combination. The clear outlying groups in Figure 5.2 are extraverted men, and especially extraverted young men. In my view, these particular effects simply make good sense. Of course, the critical lesson here is not about extraversion and demographics, but rather about the broader value inherent in attention to the possible ways that personality interacts with other determinants of political behavior. With guidance from the abundant and ever-growing literature on trait psychology, and with careful thought about plausible interrelationships among our predictors, research on personality and mass politics should help us paint a picture of the American citizen characterized by unprecedented nuance.

In addition to delineating and assessing possible conditional effects of personality, we also should be alert to circumstances in which the impact of personality may be nonmonotonic. For instance, there may be some instances in which individuals with middle values on a particular trait dimension differ in their attitudes and behaviors from those at either extreme. The second process item included on the 2006 CES may be a case in point. Recall that this question asked respondents whether members of Congress should stick to their principles no matter what, or compromise in order to get things done; respondents were divided almost evenly on this item. Of the process items examined by Hibbing, Theiss-Morse, and Whitaker (2009), this was the only question found to be unrelated to the Big Five.

In reconsidering the choice of principle versus compromise, my interest is in the possible role of conscientiousness. In the Hibbing, Theiss-Morse, and Whitaker (2009) study, this trait dimension yielded a statistically insignificant and substantively negligible negative coefficient. Starting with individuals with the lowest possible scores on conscientiousness, what answer should we expect on the 2006 CES item? At the very low end of the trait scale, individuals are sloppy, irresponsible, and slothful. At this extreme, respondents would feel no affinity for effort or achievement. Consequently, I suspect that the prospect that members of Congress could "compromise with their opponents in order to get something done" would be utterly unappealing to respondents scoring low in conscientiousness. Now consider people at the other extreme in terms of conscientiousness, those receiving the very highest marks on this trait. For these individuals, extreme conscientiousness can give rise to rigidity in thought, thereby precluding a willingness to contemplate compromise. It follows that respondents toward the middle of the conscientiousness scale may be the most interested in having members of Congress compromise in the name of accomplishment. These individuals perhaps are conscientious enough to desire achievement, yet not so conscientious as to be inflexible in the face of opposing points of view.

The logic outlined here is that of a nonmonotonic effect. The predicted relationship between conscientiousness and preference for compromise would not be an upward- or downward-sloping line, but rather an upside-down letter U. Respondents with high and low values on conscientiousness are predicted to view compromise critically, albeit for differing reasons. Support for compromise in Congress should peak for individuals toward the middle of the conscientiousness scale.

The most straightforward means to test for a hypothesized nonmonotonic effect is to include in a statistical model both the variable of interest and its squared term. Predicted values obtained from this exercise are displayed in Figure 5.3 (full statistical results for this logistic regression equation are reported in the appendix, Model B). The effect observed in Figure 5.3 is not dramatic, but the pattern is unmistakable. Medium levels of conscientiousness correspond with the highest predicted probabilities that respondents will support compromise in Congress. At its peak, preference for compromise is over twenty percentage points higher than

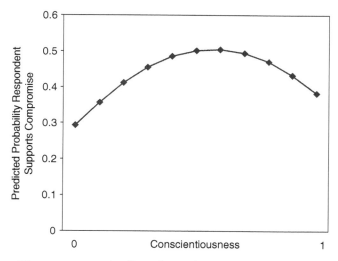

Figure 5.3 The nonmonotonic effect of conscientiousness on preference for compromise in Congress.

the mark for individuals at the bottom of the conscientiousness scale, and over fifteen percentage points higher than for those persons with the top observed levels of conscientiousness.

As with the conditional relationship between extraversion and demographics, the nonmonotonic effect of conscientiousness seen here should signal both the promise of attention to personality and the tremendous magnitude of the task at hand. This particular nonmonotonic relationship was not difficult to envision, but specification of most effects of this sort likely will come only after a great deal of additional theory building.

## CONCLUSIONS

The study of attitudes is central to research on political behavior. For decades, scholars have examined the antecedents of public opinion, the stability of attitudes over time, relationships among political predispositions and policy judgments, the psychological processes driving attitude formation and change, and a host of other related matters. This tremendous flurry of activity is quite understandable, as fundamental questions regarding citizen competence cannot be answered without research on the formation, structure, and content of political attitudes. We cannot gauge how effectively people execute the duties of citizenship if we do not know something about what opinions they hold about politics, along with how, and how well, those opinions are formed.

In this chapter, I have sought to demonstrate that attention to the psychology of individual differences can help us to uncover some of the sources of variance in mass opinion about politics and governance. I am hardly the first social scientist to suggest that personality matters for political attitudes and predispositions, nor even the first to invoke a Big Five perspective. Still, by casting the net widely, this chapter has revealed that personality is consequential at multiple levels and in multiple ways. The vastness of the playing field ensures that any single study will only scratch the surface, yet the breadth of findings reported in this chapter should bring confidence that future applications of the Big Five in this area will prove fruitful.

Three aspects of current results are particularly striking. First, citizens' political judgments have been studied broadly, yet personality effects have emerged at every turn. The territory covered in this chapter includes internal and external efficacy, partisanship and political ideology, moral traditionalism and moral judgment, attitudes about the political process, and judgments regarding several specific policies. All told, twenty-two multivariate models were estimated in this chapter; at least one Big Five indicator produced a significant effect in twenty instances, and two or more Big Five variables yielded significant coefficients in nineteen of the twenty-two models. Second, the evidence supports the desirability of a broadscale trait approach. Measures of all of the Big Five trait dimensions generated multiple statistically significant effects. Relationships between personality and political attitudes were especially common for three traits – openness to experience, conscientiousness, and agreeableness – but it is clear that all of the major trait dimensions contribute in some manner to our understanding of political attitudes and predispositions. Third, personality effects come in many forms. Most of the models estimated in this chapter searched for evidence of direct, monotonic relationships between personality and political judgments. However, we also have seen that the influence of personality in some instances can be indirect, conditional, or curvilinear.

Although considerable ground has been covered in this chapter, research on the links between personality and political attitudes remains in its infancy. One strategy for future studies would be replication and extension of current results. Further refinement of our understanding of the relationship between personality and core political predispositions certainly would be beneficial, as would be additional investigation of how personality relates to policy judgments. But the greatest payoffs likely will come with research that explores the potential role of personality in attitude formation, stability, and change. For instance, research in political cognition invokes insights from social and cognitive psychology in the study of phenomena such as information processing and decision making, and attitude formation. This body of research has taught us a great deal about how individuals' levels of motivation and ability, and their existing predispositions, influence the processing and use of new information. But it is extraordinarily rare for such works to contemplate the possible significance of personality traits. This is a glaring and unfortunate gap. Together, the results reported in this chapter and in Chapter 4 highlight the importance of personality for both political information and political attitudes. A new generation of research that integrates these insights may lead to dramatic breakthroughs in our efforts to develop holistic accounts of political behavior. Critically, such accounts necessarily would acknowledge that political behavior is not merely a product of individuals' interactions with the environment. Instead, stable forces that are in place long before people first encounter the political world also play noteworthy roles.

Examples of such future studies are easily envisioned. For instance, in recent years many interesting laboratory experiments have explored phenomena such as motivated reasoning, citizen response to heuristic cues, framing effects, the impact of misinformation on policy judgments, and so on. In each of these cases the typical laboratory experiment includes little or no effort to differentiate among participants *within* a given cell of the experimental design. However, for all of these sorts of experiments, hypotheses can be generated quite quickly as to how experimental treatments might bring more or less pronounced effects depending on the participant's personality profile. Put differently, the person's enduring psychological tendencies likely will influence how the person responds to experimentally manipulated elements of the information environment.

Future research projects in this area hold practically unlimited potential, but the significance of current results should not be minimized. Thus far, the applications of the Big Five presented in this study have revealed that personality matters for many of the central variables of interest in research on information and mass opinion. As a complement to these first two waves of tests, my final empirical task in this project entails assessment of whether personality also matters for various aspects of political participation.

Appendix 5.A *Logistic Regression Models, Citizens' Attitudes toward Political Processes*

| | Model A. Discussion versus Action | Model B. Principles versus Compromise |
|---|---|---|
| Constant | 1.20 | −1.62** |
| | (0.88) | (0.60) |
| Age | −0.01 | 0.00 |
| | (0.01) | (0.00) |
| Sex | −0.68 | −0.20 |
| | (0.43) | (0.18) |
| Education | 0.02 | 0.16*** |
| | (0.06) | (0.05) |
| Race | 1.62# | 0.13 |
| | (0.85) | (0.42) |
| Openness | 1.39* | 1.26** |
| | (0.63) | (0.46) |
| Conscientiousness | −1.22* | 3.16* |
| | (0.50) | (1.56) |
| Extraversion | −6.17** | 0.42 |
| | (1.94) | (0.34) |
| Agreeableness | 0.79 | −0.56 |
| | (0.52) | (0.39) |
| Emotional Stability | 1.53* | −0.67 |
| | (0.61) | (0.42) |
| Age × Extraversion | 0.07* | − |
| | (0.03) | |
| Sex × Extraversion | 3.69*** | − |
| | (0.95) | |
| Conscientiousness × Conscientiousness | − | −2.76* |
| | | (1.29) |
| Model $\chi^2$ | 61.63 | 43.20 |
| Number of Cases | 647 | 672 |

*Notes:* Results from these models were used to calculate the predicted probabilities reported in Figure 5.2 and Figure 5.3. Cell entries are logistic regression coefficients with standard errors in parentheses. The dependent variable in Model A is coded 1 if the respondent prefers that members of Congress engage in thorough discussion prior to action, and 0 if the respondent prefers prompt action. The dependent variable in Model B is coded 1 if the respondent prefers that members of Congress seek compromise in order to take action, and 0 if the respondent prefers that members of Congress stick with their principles no matter what.

*** $p < .001$, ** $p < .01$, * $p < .05$, # $p < .10$

# 6

## *Personality and Political Participation*

I write children's poetry and song lyrics, and also lyrics for songs in other genres. In 2008, I attended an annual gathering of songwriters in Nashville. I previously had met many of the people in attendance, whether at earlier gatherings, while working with them in their studios, or upon seeing their live performances. Several have cowritten songs with me. At this particular gathering, I attempted to round up a group to get up on stage and perform my parody of "Michael, Row the Boat Ashore," a song called "Michael Closed the Bathroom Door." The group was to be led by my friend and fellow political scientist Sergio Wals, who has often traveled with me for performances at elementary schools, bookstores, and libraries.[1] The people Sergio and I approached all are seasoned, talented songwriters and musicians, and thus we did not envision much difficulty in signing up recruits for the song.

One person we asked was "Dan." Dan told us that although he has been writing songs for thirty-five years, he had never yet played in public, and that this history certainly was not going to change in front of hundreds of people on stage in Nashville that evening. We also asked "Larry," an extraordinarily talented studio guitarist, producer, and engineer. Larry shuffled his feet a bit and mumbled, "that sounds like fun, but I don't want to." Lastly, we approached "Curt." Curt answered, "Absolutely. Anything, any time, anywhere." After quickly running through the chords and the vocals, Sergio and Curt performed as a duo about an hour later. They succeeded in getting the whole crowd singing along in what was one of the biggest hits of the evening.

Participating in an impromptu musical performance is hardly the same as participating in politics, yet my attempt to recruit performers perhaps

---

[1] Sergio Wals is a faculty member at the University of Nebraska. "Michael Closed the Bathroom Door" is the title track of Sergio's 2008 children's music CD, a compilation of songs made from some of my children's poetry.

can teach us something regarding the antecedents of political activity. If we sought to apply prominent models of political participation in an effort to explain why Curt got up on stage while Dan and Larry did not, I believe our account would come up short. For instance, Brady, Verba, and Schlozman (1995; see also Verba, Schlozman, and Brady 1995) suggest that three factors drive a lack of participation in politics: some people cannot participate due to inadequate time, money and other resources, some people are not interested in and engaged by politics, and some people have not been mobilized, or targeted, by recruitment networks. As applied to music, these factors are essentially identical for Dan, Larry, and Curt. Resources are a constant in that all already were at the club, all have the talent required to perform, and there was no financial cost to getting up on stage. As to interest and engagement, Dan, Larry, and Curt each live and breathe music on a daily basis, and have done so for years. Lastly, Sergio and I explicitly endeavored to recruit all three.

The most noteworthy difference among Dan, Larry, and Curt is personality. Curt, like Sergio, practically defines extraversion, happily bounding up on stage at every opportunity, and meeting people and working the crowd between sets. In contrast, Dan and Larry are much more reserved. I also would guess that Curt would score high in openness to experience. I have known him for several years and, except for Indian food, I have never seen him shy away from new experiences. Lastly, comparing Larry and Curt, Larry spends much more time in the studio. Anything can happen during live performances on stage, and performers learn to adapt to the mistakes of various kinds that occur all the time. But studio work tends to be considerably more precise, with meticulous attention paid to the finest of details. In light of his studio prowess, I suspect that Larry would score quite high in conscientiousness.

In this chapter, I explore the possibility that individual differences such as those demonstrated by Curt, Larry, and Dan matter for political participation. Efforts to incorporate personality variables in research on participation have been rare despite the powerful intuition that personality must play a role. All of us know people we simply cannot imagine going door to door on behalf of a petition drive or getting up and speaking in public at a city council meeting or during a local appearance by a member of Congress. And all of us know people like Curt, people who would not hesitate for an instant before engaging in these same actions. Education, interest, and networking certainly influence who participates, but it should be clear that these factors tell an incomplete story. A more comprehensive account demands attention to the impact of fundamental psychological differences.

This chapter begins with consideration of a large array of participatory acts. As in the two prior chapters, my objective is to develop a general sense of whether personality produces noteworthy direct effects on political behavior. I then offer a closer look at two instances in which the impact of personality on participation may be conditional.

## PARTICIPATION AND THE BIG FIVE

Although links between personality and political participation might seem self-evident, very few past studies have explored these relationships. One early effort, by the renowned child psychologist Paul Mussen and his collaborator Anne Wyszynski (1952), found that factors roughly similar to the Big Five's openness and extraversion trait dimensions corresponded with heightened levels of political activity, whereas tendencies toward submissiveness and deference to authority – possible correlates of high conscientiousness – were inversely related with participation. In this same era, Lasswell (1954) noted that personality contributes to success in a political career. Lasswell's discussion included factors resembling openness to experience, extraversion, and agreeableness. Sniderman's (1975) research on self-esteem offers a thorough assessment of the possible impact of this trait on participation, yielding a great deal of evidence that participation is inhibited by low self-esteem.

Despite the fact that all of these works provide evidence regarding the importance of personality for political participation, mainstream research on participation typically focuses primarily on the tangible and informal resources that may contribute to political engagement, along with motivational factors such as political interest. To my knowledge, a contemporary view of trait structure has been incorporated in only a handful of studies on participation (as opposed to studies on personality that use participation as a test case). An article by Denny and Doyle (2008) on voter turnout in Britain does not utilize a Big Five approach, although the authors do discuss the relationships between some of their trait measures and the five-factor taxonomy. The exploratory study by Gerber et al. (2008) applies the Big Five in research on participation in the 2006 elections. Some of my collaborative works examine links between the Big Five and political participation in the United States, Uruguay, and Venezuela (Mondak and Halperin 2008; Mondak et al. 2010; Mondak et al. forthcoming). Most recently, Vecchione and Caprara (2009) have used data gathered in Rome to examine the interrelationships among personality, self-efficacy, and participation.

The tests to be reported in the following sections examine the potential impact of personality on multiple aspects of political participation. Specifically, I first assess whether personality influences the tendency to contact and meet with elected officials, followed by looks at several types of campaign activity and at voter turnout. As will be seen, I posit an especially strong role for extraversion in many of these tests, but several effects of the other Big Five trait dimensions also are contemplated. It is once again important to reiterate that the results to be discussed implicitly suggest the impact of biological forces on political behavior. As I have emphasized throughout this book, the Big Five structure is highly heritable. Fowler, Baker, and Dawes (2008) report strong genetic effects on participation. Thus, any evidence that personality matters for participation will, in effect, peer inside the black box, identifying personality as a likely mechanism connecting genetics to political action.

## Contacting Elected Officials

The first aspects of participation to be considered involve interactions between citizens and their elected representatives. Some people write letters and send emails to their representatives with great frequency, whereas other people go their whole lives without ever meeting or contacting an elected official. At question is whether personality contributes to these differences. Three tests will be conducted. The 2006 CES included items on both the pre-election and postelection waves regarding efforts by respondents to contact members of Congress. The questions have three differences in format: (1) on the pre-election item, half of the respondents were asked about contacts with their House members and the other half about contacts with senators,[2] whereas the postelection item asked all respondents the same summary question about any contact with a House member or senator; (2) the pre-election item includes no time frame, but the postelection question asked about contacts within the prior two years; and (3) the pre-election item employs a categorical response format, versus a dichotomous format on the postelection survey. In addition to the two contact items, a third dependent variable is available because the postelection wave also posed an item about whether the respondent had attended a public meeting with a House member or senator in the past two years.

As will be the case with many of the models exploring possible effects of personality on participation, my strongest expectations for the contact variables concern extraversion. No bold theorizing is needed to construct or justify these fish-in-a-barrel hypotheses. Shy people avoid public meetings; people who keep to themselves tend not to be squeaky wheels. It would make little sense to expect otherwise. Beyond

---

[2] I have found no differences in response patterns for the House and Senate halves of the pre-election item, and thus all respondents will be examined simultaneously here.

extraversion, relationships between personality and contacts with public officials also are expected for openness to experience. As a general matter, openness should be linked to politicization. We have seen a great deal of evidence consistent with this point in the prior two chapters. In the present case, the confidence, inquisitiveness, and efficaciousness of individuals high in openness to experience should help prompt the willingness to contact public officials and to see those officials in action at public meetings.

My last expectations are somewhat more speculative. Setting politics aside momentarily in favor of medicine, we can consider hypochondriacs, people who continuously express excessive worry over real or imagined problems with their health. We perhaps can gain insight from the actions of hypochondriacs. Hypochondriacs often bombard their physicians with calls and visits about every conceivable matter. As anyone who has been a staff member in a legislative office is well aware, politics has its parallel to the hypochondriac. Some constituents contact their representatives with tremendous frequency, querying or opining about a great multitude of subjects. If these "political hypochondriacs" resemble their medical counterparts (or perhaps are even the very same people), then lessons learned about personality and hypochondria may be instructive for present purposes. Perhaps not surprisingly, past research has found that individuals who are highly conscientious and emotionally stable tend not to be hypochondriacs (e.g., Cox et al. 2000; Ferguson 2000, 2004). Applied to the political domain, these findings suggest that we should expect negative relationships between the frequency of contacting elected officials and both conscientiousness and emotional stability.

For these individual dependent variables, as for most indicators of political participation, the data are skewed toward a lack of engagement. Specifically, 54 percent of respondents report no contacts with members of Congress on the pre-election wave of the 2006 CES; on the survey's second wave, 59 percent report having had no contacts within the past two years. Only 14 percent of respondents indicated that they had attended public meetings with any House member or senator in the prior two years.

The empirical relationships between the Big Five and contacting behavior are summarized in Table 6.1. Impressive effects emerge for extraversion, including substantively large and statistically significant coefficients in all three models. As extraversion rises from its lowest value to its highest, the predicted probability of contact with a House member or senator increases from 0.36 to 0.65 in the first model and from 0.30 to 0.54 in the second model. The predicted probability that the respondent attended

Table 6.1 *Contacts with Elected Officials*

| | Openness to Experience | Conscientiousness | Extraversion | Agreeableness | Emotional Stability |
|---|---|---|---|---|---|
| Number of Times Respondent has Contacted House Member/Senator | 0.86* (0.42) | −0.20 (0.35) | 1.21*** (0.32) | 0.02 (0.37) | −0.67# (0.40) |
| Contacted House Member or Senator in Past Two Years | 0.70* (0.35) | −0.78* (0.30) | 0.98** (0.28) | 0.52 (0.32) | −0.57# (0.33) |
| Attended a Public Meeting with House Member or Senator in Past Two Years | 0.57 (0.46) | −1.59*** (0.43) | 2.03*** (0.38) | 0.25 (0.44) | −0.57 (0.47) |

*Notes*: Data are from the 2006 CES, with separate models estimated for each row of results; standard errors are in parentheses. Models include controls for sex, race, age and education. The dependent variable in the first model is constructed from a four-point categorical item asked on the pre-election wave of the CES, with data coded 0 (never) to 3 (frequently); cell entries are ordered logistic regression coefficients. The second and third dependent variables are coded 1 (yes) and 0 (no), with data from the post-election waves of the CES; cell entries for these models are binomial logistic regression coefficients. Personality variables range from 0 to 1. Number of cases = 764; 1,039; and 1,037.

\*\*\**p* < .001, \*\**p* < .01, \**p* < .05, #*p* < .10

a meeting with a member of Congress in the past two years increases from 0.05 to 0.27 across the observed range of extraversion.[3]

Results for the other four trait dimensions match well to expectations. First, I had no reason to foresee a link between agreeableness and contacting behavior, and agreeableness performed amenably. Second, openness to experience, conscientiousness, and emotional stability all produced coefficients with consistent signs across the three models in Table 6.1, and two of the effects for each trait dimension achieved at least minimal levels of statistical significance. Being open to experience modestly increases a person's prospects for encountering a member of Congress, and being conscientious and emotionally stable decrease these same prospects.

## Participation in Campaigns

Most Americans vote in at least some elections, but participation in campaign activities prior to Election Day is much less common. Given my expectation that extraversion will play a central role in motivating many forms of political behavior, one logical approach for organizing the study of campaign activity involves distinguishing active and social forms of participation from more passive and individualistic behaviors. As to the former, the postelection wave of the 2006 CES includes dichotomous items regarding whether respondents had tried to convince someone to vote for or against any candidate in 2006, whether respondents had worked for a candidate or party, and whether respondents had attended any campaign meetings or rallies. Categorical items regarding attendance at campaign meetings and rallies also were included on both the 1998 CS and the 2005 NJS.

Just over one-third of CES respondents reported that they had tried to convince someone to vote for or against a particular candidate in 2006. In contrast, more formal campaign activities were rare. On the CES, for instance, only 6.6 percent of respondents indicated that they had attended a campaign meeting or rally, and a mere 4.2 percent reported having worked for a party or a candidate.[4]

[3] Once again, predicted probabilities are calculated with all other variables held constant. As in the two prior chapters, the analyses reported here model political behavior on personality while controlling only for demographics. This strategy permits me to estimate in simple form the full magnitude of personality effects. It should be clear that in many instances the effects of personality on participation very likely are mediated by other factors, such as efficacy, interest in politics, and political knowledge. It follows that efforts to sort out the various pathways linking personality to participation represent a promising direction for future research.

[4] Relative to the full U.S. population, even these marks may be high. As Hibbing, Theiss-Morse, and Whitaker. (2009, 153) have noted, respondents on the CES collectively score quite well in terms of political engagement and political knowledge.

For this first group of campaign activities, extraverts should be especially engaged because all of the activities entail encounters with other people. The basis for this prediction is especially strong for attendance at campaign meetings and rallies. After all, introverts would not be introverts if they relished joining large crowds. For most individuals, working in campaigns is a form of volunteerism. Two recent studies (Elshaug and Metzer 2001; Carlo et al. 2005) identified effects of extraversion and agreeableness on volunteering, although the agreeableness effect seems less likely than the extraversion effect to travel to participation in the political arena. Beyond extraversion and possibly agreeableness, my only expectation is that the politicizing character of openness to experience will mean that individuals scoring high in openness will exhibit heightened tendencies toward campaign activity.

Table 6.2 depicts results from five models, three from the 2006 study and one each from the 1998 and 2005 surveys. Consistent with expectations, extraversion produces positive coefficients in all five models. However, only the effects for attending campaign meetings and rallies reach conventional levels of statistical significance. The impact of extraversion on these latter variables is considerable. On the 2006 survey, for example, the predicted probability that a respondent reported having attended such an event increases from 0.02 to more than 0.12 across the observed values on extraversion. Beyond extraversion, personality brings only slight and sporadic personality effects in Table 6.2. Most of the coefficients for conscientiousness, agreeableness, and emotional stability are negative, suggesting once again, as in Chapter 4, that all of these trait dimensions may be associated with a weak tendency toward depoliticization. But given that only two of these coefficients attain statistical significance, any such effects would appear to be both modest and inconsistent. Openness to experience brings no impact on the likelihood that a person will attend campaign events, but significant effects of openness do emerge for whether respondents tried to convince people to vote for or against particular candidates, and for working for a party or candidate. The first of these two significant results is especially sizeable. Specifically, the predicted probability that a respondent engaged in persuasive political discussion increases from 0.16 to 0.59 as openness to experience rises from its lowest to its highest observed values.

Three additional participatory behaviors can be juxtaposed against those examined in Table 6.2. Once again, items come from the postelection wave of the 2006 CES. Respondents were asked if they had put up a yard sign or displayed a bumper sticker or campaign button, and whether they had contributed money to a party or candidate, or whether they had given money to a group that supported or opposed any candidates in the 2006 elections. Slightly more than 17 percent of respondents reported having displayed signs, stickers, or buttons, versus marks of 14 percent

Table 6.2 *Active/Social Participation in Political Campaigns*

| | Openness to Experience | Conscientiousness | Extraversion | Agreeableness | Emotional Stability |
|---|---|---|---|---|---|
| Try to Convince People to Vote For/Against a Candidate in 2006 | 2.03*** (0.36) | −0.27 (0.31) | 0.40 (0.29) | −0.08 (0.33) | −0.79* (0.35) |
| Work for a Party or Candidate During 2006 Campaign | 1.51# (0.78) | −1.86* (0.74) | 1.24# (0.64) | −0.07 (0.76) | −0.90 (0.85) |
| Attend Meetings, Rallies, Speeches and/or Dinners During 1998 Campaign | −0.32 (0.77) | 0.37 (0.66) | 1.95** (0.60) | −0.73 (0.65) | 0.92 (0.65) |
| Attend Meetings, Rallies, Speeches and/or Dinners During 2004 Campaign | 0.19 (0.74) | −0.30 (0.79) | 1.40* (0.67) | −1.01 (0.80) | 0.30 (0.70) |
| Attend Meetings or Election Rallies During 2006 Campaign | 0.66 (0.64) | −0.40 (0.58) | 1.79*** (0.51) | −0.72 (0.61) | −0.52 (0.66) |

*Notes:* Separate models are estimated for each row of results; standard errors are in parentheses. Models include controls for sex, race, age, and education. The dependent variables in the 2006 models are drawn from the CES, and are coded 1 (yes, respondent engaged in activity) and 0 (no); cell entries are binomial logistic regression coefficients. The dependent variables in the 1998 (1998 CS) and 2004 (2005 NJS) models are four-category ordinal items with high values indicating higher levels of participation; cell entries are ordered logistic regression coefficients. Personality variables range from 0 to 1. Number of cases = 1,038; 1,040; 367; 395; and 1,040

***$p < .001$, **$p < .01$, *$p < .05$, #$p < .10$

for contributing to parties or candidates and 11 percent for contributing to other groups that supported or opposed candidates.

Indirectly, these items collectively provide for an interesting test of the link between extraversion and participation. Thus far, several strong relationships between extraversion and participation have been identified. My assumption has been that no sense of mystery accompanies these effects; extraverts, by their nature, are drawn to social activities, and the forms of participation at question in Table 6.1 and Table 6.2 necessarily involve at least some degree of social interaction. But it is conceivable that something less straightforward is at work. Perhaps, for instance, extraverts are attracted to the competitive give-and-take of partisan politics, and opportunities for actual social interaction have nothing at all to do with the relationships seen above. The questions about yard signs and financial contributions enable leverage on this possibility. People can put up yard signs or adorn their cars with bumper stickers without necessitating much, or maybe even any, interaction with other people. Likewise, contributing to candidates and political groups requires an encounter with one's checkbook or credit card, but not with another person. If the significant extraversion effects in Table 6.1 and Table 6.2 reflect the inherently social quality of the behaviors, then extraversion should turn in a much weaker showing for the more passive and individualistic actions.

Beyond extraversion, I again expect that openness to experience will predict political engagement. Openness transcends the social–individualistic divide. Consequently, unlike with extraversion, there is no reason to expect an attenuation of effects for openness as we move away from more social forms of political behavior. As to the remaining trait dimensions, it again is possible that a general tendency toward depoliticization may lead to negative effects. Research on charitable contributions and other forms of altruism reveals that these behaviors are most prevalent among individuals high in agreeableness and low in emotional stability (e.g., Ashton et al. 1998). However, given the differences between purely charitable donations and contributions to political efforts, it is not clear whether these same trait effects will be in operation in the present case.

The first noteworthy aspect of the results in Table 6.3 is that no significant effects are identified for extraversion. All three extraversion coefficients are positive, but all also fall well short of statistical significance. Viewed in conjunction with this chapter's earlier findings, along with results regarding political discussion in Chapter 4, the interpretation of the extraversion–participation link seems rather uncomplicated: extraversion operates as a strong determinant of the tendency to engage in those forms of political participation that involve social interaction,

Table 6.3 *Passive/Individualistic Participation in Political Campaigns*

| | Openness to Experience | Conscientiousness | Extraversion | Agreeableness | Emotional Stability |
|---|---|---|---|---|---|
| Respondent Put Up a Political Yard Sign or Displayed a Bumper Sticker or Campaign Button in 2006 | 1.26** (0.43) | −0.29 (0.37) | 0.04 (0.35) | −0.32 (0.41) | −0.57 (0.43) |
| Respondent Contributed Money to a Political Party or Candidate in 2006 | 0.58 (0.47) | −0.51 (0.41) | 0.54 (0.38) | 0.28 (0.44) | −0.91# (0.48) |
| Respondent Contributed Money to a Group that Supported or Opposed Candidates in 2006 | 1.78*** (0.50) | −0.41 (0.45) | 0.23 (0.42) | 0.03 (0.48) | −0.97# (0.53) |

*Notes:* Data are from the 2006 CES, with separate models estimated for each row of results; standard errors are in parentheses. Models include controls for sex, race, age, and education. The dependent variables are coded 1 (yes) and 0 (no), with data from the post-election waves of the CES; cell entries for these models are binomial logistic regression coefficients. Personality variables range from 0 to 1. Number of cases = 1,040, 1,040 and 1,036.

***$p < .001$, **$p < .01$, #$p < .10$

especially interaction in large groups, but the influence of extraversion on political participation dissipates when focus turns to more individualistic behaviors.

As expected, openness to experience produces positive coefficients in Table 6.3. Strong effects emerge for the yard sign variable and for contributions to groups that support or oppose political candidates. In both of these cases, the predicted probability that the respondent has engaged in the activity increases by 18 percentage points as openness moves from its lowest to its highest observed values. Of the remaining predictors, only the negative effects of emotional stability on the two forms of financial contributions achieve even marginal levels of statistical significance (in both cases, $p < .07$). The effects are not of idiom-generating strength,[5] but, especially when viewed in tandem with the Ashton et al. (1998) findings on emotional stability and altruism, present results suggest that people high in emotional stability may have good, solid grasps of their wallets.

Results to this point demonstrate that personality is related to political participation, but also that the linkages are anything but simple. Extraversion prompts social forms of participation. Openness to experience generally fosters political engagement, but the effects are far from universal across different participatory acts. The other three trait dimensions have produced mostly negative effects on participation, but only a handful of these have been noteworthy in terms of either statistical significance or substantive magnitude.

### Voter Turnout

Voting in elections is the most common form of political participation, and also the most studied. Here, I will comment only briefly on the possible influence of personality on voter turnout. The analyses are held to a minimum, not because personality is thought to be unrelated to electoral participation, but rather because of the notoriously questionable character of turnout data. The problem is that survey respondents claim that they voted in very high levels, much higher levels than would seem possible in light of aggregate data on voter turnout.[6] Turnout among survey participants surely is higher than among the general population, as many of the same factors that correspond with participation in a lengthy political survey presumably also correspond with showing up to vote on Election Day. Nonetheless, the 82.5 percent level of self-reported turnout

---

[5] For instance, we can put on hold for now the expression "a neurotic and his money are soon parted."

[6] For discussions, see Burden (2000); McDonald (2003), and Silver, Anderson, and Abramson (1986).

on the 2006 CES and the corresponding mark of 62.6 percent on the 1998 CS simply defy credibility.

The particular analytical problem posed by overreported turnout stems from the fact that the tendency of individuals to claim erroneously that they voted is not distributed randomly (e.g., Silver, Anderson, and Abramson 1986). Taking the CES as an example, the 82.5 percent of respondents who claimed that they voted presumably includes a mix of actual voters and people whose participation is fabricated from wishful thinking, self-delusion, and the like. If I were armed with validated turnout data, I could distinguish the two groups, but neither of my electoral surveys is accompanied by validated turnout. Thus, I have no means to differentiate the two types of "voters." Yet, our intuition surely should be that personality plays some role both in who votes and which nonvoters falsely claim to be voters. This leaves us in an especially pronounced bind, particularly if it happens that some personality traits have differing effects on actual turnout and on falsely claimed turnout. For instance, if conscientious people tend both to vote and to tell the truth about it when they do not, then current data would yield undecipherable null results. It is an interesting, vexing analytical thicket. Future applications of the Big Five in this area might generate highly illuminating findings if both personality data and validated turnout indicators are available.[7] For now, however, all I can do is identify the effects of personality on the self-reported turnout data, see if the results suggest any unambiguous lessons, and then move on.

Self-reported voter turnout in the 1998 and 2006 midterm congressional elections is modeled on personality, with results reported in Table 6.4. The findings are unremarkable. Only one coefficient each year attains even a modest level of statistical significance, and these effects – negative coefficients for agreeableness in the 1998 CS and emotional stability in the 2006 CES – are not replicated even in direction in the other year. These collectively unimpressive results give rise to multiple interpretations, but no definitive account. It may be that personality simply brings little direct influence on the decision to vote.[8] Alternatively, it may be that personality produces conditional or nonlinear effects that elude detection

---

[7] Gerber et al. (2008) make use of validated turnout data, and they do find some differences with these data versus effects in their models using self-reported turnout measures.

[8] This scenario seems unlikely. In a recent study of voter turnout in Britain, Denny and Doyle (2008) find several relationships between personality and turnout. The authors do not have indicators of the Big Five, but significant effects are produced in their models for variables that appear to be subcomponents of conscientiousness and emotional stability.

Table 6.4 *Voter Turnout*

| | Openness to Experience | Conscientiousness | Extraversion | Agreeableness | Emotional Stability |
|---|---|---|---|---|---|
| Respondent Reported Voting in the 1998 Midterm Elections | -0.04 (0.71) | -0.37 (0.63) | 0.64 (0.58) | -1.15# (0.62) | 0.33 (0.62) |
| Respondent Reported Voting in the 2006 Midterm Elections | 0.40 (0.49) | -0.47 (0.41) | 0.28 (0.40) | 0.45 (0.45) | -1.22** (0.42) |

*Notes*: Separate models estimated for each row of results; standard errors are in parentheses. Models include controls for sex, race, age, and education. The dependent variables are coded 1 (yes) and 0 (no), with data from the 1998 CS and the post-election waves of the 2006 CES; cell entries for these models are binomial logistic regression coefficients. Personality variables range from 0 to 1. Number of cases = 364 and 1,036.

** $p < .01$, * $p < .05$

in models such as those in Table 6.4. Lastly, it may be that over-reports of voter turnout hopelessly cloud efforts to identify determinants of actual voting.

In the two prior chapters, personality was found to produce rich and multifaceted influence on variables related to political information and political attitudes. In the current chapter, however, the impact of the Big Five on participation has been more restrained. The tests conducted to this point have explored whether personality yields any direct impact on political participation. We have seen that extraversion brings strong effects on the most social aspects of political behavior, and that openness to experience also prompts several forms of political action. A few statistically significant effects – which were always negative – emerged for the other three trait dimensions, but nothing in those results suggests a pivotal role in participation for conscientiousness, agreeableness, or emotional stability. What remains to be seen, of course, is whether additional effects of personality on participation will be revealed in models that contemplate more complex relationships.

## PERSONALITY AND THE FOUNDATIONS OF POLITICAL PARTICIPATION

In the previous two chapters, personality was shown to be linked both to exposure to information about politics and the holding of various political attitudes and predispositions. Building on these results, the analyses reported thus far in this chapter reveal some impact of personality on political participation, including noteworthy effects for extraversion and openness to experience. But an additional possibility is that personality somehow combines with other foundations of participation – attitudes, predispositions, and elements of the information environment – to determine the propensity to participate. Countless potential combinational effects exist, along with many conceivable indirect and nonlinear influences of personality. To demonstrate how such effects might operate, two examples will be assessed here, one involving an interrelationship between personality and political predispositions, and the second involving personality and the response to political information.

### Why Don't the Conscientious Participate?

In the first section of this chapter, thirteen tests of the impact of personality on political participation were reported. In twelve of those thirteen instances, conscientiousness produced a negative coefficient; three of these negative effects reached statistical significance. Likewise, in Chapter 4, the bulk of conscientiousness effects were negative, including statistically significant, negative coefficients for political knowledge, opinionation, and interviewer ratings of information levels and political interest. Hence, it clearly is not the case that a psychological tendency toward responsibility inclines one to become engaged in the political world. To the contrary, the evidence supports the opposite conclusion – that being conscientious is somehow at least modestly depoliticizing. But why would this be? Why doesn't conscientiousness spark political participation?

In psychology, a tremendous wealth of research, especially regarding the impact of conscientiousness on success in education and in the workplace, establishes the vital impact of this trait. We know, for instance, that the most conscientious individuals make for dutiful, hardworking students and employees. These findings hold considerable intuitive appeal. But the fact that conscientiousness performs sensibly in predicting behavior outside of the political sphere only adds to the curiosity surrounding present results. The conscientious are "good citizens" at school and at work,[9] but when it comes to politics and government they seem not to be especially good *actual* citizens.

In attempting to explain the observed mix of negative and null effects, one prospect that warrants consideration is that conscientiousness triggers political participation for some people but not for others. Under this scenario, perhaps the answer to our puzzle lies in viewing personality in combination with some additional factor. Individuals with high levels of conscientiousness demand a great deal of themselves, but they also impose high standards on other people (e.g., Organ 1994). Consequently, the impact of conscientiousness may depend on the extent to which conscientious individuals perceive that others are living up to expectations, or failing to do so. One plausible outcome is that people high in conscientiousness will be apt to participate in politics provided that they perceive the political world as being worthy of, and responsive to, their efforts. Conversely, conscientious individuals may be especially likely to react negatively if the political system is seen as falling short of expected standards of performance. A complementary thesis is that those people who are highly conscientious may be closely attuned to opportunity costs. When these individuals desire achievements, it clearly would be sensible for them to direct their efforts toward those domains where accomplishment seems most likely. From this perspective, individuals high in conscientiousness would be unlikely to expend effort in politics unless they feel that such effort hold good prospects for producing meaningful results.

---

[9] The relevant literature in psychology even employs "citizenship" as a metaphor in explorations of the impact of personality on behavior in school and the workplace. See, for example, Borman et al. 2001; Deluga 1995; Organ and McFall 2004.

Likewise, if political engagement is not seen as a duty or obligation, there would be no reason to expect conscientiousness to predict participation.

External efficacy is well-suited to test the two-part thesis outlined here. Citizens perceive themselves to have high levels of external efficacy to the extent that they believe that public officials care what people think. Where external efficacy is low, political participation very likely would be seen as futile, and thus a depoliticizing effect is likely. After all, why expend effort on politics if your actions will not be acknowledged by elected officials?[10] My contention is not merely that external efficacy will matter for levels of political participation, but that the effects of efficacy will be especially pronounced for individuals scoring high in conscientiousness. Where they see that their efforts can be productive, the conscientious will work with noteworthy diligence and intensity. But where they perceive that their efforts will be fruitless, I expect the conscientious to turn their attention elsewhere.

Recall that the direct relationship between conscientiousness and external efficacy was explored in Chapter 5. There, we saw that conscientiousness exerted very different effects on my two national surveys. Among citizens called in for jury duty, conscientiousness corresponded with strong feelings of external efficacy. In contrast, in the context of the 2006 elections, high conscientiousness predicted low external efficacy. Consistent with the thesis outlined here, those findings suggest that conscientiousness signals a contextual sensitivity to efficacy: Where the context supports the inference that citizens' views matter, individuals high in conscientiousness respond enthusiastically, but these same individuals respond critically in the context of more impersonal national elections. Building on those results, whether perceptions of efficacy are prerequisites before conscientious citizens will become active political participants is at question now.

The relevant tests entail revisiting the models estimated previously in this chapter, this time adding two new variables as predictors, external efficacy and the interaction between external efficacy and conscientiousness. The expected pattern of results includes two central components. First, the main effects for conscientiousness should be more strongly negative than in the earlier tests. Previously, the coefficients for this trait dimension represented the average impact across all levels of efficacy. In the new specifications, the conscientiousness effects will capture the impact of this trait when efficacy is at its lowest value. Where efficacy has a value of zero – that is, where respondents feel strongly that public

---

[10] The one obvious exception, of course, is if citizens feel that by participating in politics they can help secure the election of new representatives who *do* care what people think.

officials do not care about citizens' views – people scoring high in conscientiousness should exhibit a marked reluctance to enter the political sphere. Second, coefficients for the efficacy × conscientiousness interaction term should be positive. This outcome would mean that the conscientious become more politically engaged (or less unengaged) as their perceptions of external efficacy rise.

All ten models using data from the 2006 CES were rerun in variants that added external efficacy and the efficacy × conscientiousness interaction. Recall that conscientiousness always produced a negative coefficient in the original versions of these models, with three of those ten coefficients attaining statistical significance. In the new renditions (full results are reported in part A of this chapter's appendix), it is again the case that all ten coefficients are negative. This time, however, six are statistically significant. Two more, those for displaying yard signs and for contributing money to political candidates, approach significance ($p < .13$). As to the efficacy × conscientiousness interactions, the expected positive coefficient is obtained in all ten models. Five of these effects meet conventional levels of statistical significance,[11] and three additional effects approach significance ($p < .17$).

The strongest results from these tests are not distributed randomly across the ten models. Instead, the sharpest effects emerge for those dependent variables that involve some mix of formal and social activity. Conscientiousness and the efficacy × conscientiousness interaction each reach statistical significance in both of the models concerning contacting members of Congress and in the models for working for a candidate or party and attending a political meeting or rally. The two key predictors also turn in relatively strong showings in the models for attending meetings with members of Congress and for displaying yard signs, buttons, and bumper stickers. Effects are much weaker, and short of statistical significance, for the remaining models, that is, those concerning financial contributions to candidates and political organizations, informal efforts to persuade others to support or oppose a candidate, and voter turnout. Conscientiousness and external efficacy do apparently work in tandem to influence patterns in political participation, but primarily for those participatory acts that require the citizen to make tangible commitments of time and effort.

To provide a sense of the substantive magnitude of the efficacy × conscientiousness effects, Figure 6.1 depicts predicted probabilities for four of the dependent variables measured on the postelection wave of the 2006 CES: contacting a member of Congress; working for a political

---

[11] This is a slightly generous interpretation, as the interaction in the yard signs model is significant at a level of $p < .052$.

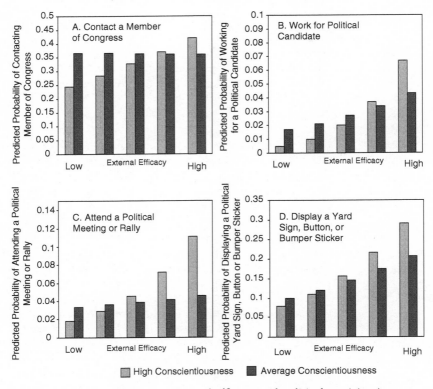

Figure 6.1 Conscientiousness, external efficacy, and political participation.

party or candidate; attending a political meeting or rally; and displaying a political yard sign, button, or bumper sticker.[12] In each panel, the dark, solid bars represent the predicted probability of participation across efficacy for individuals with average levels of conscientiousness, whereas the lighter bars report the corresponding effects for the highly conscientious (values of one standard deviation greater than the mean).

Two points of contrast in each panel warrant notice. First, a comparison of the left-most and right-most light bars in each panel provides a sense of the impact of external efficacy among the highly conscientious. In panel A, for instance, the predicted probability that a highly conscientious respondent contacted a member of Congress in the past

---

[12] To minimize redundancy, estimates for the model for contacting a member of Congress as calculated using data from the pre-election survey are omitted; the pattern is highly similar to that for the postelection contacting model as seen in panel A of Figure 6.1.

two years increases from 0.25 to 0.42 across efficacy. In panel B, the corresponding marks for working for a political candidate are less than 0.01 versus nearly 0.07. Second, a comparison of the final two bars in each figure indicates the value of conscientiousness in sparking participation among individuals with high levels of external efficacy. Here, the effect is most pronounced in panel C, with predicted values of below 0.05 for efficacious citizens with average levels of conscientiousness, versus 0.11 for respondents who are both efficacious and highly conscientious. These results establish that external efficacy alone does not necessarily prompt participation. The perception that public officials care what they think does little to engage people who are lacking in conscientiousness, yet this same efficaciousness resonates strongly with the highly conscientious.

This exercise has been motivated by the question of why people who are highly conscientious do not participate in politics at high levels. Present findings provide at least a partial answer. When it comes to investing time and effort in politics, the conscientious will do so if they perceive that the political system will be responsive to their actions. Conversely, if prospects for a pay off are seen as dim – if people think that public officials do not care what citizens think – then the highly conscientious will tend to withdraw from the political arena, quite possibly so that their time and effort can be directed toward domains in which greater achievement is possible. For those political observers who thirst for a more participatory citizenry, the lesson here is clear. There is a tendency among the highly conscientious to believe, whether rightly or wrongly, that their voices are ignored by public officials. This belief discourages political involvement. Present findings suggest that conscientious individuals can be enthusiastic, active political participants, but also that this promise will be unfulfilled so long as these citizens perceive that their efforts would be for naught.[13]

---

[13] A related explanation to the account tested here, although a much simpler one, is that political engagement is not seen as a duty or obligation, meaning that the tendency of the conscientious to be diligent in the execution of their duties never comes into play. On the first wave of the 2006 survey, respondents were asked seven three-category items regarding the importance of various facets of civic involvement. Conscientiousness was not related to response patterns on any of the seven individual items or to a composite scale. Because individuals high in conscientiousness attribute no particular importance to civic engagement, the basis of the hypothesized positive impact of this trait on political involvement has been undercut. For the conscientious, time spent on politics is perhaps viewed as time spent neglecting family or career. This possibility is tested in Mondak et al. (2010). There, we find that among respondents who see being involved in election campaigns as important, there is a slight rise in political participation across conscientiousness. However, among respondents who see electoral activity as not very important, there

## Personality, Information, and Electoral Mobilization

Among the analyses conducted in this chapter, the greatest frustration arises from those regarding levels of voter turnout. The choice of whether to vote arguably constitutes the most pivotal act of political behavior, and intuition certainly suggests that personality matters for this decision. Yet, intuition notwithstanding, the tests reported in the previous discussion yielded no compelling evidence of a link between personality and turnout. The available data do not permit a more thorough test of the possible personality–turnout link, but one facet of this potential relationship can be examined more closely. Past research establishes that some information disseminated during political campaigns may be either mobilizing or demobilizing. Hence, we can ask if the way in which voters respond to this campaign information – and any resulting impact on turnout – hinges partly on personality.

Much of the literature on voter turnout considers the influence of relatively stable aspects of the individual or context, examining factors including age, education, political culture, and so on (e.g., Wolfinger and Rosenstone 1980). Other research incorporates variables that are campaign specific, such as the competitiveness of the campaign and partisan efforts to mobilize voters (e.g., Huckfeldt et al. 2007; Huckfeldt and Sprague 1992; Jackson 2002). One aspect of campaigns that has attracted particular attention in recent years is tone, and especially the possible impact of negative advertisements. It is here that I will reexamine whether personality plays any role in who votes.

In their 1995 book *Going Negative*, a work that relies primarily on data from laboratory experiments, Ansolabehere and Iyengar report that exposure to negative campaign advertisements produces a demobilizing effect. People apparently find negative advertisements to be off-putting, and, at least in the laboratory, many respond by opting out of participation in elections. These results comport well with those from later research, also from the laboratory, showing that exposure to televised political incivility adversely affects people's perceptions of government, and especially their levels of trust (Mutz and Reeves 2005). The Ansolabehere and Iyengar study set off a flurry of research in response. A central question in the ensuing debate has been whether any demobilization identified in the laboratory also will be evident in analyses of individual-level and aggregate-level survey data. It is possible, as one example, that any antagonistic

---

is a sharp drop in participation as conscientiousness rises. This finding is consistent with the view that many conscientious individuals refrain from what is perceived as unimportant political activity, perhaps so that they can focus their energies on what are seen as more pressing responsibilities.

reaction to negative campaigns may be offset by indirect positive effects of campaign tone on voters' levels of political information and interest (e.g., Finkel and Geer 1998).[14]

My approach to studying the impact of campaign tone on turnout side steps many of the issues that have generated debate since the publication of *Going Negative*. In a laboratory setting, I believe the evidence shows that people typically find negative advertisements to be disconcerting. Other forces operating in actual campaigns very likely counter, mute, or even reverse these effects. The existence of such forces apparently minimizes any real-world demobilization associated with exposure to negative ads. Nonetheless, laboratory tests reveal that, on balance, the immediate psychological response to attack ads is not positive. My interest is with this point. With focus on personality, my present concern is not with the cumulative impact of negative ads on voter turnout, but rather with which people respond in what manner following exposure to information from a heated political campaign.

In the most straightforward of experimental designs, participants first would encounter campaign advertisements, with different groups of participants observing ads that are positive, neutral, or negative in tone. Then, projected voter turnout would be measured. Drawing on Ansolabehere and Iyengar (1995), we should expect that participants who were exposed to the most positive advertisements would report the greatest proclivities to vote. My question concerns not whether this basic relationship exists, but rather whether it holds to a similar extent for all participants. More specifically, does personality influence any demobilizing impact of exposure to negative advertisements?

Research in psychology offers no clear guidance on this question. Nonetheless, it is not difficult to conceive of possible effects of the Big Five. Some people view negative ads and apparently become so perturbed that their immediate reaction is to boycott the subsequent election. Other people view negative advertisements and either are not disturbed at all or do not translate an adverse reaction into electoral demobilization. So, which people are which? My first expectation is that any effects of ad tone on turnout will be weak among individuals high in openness to experience. Openness to experience encompasses sophistication and perceptiveness, and, in the extreme, an "anything goes" mindset. Thus, people with high openness scores should be capable of looking past any given advertisement and of seeing the bigger picture. I also expect that

---

[14] Some of the key studies in the immediate debate regarding the Ansolabehere and Iyengar findings include Ansolabehere, Iyengar, and Simon (1999); Brooks (2006); Geer (2006); Kahn and Kenney (1999); Lau et al. (1999); and Wattenberg and Brians (1999).

the impact of ad tone will be muted for individuals high in emotional stability, given that, by definition, they are relatively unflappable and not prone to agitation. Conversely, I expect that the effects of ad tone on turnout will be especially pronounced among people with high marks in conscientiousness, extraversion, and agreeableness. The conscientious person possesses a strong sense of right and wrong, and thus may well be disturbed and possibly offended by unduly critical or inflammatory campaign ads. The extravert – the people person – seeks to direct energy toward positive social experiences. When politics turns ugly, the extravert likely turns elsewhere. Finally, the last thing the agreeable person wishes to do is to become mired in matters that are disagreeable.

To test these hypotheses, an experiment on negative advertising and voter turnout was included as part of the 2005 NJS, with roughly one-third of survey respondents assigned to this particular experimental group.[15] The experiment was uncomplicated in form. Participants were randomly assigned to one of three treatment conditions: positive tone, neutral tone, and negative tone. In each condition, participants read what were described as transcripts from radio ads run as part of a recent U.S. House campaign; four transcripts, two from each candidate, were presented. In actuality, the text used in these treatments was drawn with only very minor editing from actual ads run as part of 2004 House campaigns. Participants then were asked to indicate, using eleven-point (zero to ten) scales, "Knowing what you do about the candidates, were you a resident of this U.S. House district, how likely would you have been to turnout to vote in this election?"[16] and "How negative or positive do you feel the

---

[15] The 2005 NJS was fielded as the centerpiece of a graduate research seminar I taught at Florida State University. I am tremendously appreciative of the efforts of all of the students in that course, as their contributions ensured the survey's success. Particular thanks go to Dona-Gene Mitchell, who served as the project supervisor for the 2005 NJS. As part of this project, I designed the negative-advertising experiment in collaboration with Karen Halperin. I am especially grateful to Karen for working with me on this portion of the NJS, and for agreeing to my reporting of some of the data from this experiment as part of the present study.

[16] Although voting versus nonvoting ultimately is a dichotomous choice, use of an eleven-point scale permits me to capture variance in the underlying intensity of participatory preferences. Also, pragmatically, these data are characterized by considerably more variance than are dichotomous self-report data from actual elections, such as the available items from the 1998 CS and the 2006 CES. On the NJS, the mean on the turnout item is 6.24 (s.d. = 3.27). The mean for the indicator of perceived campaign tone is 3.86 (s.d. = 2.76). This latter mean is well to the negative side of neutral. Initially, I was concerned that perhaps participants viewed the would-be neutral treatment condition in unduly negative terms, thereby suppressing any tendency to view the campaign as neutral or positive. This appears not to be the case. A separate eleven-point item on the NJS asked respondents how positive

climate of this campaign was?" Scores of zero indicate, respectively, a very low likelihood of turnout and a perception of the campaign as very negative. At question, of course, is whether any impact of campaign tone on turnout varies as a function of personality.

The first step in examining these data involves testing whether the manipulation of ad tone actually resonated with the study's participants. It did. I regressed the eleven-point indicator of perceived campaign tone on two dummy variables designed to capture the experiment's three treatment conditions. Both variables yielded highly significant ($p < .001$) coefficients. On average, respondents in the positive-ad cell reported campaign tone perceptions that were 2.64 points higher than those of participants in the neutral condition, and 5.16 points higher than those of participants exposed to negative ads. The $R^2$ value from this simple two-variable model is 0.58. Thus, as expected, perceptions of the campaign as being positive or negative were shaped to an overwhelming extent by the manipulation of ad tone.[17]

The second, and more critical, step requires that projected voter turnout be modeled on perceptions of campaign tone, personality, and interactions between the two. As a prelude to this exercise, I first regressed projected turnout on just the perceived tone variable and four demographic measures: age, education, sex, and race. Results corroborate Ansolabehere and Iyengar's central finding: In the laboratory, exposure to negative ads leads participants to view campaigns as negative, adversely affecting prospects for voter turnout.[18] The coefficient on the indicator of perceived campaign tone produces a highly significant ($p < .001$) positive coefficient with a value of 0.33. Hence, across the full zero-to-ten range of the independent variable, predicted values on the turnout scale swing by 3.3 points. Given that the experiment's manipulations induced

---

or negative they perceived the average House campaign to be. On this question, the mean is 2.96 (s.d. = 1.99). Thus, although perceptions of the experiment's hypothetical campaign were negative on balance, they actually were somewhat positive relative to the typical respondent's baseline appraisal of congressional elections.

[17] In a second model, I included the Big Five indicators, along with interactions between these measures and the dummy variables for treatment condition. I did so to test whether personality influences people's perceptions of negativity. No statistically significant effects were identified. Thus, regardless of personality, it appears that all citizens are on roughly the same page when it comes to labeling a given campaign as positive or negative.

[18] Full regression results are reported in this chapter's appendix, part B. As an alternate to modeling turnout on perceived tone, I could have modeled turnout on the two dummy variables for experimental treatment condition. I did not do so because any impact of actual campaign negativity necessarily is mediated by respondents' perceptions; if no one thought a given ad was negative, there could be no demobilizing reaction to that ad.

an average shift of 5.16 points in views of campaign tone for participants exposed to positive rather than negative ads, it follows that the experiment itself caused predicted values on the projected turnout dependent variable to move by an average of 1.70 points (0.33 × 5.16).

These average effects fail to differentiate in any way among participants within each of the experiment's three treatment conditions. All participants naturally did not respond identically, either when asked to evaluate campaign tone or when asked to indicate a projected likelihood of turnout. Any variance may have been unsystematic, in which case no meaningful lessons can be gleaned beyond the basic corroboration of demobilization in a laboratory setting. However, by adding the Big Five indicators along with their interactions with perceived campaign tone, we can determine if personality influences the nature of the negativity-demobilization effect.

Addition of the personality variables generates evidence of three personality effects. First, a modest ($p < .10$) negative main effect emerges for agreeableness. Consistent with some of the results reported both earlier in this chapter and in Chapter 4, this suggests that agreeableness may be slightly depoliticizing. However, the agreeableness × campaign tone effect is substantively negligible and statistically insignificant; likewise, the interactions for conscientiousness and emotional stability offer no evidence that these traits condition the relationship between campaign tone and electoral participation. The remaining two interactions, those for openness to experience and extraversion, do produce significant effects, with patterns consistent with expectations. Specifically, the impact of campaign tone on turnout is relatively slight for individuals high in openness to experience, but quite pronounced for participants with high marks in extraversion.

Figure 6.2 displays estimated effects for openness to experience and extraversion. In both panels, the horizontal axis captures the full range of values on perceived campaign tone, from very negative (a scale value of zero) to very positive (a value of ten). Likewise, the two lines in each panel represent effects for the highest and lowest values of the relevant trait dimensions. All four lines in Figure 6.2 slope upward from left to right, indicating that projected voter turnout always is higher for participants exposed to positive campaigns than for participants exposed to negative campaigns. However, the slopes are slight for people who are highly open to experience and highly introverted. With openness, for instance, projected values on the turnout variable rise from 7.43 to only 8.87 as campaign tone is perceived to grow dramatically more positive. People high in openness to experience seemingly are only mildly concerned about campaign tone. Collectively, they have a quite high likelihood of voting, and they are able to dismiss negative ads as a basis to defer from participation. In contrast, the influence of campaign tone is extremely sharp among participants who are low in openness to experience, moving from

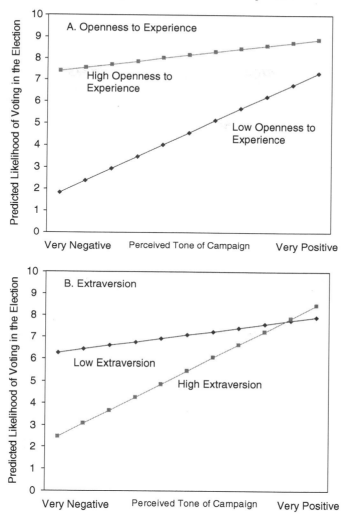

Figure 6.2 Personality and the impact of campaign tone on projected voter turnout.

a mere 1.85 to 7.32 as perceptions of the campaign grow from negative to positive.

The pattern for extraversion resembles that for openness to experience, except this time participants high in the trait dimension exhibit the greatest responsiveness to campaign tone. These results match well with expectations. Extraverts who perceive campaigns as especially negative react by turning their attentions elsewhere and they opt out of electoral participation. This point gains particular significance when viewed in conjunction with this chapter's earlier findings. Previously, we saw that extraverts gravitate toward social forms of political participation, but present results reveal that perceptions of negativity slam the brakes on at least one aspect of political involvement. Thus, a group of citizens whose psychological predispositions suit them well for political engagement can be dissuaded from voting if the campaign's information context is characterized by a high degree of negativity.

Earlier, no clear evidence of a link between personality and voter turnout was observed in tests involving self-reported turnout in the 1998 and 2006 midterm congressional elections. Present findings cast those initial results in a new light. Irrespective of any direct connection, it is now clear that personality does matter for turnout in at least one important way. Further, the effects depicted in Figure 6.2 are hardly subtle. Personality makes the difference for whether variance in campaign tone translates into marginal or dramatic effects on electoral participation. As was the case in prior chapters, the results presented here on conscientiousness and efficacy and on personality and campaign tone are interesting in their own right, but their primary value relates to what they suggest for future inquiry. Throughout this study, I have argued that the greatest value of incorporating personality in research on political behavior will come when we move beyond a one-size-fits-all depiction of citizens and politics. For many well-established relationships outside of the realm of personality, it is entirely plausible that effects vary markedly in magnitude for introverts and extraverts, the agreeable and the disagreeable, and so on. Present results provide a brief glimpse at the promise of systematic attention to such possibilities. What is especially noteworthy about the final results, those for personality and campaign tone, is that they capture interactions between core psychological traits and an aspect of the information environment. Such personality–environment interactions demonstrate that isolated attention to either personality or context risks yielding an incomplete account of political behavior.

## CONCLUSIONS

The behaviors examined in this chapter collectively constitute the central acts of citizenship. If people did not contact their representatives, become involved in political campaigns, or vote in elections, the underlying elements of political behavior – such as information acquisition and attitude formation, the subjects of the two previous chapters – would be of dramatically lessened consequence. In light of its importance, it is understandable that a tremendous amount of scholarly effort has been devoted to discovering the underpinnings of political participation. What is less understandable, however, is why so many prominent accounts have neglected to consider the possible role of core psychological differences. Those few studies that have incorporated personality measures consistently have found that variance in personality does matter for the tendency to participate in politics, yet the field as a whole has not acknowledged that psychological differences may bring influences on participation of a magnitude comparable to those of age, education, and political interest.

The various tests reported in this chapter demonstrate that the Big Five trait dimensions do not contribute equally to political participation. Many forms of participation inherently entail social interaction. For these, extraversion exerts a powerful influence. It is not news that people differ dramatically in how talkative, outgoing, and adventurous they are, and it is not shocking that these differences matter for politically relevant social interaction. Nonetheless, the significance of present findings should not be minimized. For decades, social scientists have sought to explain variance in political participation. This chapter's extraversion effects reveal that one of the most obvious answers long has escaped notice while standing in plain view. Accounts of social forms of political participation will be incomplete until attention to core psychological differences becomes widespread.

Beyond extraversion, the only other Big Five trait dimension that produced noticeable impact on multiple forms of political participation in this chapter's tests is openness to experience. For openness, the attraction of politics appears not to be social interaction, but rather cognitive and psychological engagement. Extraversion matters tremendously for social acts and not at all for individualistic behaviors. In contrast, openness plays a steady role in influencing multiple aspects of participation.

Results from thirteen models were reported in this chapter's first four tables. Among the thirty-nine coefficients for conscientiousness, agreeableness, and emotional stability, twenty-nine were negative, and ten of these reached at least minimal levels of statistical significance. The collective impact of these trait dimensions on participation is modest and inconsistent at best, yet the pattern warrants comment. Something about politics appears to be uninviting to people who are responsible, sympathetic, and level headed. Given the nature of politics in the 1998–2006 period in which my data were gathered, my guess is that most observers would find this pattern to be both understandable and lamentable.

As in the two previous chapters, this chapter's final tests – those involving the interplay between conscientiousness and external political efficacy and the importance of personality for response to campaign tone – highlight the value of analyses that contemplate some of the intricacies of political behavior. This point takes on particular significance for those analysts who seek to foster higher levels of political engagement in the citizenry. Good coaches learn that players have different attributes and skills, and players are positioned – and counseled – accordingly. For civic leaders who wish to mobilize political action, one challenge involves managing the psychology of individual differences. Conscientious individuals need to be convinced that their contributions will be meaningful. Extraverts must be coached to look past the disconcerting momentary aspects of negative campaigns, and focus on the big picture. Introverts should not be cast into uncomfortable social forms of participation. In short, there will be greater success in recruiting and retaining political activists if fundamental psychological differences are recognized. My point is not that everyone should devote high levels of effort to political engagement. However, opportunities are lost to both the individual and to society if a failure to acknowledge the importance of personality leads some people to be discouraged from joining the political sphere.

A considerable amount of ground has been covered both in the present chapter and throughout this study. The many tests that have been reported combine to demonstrate the insight that can be gained with greater attention to fundamental psychological differences in research on political behavior. Large numbers of noteworthy effects have been identified, yet my belief is that most of the significance of personality in this area remains to be discovered. Creative, forward-looking applications of the Big Five hold particular promise, but certainly the value of incorporating innate differences in our research is not limited to the Big Five framework. These issues are discussed and explored more thoroughly in the concluding chapter.

Appendix 6.A *Conscientiousness, External Efficacy, and Political Participation*

| | Contact with House Member or Senator (Pre-election Survey) | Contact with Any Member of Congress in Past Two Years (Postelection Survey) | Attend a Meeting with a Member of Congress in Past Two Years | Work for a Political Candidate or Party | Attend a Political Meeting or Rally |
|---|---|---|---|---|---|
| Age | 0.02*** | 0.01 | −0.01 | −0.01 | −0.01 |
| | (0.00) | (0.01) | (0.01) | (0.01) | (0.01) |
| Sex | −0.01 | −0.30 | −0.68** | −0.48 | −0.58# |
| | (0.17) | (0.18) | (0.25) | (0.44) | (0.35) |

| | Display Yard Signs, Buttons, or Bumper Sticker | Contribute Money to a Political Candidate or Party | Contribute Money to a Group that Supported or Opposed a Political Candidate | Try to Persuade Another Person to Vote for or Against a Candidate | Voter Turnout in the 2006 Midterm Elections |
|---|---|---|---|---|---|
| Education | 0.16*** (0.04) | 0.12* (0.05) | 0.14* (0.07) | 0.14 (0.11) | 0.27** (0.10) |
| Race | −1.51** (0.52) | −1.38* (0.57) | 0.28 (0.57) | −0.80 (1.77) | −0.01 (0.90) |
| External Political Efficacy | −0.35* (0.17) | −0.48** (0.18) | −0.20 (0.23) | −0.67# (0.39) | −0.82* (0.35) |
| Openness | 0.95* (0.42) | 0.72 (0.46) | 0.81 (0.60) | 1.05 (1.04) | 1.63* (0.82) |
| Conscientiousness | −1.01* (0.48) | −2.31*** (0.54) | −2.65** (0.78) | −4.51** (1.51) | −2.49* (1.06) |
| Extraversion | 1.22*** (0.32) | 1.14 (0.36) | 1.83*** (0.47) | 0.95 (0.84) | 1.52* (0.64) |
| Agreeableness | −0.06 (0.37) | 0.74# (0.41) | 0.40 (0.56) | 0.66 (0.98) | −1.62* (0.78) |
| Emotional Stability | −0.70# (0.40) | −0.79# (0.45) | −0.01 (0.61) | −1.86 (1.19) | −0.60 (0.88) |
| Conscientiousness × External Political Efficacy | 0.62* (0.27) | 0.83** (0.30) | 0.54 (0.39) | 1.60* (0.66) | 1.58** (0.55) |
| Model $\chi^2$ | 77.30 | 57.30 | 49.00 | 22.44 | 42.23 |
| Number of Cases | 676 | 685 | 683 | 686 | 686 |
| Age | −0.01 (0.01) | 0.02# (0.01) | 0.01 (0.01) | 0.00 (0.01) | 0.05*** (0.01) |
| Sex | −0.09 (0.24) | −0.19 (0.27) | 0.27 (0.29) | −0.10 (0.18) | −0.01 (0.26) |
| Education | −0.02 (0.06) | 0.31*** (0.07) | 0.24** (0.08) | 0.07 (0.05) | 0.27*** (0.07) |
| Race | 0.81 (0.50) | −19.00 (7448.98) | −18.97 (7395.76) | −0.94# (0.50) | 0.58 (0.62) |
| External Political Efficacy | −0.21 (0.23) | −0.10 (0.25) | −0.29 (0.28) | −0.03 (0.18) | −0.13 (0.29) |
| Openness | 1.62** (0.59) | 1.08# (0.65) | 0.98 (0.70) | 1.05 (1.04) | 0.05 (0.66) |

*(continued)*

Appendix 6.A *(continued)*

| | Display Yard Signs, Buttons, or Bumper Sticker | Contribute Money to a Political Candidate or Party | Contribute Money to a Group that Supported or Opposed a Political Candidate | Try to Persuade Another Person to Vote for or Against a Candidate | Voter Turnout in the 2006 Midterm Elections |
|---|---|---|---|---|---|
| Conscientiousness | −1.13 | −1.35 | −1.65# | −0.26 | −0.82 |
| | (0.73) | (0.82) | (0.88) | (0.53) | (0.72) |
| Extraversion | −0.43 | 0.73 | 0.69 | 0.71* | 0.02 |
| | (0.48) | (0.51) | (0.54) | (0.35) | (0.50) |
| Agreeableness | −0.14 | 0.28 | −0.22 | 0.11 | −0.20 |
| | (0.55) | (0.60) | (0.65) | (0.41) | (0.58) |
| Emotional Stability | −1.48* | −1.30# | 0.18 | −0.82# | −0.82 |
| | (0.63) | (0.71) | (0.70) | (0.45) | (0.59) |
| Conscientiousness × External Political Efficacy | 0.74# | 0.37 | 0.66 | 0.05 | 0.73 |
| | (0.38) | (0.42) | (0.45) | (0.30) | (0.48) |
| Model $\chi^2$ | 26.92 | 52.89 | 30.69 | 39.25 | 67.75 |
| Number of Cases | 686 | 686 | 684 | 685 | 684 |

*Notes:* Data are from the 2006 CES. Cell entries from the first model are ordered logistic regression coefficients and cell entries for all other models are binomial logistic regression coefficients, with separate models estimated for each column; standard errors are in parentheses. Each model also includes threshold estimates (column one) or a constant term (all other models). Higher values on the dependent variables indicate greater levels of participation. Results from some of these models were used to calculate the predicted probabilities reported in Figure 6.1.

*** $p < .001$, ** $p < .01$, * $p < .05$, # $p < .10$

Appendix 6.B *Campaign Tone, Personality, and Voter Turnout*

| | Model 1. Campaign Tone | Model 2. Campaign Tone and Personality |
|---|---|---|
| Age | 0.04** | 0.04** |
| | (0.01) | (0.01) |
| Sex | −0.76* | −0.56# |
| | (0.31) | (0.33) |

| | | |
|---|---|---|
| Education | 0.33*** | 0.27** |
| | (0.09) | (0.09) |
| Race | 0.62 | 1.00# |
| | (0.57) | (0.60) |
| Perceived Campaign Tone | 0.33*** | 0.35 |
| | (0.06) | (0.23) |
| Openness | | 5.58** |
| | | (1.74) |
| Conscientiousness | | 1.94 |
| | | (1.77) |
| Extraversion | | −3.80** |
| | | (1.45) |
| Agreeableness | | −3.19# |
| | | (1.82) |
| Emotional Stability | | 1.92 |
| | | (1.67) |
| Perceived Campaign Tone × Openness | | −0.40* |
| | | (0.16) |
| Perceived Campaign Tone × Conscientiousness | | −0.03 |
| | | (0.16) |
| Perceived Campaign Tone × Extraversion | | 0.43** |
| | | (0.14) |
| Perceived Campaign Tone × Agreeableness | | 0.05 |
| | | (0.16) |
| Perceived Campaign Tone × Emotional Stability | | 0.02 |
| | | (0.16) |
| Constant | 2.00** | 0.82 |
| | (0.75) | (1.33) |
| $R^2$ | 0.15 | 0.23 |
| Number of Cases | 396 | 373 |

*Notes:* Data are from the 2005 NJS. Cell entries are OLS regression coefficients; standard errors are in parentheses. The dependent variable is coded 0 (very unlikely respondent will vote) to 10 (very likely respondent will vote). Results from the second model were used to calculate the predicted values reported in Figure 6.2.

*** $p < .001$, ** $p < .01$, * $p < .05$, # $p < .10$

# 7

## The Multiple Bases of Political Behavior

The term "political behavior" encompasses a wide array of phenomena, most of which convey a sense of people interacting with, and responding to, the political stimuli that surround them. People follow contemporary political events by reading today's newspaper or watching this evening's TV news; they approve or disapprove of the job the president currently is doing; and they vote for candidates in this year's election. In light of this immediacy, it is understandable that most accounts of political behavior contemplate how people may be influenced by environmental forces, and especially by forces in operation just prior to the behaviors in question. Thus, a great deal of research examines matters such as the impact of news media on political attitudes, of partisan mobilization on voter turnout, and of campaign content on candidate choice. Or, reaching back to earlier influences, studies consider the effects of childhood political socialization, education, and the person's exposure to others within various social contexts.

To the extent that such research calls attention to one key set of determinants of political behavior, we should have no qualms about a focus on the influence of environmental forces. However, diligence is needed to ensure that such a focus does not produce analytical myopia. Any account of political behavior positing, either explicitly or implicitly, that *only* environmental forces matter necessarily assumes that people first encounter the world of politics as political blank slates. And that assumption is wrong. A full, holistic theory of political behavior must recognize the impact of three broad sets of variables: environmental factors, innate biological or biologically influenced factors, and interactions between environmental and innate forces. My purpose in this book has been to help bring the second and third of these sets of variables into the mix by highlighting the importance of personality as an influence on political behavior. In pursuing this objective, I have sought to emphasize that personality is significant in itself as a persistent force, but also that any effect of personality implicitly signals the underlying role of biology. Empirically, this study has shown that fundamental psychological differences contribute to variance in political behavior both directly and through interaction with environmental influences. Hence, by considering the role of personality, a much richer and more nuanced depiction of the bases of political behavior becomes possible.

Although the theory I have advanced facilitates development of a more intricate view of the influences on human behavior, such a view may bring consternation to some. The present discussion is hardly the first time this issue has been confronted. In her biography of the writer Alice Sheldon,[1] Julie Phillips recounts the nervous skepticism some of Sheldon's psychological research had faced in the 1960s, commenting that (2006, 204) "There is a side to behaviorism that's very liberating: if the human psyche begins as a blank slate, then we can change anything. But what if you can't change things in yourself?" I have posited that personality is a stable, biologically influenced psychological structure. It changes very little, if at all, during one's adult years. This implies, as one example, that introverts cannot refashion their psychological compositions into those of extraverts. Introverts may endeavor to become more outgoing and talkative in their behavior, but they will not do so by transforming their basic psychological tendencies; instead, they can only strive to adjust their behavior *despite* the inertial force of their core personality traits.

Two facets of this discussion require further elaboration. First, my thesis is *not* one of biological or psychological determinism. Under my conceptualization, personality traits are psychological structures that give rise to certain tendencies in behavior, but traits do not predetermine that such behavior must and will occur. The trait literature abounds with evidence consistent with my perspective. For each of us, personality traits establish central tendencies, but actual behavior can and does vary markedly around these central tendencies. Recall, for example that Mischel (1979), a chief critic of trait approaches, found an average correlation of 0.30 in trans-situational behavior. Although the precise estimate can be debated, I agree with Mischel's broader point that traits are not absolute determinants of behavior. As applied to politics, my argument is not that people are born to be well informed, conservative, or politically engaged, but instead that biologically influenced psychological structures exert meaningful and systematic impact on the likelihood of these and other forms of political behavior. Tendencies matter, but tendencies are not requirements.

---

[1] Alice Sheldon gained fame as a science fiction writer, writing primarily under the name James Tiptree, Jr. Earlier in her life, she had been an African explorer, painter, WAC, poultry farmer, CIA operative, and, in the period that gave rise to Phillips's comment, a graduate student who earned a doctorate in psychology in 1967.

A second critical point is that what I advocate is much more than the mere addition of some new variables to our models. Implicit in my approach is the belief that students of political behavior require a new, expansive, and multifaceted way of thinking about the bases of political action. We must recognize that basic psychological differences exist. We must recognize that these differences often exert influence on political behavior in a manner that is causally prior to the effects of environmental forces. Lastly, we must recognize that environmental factors will not always produce identical effects on all individuals, but instead that these effects often will vary as a function of people's deep-rooted psychological tendencies. Once we consider the possible impact of personality, our theories of political behavior expand from one constellation of explanatory factors to three.

The thesis advanced here implies the need for considerable initiative in terms of theory building, methodological advances, and substantive inquiry. The present effort has centered on the dominant contemporary model of personality trait structure, the five-factor approach. Indicators of the Big Five have been developed, and the implications of these trait dimensions for a large number of dependent variables have been considered. The tests have explored both direct effects and numerous forms of indirect, nonmonotonic, and conditional relationships. At virtually every turn, we have seen that personality does indeed constitute a key foundation of political behavior. Although the substantive ground covered in this book has been expansive, it should be clear that anything accomplished here represents only the very first step in pursuit of what promises to be an extremely rich stream of scholarly research. My hope is that this book will have persuaded at least some readers that there is value in studying the political effects of fundamental psychological differences, and will have sparked interest in further research on the multiple bases of political behavior. In the remainder of this chapter, I discuss a few of the lingering questions and future directions suggested by the analyses reported in the preceding pages.

## THE ROLE OF PERSONALITY IN THEORIES OF POLITICAL BEHAVIOR

The most immediate need in further contemplating the possible impact of personality on political behavior is for theory building and the careful derivation of additional hypotheses. For direct effects, this matter is not especially daunting because past research in trait psychology offers ample guidance regarding the likely consequences of variance in the Big Five trait dimensions. In the preceding chapters, numerous hypotheses have been tested, offering a solid foundation for subsequent study of direct effects. However, in moving beyond these direct effects, a great deal of theorizing will be required before the full significance of enduring psychological differences will be realized. In particular, creative and diligent effort will be needed to specify the many possible indirect and conditional effects of personality.

In the three prior chapters, examples were offered of the chief types of personality effects for which I believe additional hypotheses must be crafted. First, in many instances, it seems likely that the influence of personality will operate through mediating factors. For political attitudes, one plausible path, as tested in Chapter 5, includes personality effects on political predispositions such as partisanship and ideology, with those predispositions, in turn, shaping political attitudes. This same line of reasoning must be applied in theory building pertinent to other sorts of dependent variables. For instance, in Chapters 4 and 6, openness to experience and extraversion were found to exert positive effects on numerous forms of political engagement, but it is not yet known what intermediary factors, if any, must be added for the causal path to be complete.

The second possibility that requires further theorizing concerns nonmonotonic effects of personality. In most of the tests reported in the prior three chapters, indicators of the Big Five were modeled in simple additive form. It is conceivable, however, as was demonstrated by the case of conscientiousness and preference for legislator action in Chapter 5, that many personality effects will be nonmonotonic. As one example, extraversion influences the inclination to engage in social forms of political participation, but the impact of this trait dimension does not necessarily rise steadily across the introversion–extraversion scale. One obvious alternate is that there may be some sort of threshold effect, either in which extraversion must be very low before social forms of participation become unlikely or in which only the very most outgoing individuals gravitate toward these behaviors. Positing the existence and direction of a relationship are much easier matters than specifying its form, but our theoretical and empirical models will remain imprecise absent the latter.

Additional work also is required to construct hypotheses regarding possible conditional effects of personality. One type of conditional relationship involves interactions between two or more of the Big Five trait dimensions. We saw examples of this in Chapter 4 with the interaction between openness to experience and conscientiousness in two models of political knowledge. Research in trait psychology often hypothesizes interactions between Big Five traits, but applications of the five-factor framework in the study of political behavior must advance beyond the present fledgling state for such conditional effects to become routine components of theory-driven inquiry.

A second type of conditional relationship involves the interaction between personality traits and environmental factors. My thesis holds, first, that both biologically influenced forces and environmental factors matter for political behavior, and second, that specific elements from these two broad categories of variables likely operate in interaction with one another. Simply put, variance in personality often leads people to respond differently to environmental stimuli. It is one thing, however, to embrace the intuition that personality and environment interact, and quite another to delineate and test specific hypotheses regarding the nature and form of such relationships. For decades, scholars in the field of trait psychology have mentioned possible interactions between trait variables and situational forces, yet theory-driven empirical study of such effects remains disappointingly rare. It may be that scholars conducting applied research will need to take the lead role in identifying these conditional effects. Two examples of personality–environment interactions were reported in the prior chapters, that is, concerning the size of discussion networks and exposure to cross-cutting discourse, and negative campaign tone and projected voter turnout. Countless additional relationships such as these are possible. In virtually any laboratory experiment in political psychology, for example, we should at least pause to consider whether our manipulations may produce effects that vary as a function of participants' personality traits. Absent attention to personality–environment interactions, our explanations of political behavior tend to have a simplistic "one-size-fits-all" character. Moving beyond that point will require rigorous effort, but the pay off promises to be more elaborate and powerful theories of how citizens engage the political world.

In addition to theorizing regarding the form of personality effects, further attention must be directed to how personality fits within broader accounts of political behavior. One matter is whether research on personality and politics should be wedded to the Big Five. The emergence of five-factor models in the late 1980s genuinely revolutionized the study of trait psychology, and it is an extreme understatement to note that research on the Big Five in the past two decades has been impressive in its scope and quality. Scholars in many fields have conducted applied work drawing on the Big Five. In this sense, political science has come late to the game. As discussed in Chapter 2, most of the lingering dispute about five-factor taxonomies does not challenge the centrality of openness, conscientiousness, extraversion, agreeableness, and emotional stability. Instead, some psychologists disagree regarding whether there might be greater utility in either reducing the Big Five to two higher-order trait dimensions, or splitting some or all of the Big Five traits into multiple subsidiary factors. Given that consensus strongly supports the Big Five, my belief is that this approach presently offers the most useful and well-grounded starting point for political scientists interested in conducting applied research on personality and politics.

Although I advocate focus on the Big Five, we should not invoke this approach while wearing blinders. Three points warrant mention. First, for some purposes it may be adequate, and perhaps even desirable, to account only for the two higher-order trait dimensions that apparently encompass the Big Five. Digman (1997) suggests that a hierarchical view connects openness and extraversion in one higher-order trait dimension, and conscientiousness, agreeableness, and emotional stability in another. Digman further argues that these higher-order factors are easily linked with several traditional theories of personality. In many of the tests reported in the prior three chapters, and especially those concerning information in Chapter 4 and participation in Chapter 6, openness and extraversion yielded strong positive effects while the remaining trait dimensions produced a great number of modest negative effects. This pattern is at least loosely consistent with Digman's empirical observations. It would be extremely premature to conclude that research in political science should forego the Big Five in favor of a "Big Two" approach. Still, the pattern emerging from present empirical tests is suggestive, and thus, at a minimum, we would be wise to be receptive to the possibility that some of the Big Five trait dimensions bring reinforcing influences, yielding general patterns consistent with Digman's claimed higher-order trait dimensions.

A second possibility, one with the opposite logic of a move to two global factors, is that applied research on personality and political behavior will be most fruitful when the Big Five dimensions are parsed into subsidiary traits. In psychology, a typical progression begins with identification of effects of one or more of the Big Five dimensions, followed by subsequent research that seeks to pinpoint the specific elements of the dimension that are most important for the phenomenon in question. For instance, if initial tests show that conscientiousness matters for some aspect of job performance, follow-up work might explore which subcomponents of conscientiousness drive this relationship. I see it as highly likely that political scientists will find value in pursuing a similar course. But, first things first, more work is needed to posit and test effects of the Big Five. Down the road, refinements centered on subsidiary traits are to be welcomed.

A final point to reiterate concerning the Big Five is that even the framework's most ardent advocates recognize that the taxonomy does not capture the entirety of variance in psychological differences (e.g., Saucier and Goldberg 1998). In most research on politics, the starting point in incorporating personality in our theories should be the Big Five. However, we should remain receptive to the possibility that particular trait factors not encompassed by the five-factor framework also may be consequential. For instance, Saucier and Goldberg (1998) identified a handful of traits that are not fully captured by the Big Five, including at least two – religiousness and prejudice – that may be of relevance in many studies of political behavior.

Moving beyond the immediate confines of the Big Five, one topic to consider more closely involves the interrelationship among genetics, personality, and politics. At present, we know that variance in genes corresponds with variance in both personality and political behavior, and that differences in personality also correspond with variance in political behavior. A reasonable inference to derive from this array of findings is that biological effects on political behavior operate at least partly through personality. Genes shape basic psychological differences that, in turn, influence patterns in political behavior.

The evidence regarding these three relationships is strong. Nonetheless, the implications of extant work should not be exaggerated. First, the claim that personality functions as a mechanism connecting genes and politics has been established only by inference. Additional work is needed to provide direct evidence of personality's mediating role. This presumably will require analysis of twin or molecular data from a dataset that also includes indicators of personality and political engagement. Second, although biological influences on politics may operate partly through personality, it should not be assumed that personality is the only intervening mechanism. Thus far, students of biology and politics have been much more active in identifying genetic influences on political behavior than in explaining how and why these influences operate. I believe personality to be one key linkage mechanism, but we should not permit the study of personality to foreclose consideration of other alternates. Third, if genetic effects do operate through personality, we should not assume that the causal chain includes only genes, traits, and the political variables under consideration, nor should we assume a simple and direct causal chain. As noted previously, for instance, personality may influence long-term political predispositions that then shape more immediate attitudes and behaviors. Further, even granting a strong influence of biology on both personality and political behavior, the precise expression of these effects may hinge on complex interactions involving environmental factors. Lastly, one conceivably also could extend the causal chain in the opposite direction, specifying those factors that give rise to biological differences.

This last point raises a question about just how far back we must reach to devise satisfactory accounts of political behavior. This is a reasonable query. On the one hand, it would not be especially revealing to model attendance at the February 17th PTA meeting solely on attendance at the February 3rd meeting. On the other hand, students of politics surely should not be forced to anchor our causal theories in a discussion of the Big Bang. Some might argue that there is no need for our explanations to incorporate biology, or even personality, and that focus on what happens just prior to the behavior in question is adequate. I obviously disagree. My view is that we must reach back far enough to include fundamental, biologically influenced differences because only by doing so can we acknowledge the effects of the three central bases of political behavior: innate forces, environmental forces, and their interactions. It follows that precisely how far back we must reach is not yet known. If we were to find, for instance, that biological influences on politics operate exclusively via personality, then I would contend that students of politics could fare well without incorporating processes prior to personality effects in our empirical accounts; in this scenario, personality variables would be sufficient to capture the influence of deep-rooted forces. Conversely, if, as seems likely, personality is found to be only one of a set of mechanisms linking biology and politics, then a comprehensive treatment of biological influences clearly would require data on personality's fellow mechanisms.

A related issue concerns the appropriate division of labor among scholarly disciplines.[2] For instance, the impact of biology on personality clearly is relevant for political scientists, yet empirical examination of the biology–personality link arguably should be left to behavioral geneticists and trait psychologists. Some line has to be drawn. After all, absent some reasonable division of labor, we fall prey to an infinite regress. Genes matter for personality, but what factors lead to variance in genetics? Prenatal exposure to certain chemicals may influence genes, but what factors cause prenatal exposure to those chemicals? The composition of local soil partly determines environmental exposure to certain chemicals, but what affected the composition of the soil? Continuing on this path, it would not be long before we found ourselves asking what caused indigestion among dinosaurs. But the way to escape this infinite regress is not to draw an arbitrary line. Instead, where we draw the line must be guided by the tenets of our theories. If we theorize a biological basis to political behavior, then our causal chain necessarily must include indicators – such as measures of personality traits – that capture biological forces and that differentiate those forces from environmental influences. But we reasonably can leave to other disciplines the task of identifying the processes that gave rise to our predictors.

The impact of personality on political attitudes suggests a need to rethink other long-standing theories of political behavior. For instance, what does it imply for rational-actor perspectives if, due to differences in their

---

[2] I thank Paul Quirk for suggesting this point.

personalities, two identically situated individuals form disparate policy preferences or choose different courses of political engagement? If variance in personality traits influences behaviors or preferences, can we reconcile this with traditional conceptions of utility maximization? Suppose, for example, that two neighbors, one a trembling introvert and the other a boisterous extravert, hold identical stakes in an upcoming city council discussion of a zoning ordinance. Based on findings in Chapter 6 (and sheer common sense), we surely would expect that the extraverted neighbor would be more likely to attend the council meeting, yet an exclusive focus on economic self-interest seemingly would be silent on this matter.

Partisanship offers a related test case. The "running tally" view of partisanship (e.g., Downs 1957; Fiorina 1981) casts partisan preference as the fluid outcome of a person's ongoing assessment of party performance. This perspective admits no enduring basis to partisan attachment. Under such a framework, why would partisan affiliation vary as a function of stable personality traits such as openness to experience, conscientiousness, and agreeableness, as was found in Chapter 5? Following these models, people with identical utility functions should not differ in partisan preference merely because one person is more conscientious than another, yet we have seen personality effects of precisely this sort.

Personality traits logically serve as sources of stability for political judgments. For instance, a high level of conscientiousness should act in a consistent, persistent manner to nudge a person toward ideological conservatism. Personality similarly may constitute a stabilizing influence on assessments of policy. Since at least the time of Converse (1964), preference stability has been championed as a desirable property in citizens.[3] But adulation of attitudinal stability presupposes that that stability arises from well-informed deliberation, not from a biologically influenced psychological tendency. Personality exerts strong influence on political preferences, including, as was reported in Chapter 5, a noteworthy influence on ideology. If this effect contributes to attitudinal stability, as seems likely, then the significance conventionally attributed to such stability must be reconsidered. A person with a very high level of openness to experience and a very low level of conscientiousness may persistently claim to be a staunch liberal, but it surely would require a definitional stretch to suggest that stability in this case signifies sophistication.

To some extent, these matters merely represent concrete instances in which exclusively environmental perspectives offer incomplete accounts of political behavior. Running tally models of partisan preference are purely environmental, treating actors as blank slates who calculate party

---

[3] For a recent example of research in this tradition, see Ansolabehere, Rodden, and Snyder (2008).

assessments after compiling and tabulating evidence of a party's successes and failures. Adding the impact of personality to the mix results in a more comprehensive and realistic depiction of partisan choice. As to what constitutes self-interested behavior, any impact of personality on political judgment implies that there is not a single right answer for all individuals. Under economic definitions of rationality, we may struggle to explain why two seemingly similar individuals hold fundamentally different political views, or why our hypothetical introvert stayed home while the extraverted neighbor attended the city council meeting. But once we factor in personality, a different interpretation of what constitutes rational behavior may emerge. We may recognize that a preference for limited, cautious policymaking is right given one person's personality, while a preference for more aggressive governmental action is right for the other, just as a quiet evening at home makes more sense for the introvert than for the extravert.

These various questions of theory clearly are not all answerable as yet. I have called attention to them to provide a sense of what a personality approach implies for alternate perspectives, and to suggest areas in which refinements in theory may be needed. For what it is worth, my own tendency is to see different scholarly points of view as potential complements, not as competitors, and such is the case here. Although I believe research on political behavior must account for fundamental psychological differences, I do not advocate a focus on personality as a replacement for prior approaches. Instead, as I have emphasized throughout this chapter, I believe that simultaneous attention to stable psychological factors, environmental factors, and interactions between the two is necessary if we are to develop a comprehensive treatment of the multiple bases of political behavior.

## THE EMPIRICAL STUDY OF PERSONALITY AND POLITICS

Issues in measurement are perhaps more mundane than questions of theory, but issues in measurement still must be addressed. I strongly advocate that research on political behavior include a focus on personality traits, and I believe that the Big Five presently affords our best opportunity to pursue this objective. However, I am less wedded to particular indicators of the Big Five. The good news on this front is that data gathered via univocal, bipolar, and questionnaire formats consistently yield evidence of a five-factor trait structure. In an important sense, it follows that it is difficult to go wrong when selecting Big Five measures from among those already tested by trait psychologists, particularly if it is possible for respondents to complete large, multi-item batteries.[4]

---

[4] For a good, recent discussion of the properties of various Big Five measures, see John, Naumann, and Soto (2008, 130–8).

As political applications of the Big Five proceed, two methodological issues will require further attention. First, although it is true that multiple-item formats can be used to develop functional measures, it is not clear that ideal brief measures of the Big Five have been identified. As we have seen, my own approach on this point has been to use bipolar items, and, as a simple check on the robustness of results, to vary some of the particular item pairs from one survey to the next. The two-item scales developed here functioned well, and the same can be said of the brief Big Five measures reported by Gosling, Rentfrow, and Swann (2003), Woods and Hampson (2005), and Rammstedt and John (2007). Still, there is a clear difference between "good enough" and "best possible." With further research on measurement, and especially with direct tests of various competing measures, it should be possible to identify the unique attributes of our best contenders, and ultimately to propose a preferred battery for use on future surveys. Validity should be the chief concern, but we also must be attentive to how much survey time is required to obtain Big Five data and whether inclusion of trait items adversely affects interview rapport. Ideally, our long-term objective should be for a common trait battery to gain regular use on a wide array of surveys and experiments. Once this goal is met, it will be possible for scholars to incorporate basic psychological differences in their empirical research as a matter of routine, facilitating ongoing attention to the multiple bases of political behavior. As this research takes place, use of a well-established common trait battery will help the work to be cumulative and mutually reinforcing, thus hopefully avoiding a return to the idiosyncratic, piecemeal approach rightly criticized by Sniderman (1975).

A second, and more complicated, challenge will be in the development of high-quality Big Five indicators for use in cross-national research. As noted in Chapter 2, psychologists have reported a great deal of evidence regarding the universality of the five-factor structure. Big Five batteries have been translated into multiple languages, and the scales have performed well. Hence, working *within* any given country, it should not be problematic for political scientists to devise good indicators of the Big Five. However, it is a considerably more difficult matter to represent the Big Five in a comparable manner *across* nations, and especially across languages. The development of good indicators for use in comparative research is an age-old problem, and there is no need to belabor the point here. It is sufficient to note that, as in all cross-national research on political behavior, it will be important for analysts to be particularly cautious in matters concerning measurement.

## PERSONALITY AND POLITICS

A deepening of our understanding of citizens and politics stands as the ultimate goal of research on personality and political behavior. As emphasized throughout this book, I believe that a much richer and more nuanced appreciation of the underpinnings of political behavior will emerge once we incorporate both innate and environmental forces, along with their interactions, in our accounts. As this research proceeds, a great number of specific substantive questions can be pursued. At this early stage, I neither wish to foreclose research avenues nor to suggest that some topics are more pressing than others. Hence, in calling attention to a few possible issues, I do so with the intent of providing examples of the sorts of substantive questions future research on personality and politics might pursue, not to imply that these particular questions should be awarded any privileged status.

One issue to consider is whether any influence of personality on patterns in civic engagement yields an inadvertent partisan or ideological imbalance in political discourse. In the prior three chapters, we observed numerous instances in which openness to experience produced a positive effect and in which conscientiousness produced a negative effect in models regarding many facets of civic engagement. This pattern was seen in tests concerning political discussion, political knowledge, opinionation, interest in politics, efficacy, and working in campaigns. In several additional cases, either a significant positive effect of openness or a significant negative effect of conscientiousness was observed. In themselves, these results establish that personality matters for civic engagement, but the findings carry no overt political importance. However, these findings are placed in a new light when we recall from Chapter 5 that openness predicts ideological liberalism and a Democratic partisan affiliation, and that conscientiousness predicts the opposite. Putting these results together, the possibility emerges that liberal Democratic voices speak more loudly in the American political scene than do conservative Republican voices, purely due to what may be nothing more than a coincidental correspondence in the traits that influence political predispositions and those that influence engagement.[5]

Future research might examine the magnitude of any such personality-based effect in an effort to gauge its aggregate strength.[6] For any given individual, the effect may well be modest, but even marginal individual-level influences can take on considerable systematic importance when aggregated across tens of millions of citizens. Also, further research could find that the effect suggested here is transient, linked somehow to political developments at the time this book's data were gathered rather than to more lasting features of the American political system. Lastly, it should be clear that if there is a personality-based tilting of the playing field, this

---

[5] My thanks to John Zaller for suggesting this possibility.
[6] A variant of the simulation techniques used by Althaus (2003) and Bartels (1996) to study information effects could be employed.

effect may well be offset by differences in mobilization efforts. That is, we might find that any advantage for liberals and Democrats we observe when personality is studied in isolation vanishes, or even reverses, when environmental factors are added to the mix.

A second substantive concern that may warrant further attention involves the interplay between the personalities of citizens and those of candidates for elected office.[7] As just reiterated, we have seen that openness to experience and conscientiousness produce opposite effects in terms of ideology and partisan preference. My assumption in interpreting these findings has been that these trait dimensions correspond with characteristic views regarding what it means to be liberal or conservative, and what it means to be a Democrat or a Republican. For instance, people who are high in conscientiousness tend toward caution and personal responsibility, attributes that should attract these individuals to the principles of small government. But an alternate possibility is that people value the traits they themselves possess, seek out those traits in others, and find them in fellow partisans.[8]

I have long been interested in the influence of candidate character on candidate evaluation (e.g., McCurley and Mondak 1995; Mondak 1995a). Previously, I have focused on candidate traits such as competence and integrity, traits that all voters presumably value. But if, as posited here, there is also a personality connection, it might be that voters differ in the personality traits they find desirable in candidates. All voters should prefer candidates who are honest, but all voters will not necessarily prefer candidates who are extraverts. The person who is open to experience may be averse to dogmatic politicians, and the person who is careless or dishevelled may be unimpressed by a candidate's conscientiousness.

If there is such a personality-based affinity between voters and candidates – and at this point, definitive demonstration of the existence of this link requires further research – it would suggest two noteworthy implications. First, an impact of personality on candidate preference generally would have the effect of reinforcing partisan and ideological preferences, but for a reason unrelated in any direct manner to policy. In the extreme case, if a conscientious individual votes solely on the basis of which candidate is the most responsible, then the fact that both the voter and the candidate are Republicans would be a coincidence. But second, because

[7] Important first steps toward studying this matter have been taken by Caprara and colleagues (see especially Caprara, Barbaranelli, and Zimbardo 2002; Caprara et al. 2003).

[8] A related, but somewhat different, possibility is that voters derive ideological inferences from assessments of candidates' traits. For instance, if the candidate appears a bit dishevelled, might a voter equate this with a low mark on conscientiousness, and thus with the assumption that the candidate is not a conservative?

it is not set in stone that all Democrats are open to experience or that all Republicans are conscientious, evidence that voters seek out candidates similar to themselves in personality would suggest a campaign strategy for candidates from the political minority. For instance, Democratic nominees in strongly Republican districts might improve their prospects, even if only on the margins, by emphasizing their work ethic and sense of personal responsibility, and by omitting from their personal histories any mention of their surfing accolades, skill at cooking Tibetan cuisine, and experiences as a street performer. In short, candidates may find that the personality attributes that go over well in one district may not in another, and that by highlighting those traits the voters find to be most desirable, the candidates can make inroads even where partisan forces are unfavorable.

The third possible research stream I will note concerns cross-national work on political behavior, and especially on politics and culture. Students of comparative political behavior have long been intrigued by the significance of political culture, with Ronald Inglehart's research achieving particular prominence (e.g., Inglehart 1988, 1989). Recent contributions in this area suggest a possible role for personality. First, some works have commented on a possible interplay between genetic and cultural influences (e.g., Inglehart and Klingemann 2003). Second, in a very interesting discussion, Hofstede and McCrae (2004) report and analyze correlations between the Big Five and Hofstede's cultural dimensions. Hofstede and McCrae posit numerous possible accounts for these relationships, including that the distribution of genetically influenced personality traits may vary by nation, and thus that "there are innate temperamental differences between ethnic populations that give rise to cultural differences" (Hofstede and McCrae 2004, 77). Hofstede and McCrae rightly note that extant data do not support conclusive statements regarding the causal connection between personality and culture, but the authors also emphasize the importance of future research on this matter. As this work proceeds, it may be of particular value for students of comparative political behavior if it provides new insight on the origins, meaning, and significance of culture. Hence, simultaneous attention to personality and political culture exemplifies well the promise I see in incorporating fundamental psychological differences in our substantive examinations of political behavior.[9]

The examples of possible research streams outlined here suggest two general lessons about personality and politics. First, opportunities abound for dramatic breakthroughs in the depth and sophistication of both our theories and our substantive explanations of political behavior.

---

[9] As this research proceeds, it will be important for scholars to be attentive to issues in cross-level inference as work moves between an individual-level and a national-level focus (e.g., Seligson 2002).

Second, achieving these breakthroughs will require considerable effort, however. Research on personality and mass politics – indeed, research on all innate influences on political behavior – remains in a fledgling state. Noteworthy inroads in the study of genetics and politics have been accumulating at a rapid pace, and the present effort to call attention to the significance of personality hopefully has succeeded in highlighting the corresponding importance of psychological differences. Nonetheless, the combined body of extant research in these areas is minute relative to what can and should be achieved with further effort. For this research to realize its full potential, scholars must embrace a new perspective, a perspective that fully acknowledges the significance of the multiple bases of political behavior.

# References

Adorno, T. W., E. Frankel-Brunswick, D. J. Levinson, and R. N. Sanford. 1950. *The Authoritarian Personality*. New York: Harper.

Alford, J. R., C. L. Funk, and J. R. Hibbing. 2008. "Beyond Liberals and Conservatives to Political Genotypes and Phenotypes." *Perspectives on Politics* 6: 321–8.

2005. "Are Political Orientations Genetically Transmitted?" *American Political Science Review* 99:153–67.

Alford, J. R., and J. R. Hibbing. 2007. "Personal, Interpersonal, and Political Temperaments." *The Annals of the American Academy of Political and Social Science* 614: 196–212.

Allen, B. P. 1994. *Personality Theories*. Boston: Allyn and Bacon.

Allik J., and R. R. McCrae. 2004. "Toward a Geography of Personality Traits: Patterns of Profiles across Cultures." *Journal of Cross-Cultural Psychology* 35: 13–28.

Allport, G. W. 1937. *Personality: A Psychological Interpretation*. New York: Holt.

Allport, G. W., and H. S. Odbert. 1936. "Trait-Names: A Psycho-Lexical Study." *Psychological Monographs* 47 (Whole No. 211).

Altemeyer, B. 1996. *The Authoritarian Specter*. Cambridge: Harvard University Press.

1988. *Enemies of Freedom: Understanding of Right-Wing Authoritarianism*. San Francisco: Jossey-Bass.

Althaus, S. L. 2003. *Collective Preferences in Democratic Politics: Opinion Surveys and the Will of the People*. New York: Cambridge University Press.

Anderson, C. J., and A. Paskeviciute. 2005. "Macro-Politics and Micro-Behavior: Mainstream Politics and the Frequency of Political Discussion in Contemporary Democracies." In A. S. Zuckerman, ed., *The Social Logic of Politics: Personal Networks as Contexts for Political Behavior*. Philadelphia: Temple University Press, pp. 228–48.

Ansolabehere, S., and S. Iyengar. 1995. *Going Negative: How Political Advertising Shrinks and Polarizes the Electorate*. New York: Free Press.

Ansolabehere, S. D., S. Iyengar, and A. Simon. 1999. "Replicating Experiments Using Aggregate and Survey Data: The Case of Negative Advertising and Turnout." *American Political Science Review* 93: 901–09.

# References

Ansolabehere, S., J. Rodden, and J. M. Snyder, Jr. 2008. "The Strength of Issue: Using Multiple Measures to Gauge Preference Stability, Ideological Constraint, and Issue Voting." *American Political Science Review* 102: 215–32.

Arias, J. L. P., and M. Spinka. 2005. "Associations of Stockpersons' Personalities and Attitudes with Performance of Dairy Cattle Herds." *Czech Journal of Animal Science* 50: 226–34.

Arthur, W., and W. G. Graziano. 1996. "The Five-Factor Model, Conscientiousness, and Driving Accident Involvement." *Journal of Personality* 64: 593–618.

Ashton, M. C., S. V. Paunonen, E. Helmes, and D. N. Jackson. 1998. "Kin Altruism, Reciprocal Altruism, and the Big Five Personality Factors." *Evolution and Human Behavior* 19: 243–55.

Barbaranelli, C., G. V. Caprara, M. Vecchione, and C. R. Fraley. 2007. "Voters' Personality Traits in Presidential Elections." *Personality and Individual Differences* 42: 1199–208.

Barber, J. D. 1992. *The Presidential Character: Predicting Performance in the White House*, 4th ed. Englewood Cliffs, NJ: Prentice-Hall.

Barrick, M. R., and M. K. Mount. 1991. "The Big Five Personality Dimensions and Job Performance: A Meta-Analysis." *Personnel Psychology* 44: 1–26.

Bartels, L. M. 1996. "Uninformed Votes: Information Effects in Presidential Elections." *American Journal of Political Science* 40: 194–230.

Bassili, J. N. 2000. "Editor's Introduction: Reflections on Response Latency Measurement in Telephone Surveys." *Political Psychology* 21:1–6.

Basu, A. K. 1968. "Correlates of Political Conservatism." *Western Political Quarterly* 21: 725–30.

Bekkers, R. 2005. "Participation in Voluntary Associations: Relations with Resources, Personality and Political Values." *Political Psychology* 26: 439–54.

Berkowitz, L., and K. G. Lutterman. 1968. "The Traditional Socially Responsible Personality." *Public Opinion Quarterly* 32: 169–85.

Bernardin, H. J., D. K. Cooke, and P. Villanova. 2000. "Conscientiousness and Agreeableness as Predictors of Rating Leniency." *Journal of Applied Psychology* 85: 232–6.

Bilalic, M., P. McLeod, and F. Gobet. 2007. "Personality Profiles of Young Chess Players." *Personality and Individual Differences* 42: 901–10.

Bizer, G. Y., J. A. Krosnick, A. L. Holbrook, S. C. Wheeler, D. D. Rucker, and R. E. Petty. 2004. "The Impact of Personality on Cognitive Behavioral, and Affective Political Processes: The Effects of Need to Evaluate." *Journal of Personality* 72: 995–1027.

Bizer, G. Y., J. A. Krosnick, R. E. Petty, D. D. Rucker, and S. C. Wheeler. 2000. *Need for Cognition and Need to Evaluate in the 1998 National Election Survey Pilot Study*, NES Pilot Study Report, No. nes008997.

Block, J., and J. H. Block. 2006. "Nursery School Personality and Political Orientation Two Decades Later." *Journal of Research in Personality* 40: 734–49.

Bloeser, A. J., C. McCurley, and J. J. Mondak. 2009. "The Nature of Civic Duty: Political Science, Life Science, and the Determinants of Juror Compliance." Presented at the Annual Meeting of the American Political Science Association, Toronto.

Bolger, E. A., and E. A. Schilling. 1991. "Personality and the Problems of Everyday Life: The Role of Neuroticism in Exposure and Reactivity to Daily Stressors." *Journal of Personality* 59: 335–86.

# References

Booth-Kewley, S., and R. R. Vickers. 1994. "Associations between Major Domains of Personality and Health Behavior." *Journal of Personality* 62: 281–98.

Borgatta, E. F. 1964. "The Structure of Personality Characteristics." *Behavioral Science* 9: 8–17.

Borkenau, P. 1992. "Implicit Personality Theory and the Five-Factor Model." *Journal of Personality* 60: 295–327.

Borman, W. C., L. A. Penner, T. D. Allen, and S. J. Motowidlo. 2001. "Personality Predictors of Citizenship Performance." *International Journal of Selection and Assessment* 9: 52–69.

Bouchard, T. J. 1994. "Genetic and Environmental Influences on Adult Personality: Evaluating the Evidence." In J. Hettema ed., *Foundations of Personality*. Dordrecht, The Netherlands: Kluwer Academic Publishers, pp. 15–44.

Bouchard, T. J., and J. C. Loehlin. 2001. "Genes, Evolution, and Personality." *Behavior Genetics* 31: 243–73.

Bouchard, T. J., Jr., D. T. Lykken, M. McGue, N.L. Segal, and A. Tellegen. 1990. "Sources of Human Psychological Differences: The Minnesota Study of Twins Reared Apart." *Science* 250: 223–50.

Boyle, G. J. 1989. "Reexamination of the Major Personality-Type Factors in the Cattell, Comrey, and Eysenck Scales: Were the Factor Solutions by Noller et al. Optimal?" *Personality and Individual Differences* 10: 1289–99.

Brady, H. E., S. Verba, and K. L. Schlozman. 1995. "Beyond SES: A Resource Model of Political Participation." *American Political Science Review* 89; 271–94.

Brooks, D. J. 2006. "The Resilient Voter: Moving Toward Closure in the Debate over Negative Campaigning and Turnout." *Journal of Politics* 68: 684–96.

Burden, B. C. 2000. "Voter Turnout and the National Election Studies." *Political Analysis* 8: 389–98.

Burke, R. J., S. B. Matthiesen, and S. Pallesen. 2006. "Personality Correlates of Workaholism." *Personality and Individual Differences* 40: 1223–33.

Butler, J. C. 2000. "Personality and Emotional Correlates of Right-Wing Authoritarianism." *Social Behavior and Personality* 28: 1–14.

Campbell, A., P. E. Converse, W. E. Miller, and D. E. Stokes. 1960. *The American Voter*. New York: John Wiley & Sons.

Canli, T., ed. 2006. *Biology of Personality and Individual Differences*. New York: Guilford.

Caprara, G. V., C. Barbaranelli, C. Consiglio, L. Picconi, and P. G. Zimbardo. 2003. "Personalities of Politicians and Voters: Unique and Synergistic Relationships." *Journal of Personality and Social Psychology* 84: 849–56.

Caprara, G. V., C. Barbaranelli, and P. G. Zimbardo. 2002. "When Parsimony Subdues Distinctiveness: Simplified Public Perceptions of Politicians' Personality." *Political Psychology* 23: 77–95.

1999. "Personality Profiles and Political Parties." *Political Psychology* 20: 175–97.

Caprara, G. V., S. Schwartz, C. Capanna, M. Vecchione, and C. Barbaranelli. 2006. "Personality and Politics: Values, Traits and Political Choice." *Political Psychology* 27: 1–28.

Carlo, G., M. A. Okun, G. P. Knight, and M. R. T. de Guzman. 2005. "The Interplay of Traits and Motives on Volunteering: Agreeableness, Extraversion and Prosocial Value Motivation." *Personality and Individual Differences* 38: 1293–305.

# References

Carmen, I. H. 2004. *Politics in the Laboratory: The Constitution of Human Genomics*. Madison: University of Wisconsin Press.

Carney, D. R., J. T. Jost, S. D. Gosling, and J. Potter. 2008. "The Secret Lives of Liberals and Conservatives: Personality Profiles, Interaction Styles, and the Things They Leave Behind." *Political Psychology* 29: 807–40.

Caspi, A. 2000. "The Child is Father of the Man: Personality Correlates from Childhood to Adulthood." *Journal of Personality and Social Psychology* 78: 158–72.

Caspi, A., E. Chajut, K. Saporta, and R. Beyth-Marom. 2006. "The Influence of Personality on Social Participation in Learning Environment." *Learning and Individual Differences* 16: 129–44.

Cattell, R. B. 1973. "Personality Pinned Down." *Psychology Today* 7 (July) 41–42, 44–46.

——— 1956. "Validation and Interprettion of the 16 P. F. Questionnaire." *Journal of Clinical Psychology* 12: 205–14.

——— 1947. "Confirmation and Clarification of the Primary Personality Factors." *Psychometrika* 12: 197–220.

——— 1946. *Description and Measurement of Personality*, New York: World Book.

——— 1944. "Interpretation of the Twelve Primary Personality Factors." *Character and Personality* 13: 55–91.

——— 1943. "The Description of Personality: Basic Traits Resolved into Clusters." *Journal of Abnormal and Social Psychology* 38: 476–507.

——— 1933. "Temperament Tests." *British Journal of Psychology* 23: 308–29.

Cattell, R. B., H. W. Eber, and M. M. Tatsuoka. 1970. *Handbook for the Sixteen Personality Factor Questionnaire*. Champaign, IL: Institute for Personality and Ability Testing.

Charney, E. 2008a. "Genes and Ideologies." *Perspectives on Politics* 6: 299–319.

——— 2008b. "Politics, Genetics, and 'Greedy Reductionism.'" *Perspectives on Politics* 6: 337–43.

Cheung, F. M., and K. Leung. 1998. "Indigenous Personality Measures: Chinese Examples." *Journal of Cross-Cultural Psychology* 29: 233–48.

Chowdhury, M. S., and M. N. Amin. 2006. "Personality and Students' Academic Achievement: Interactive Effects of Conscientiousness and Agreeableness on Students' Performance in Principles of Economics." *Social Behavior and Personality* 34: 381–8.

Christal, R. E. 1992. "Author's Note on 'Recurrent Personality Factors Based on Trait Ratings." *Journal of Personality* 60: 221–4.

Christie, R., and M. Jahoda, eds. 1954. *Studies in the Scope and Method of "The Authoritarian Personality": Continuities in Social Research*. Glencoe, IL: Free Press.

Church, A T. 2001. "Personality Measurement in Cross-Cultural Perspective." *Journal of Personality*, 69: 979–1006.

——— 2000. "Culture and Personality: Toward an Integrated Cultural Trait Psychology." *Journal of Personality* 68: 651–703.

Clark, J., M. T. Boccaccini, B. Caillouet, and W. F. Chaplin. 2007. "Five Factor Model Personality Traits, Jury Selection, and Case Outcomes in Criminal and Civil Cases." *Criminal Justice and Behavior* 34: 641–60.

Conn, S. R., and M. L. Rieke, eds. 1994. *The 16PF Fifth Edition Technical Manual*. Champaign, IL: Institute for Personality and Ability Testing.

# References

Connolly, J. J., E. J. Kavanagh, and C. Viswesvaran. 2007. "The Convergent Validity between Self and Observer Ratings of Personality: A Meta-Analytic Review." *International Journal of Selection and Assessment* 15: 110–7.

Conte, J. M., and J. N. Gintoft. 2005. "Polychronicity, Big Five Personality Dimensions, and Sales Performance." *Human Performance* 18: 427–44.

Converse, P. 1964. "The Nature of Belief Systems in Mass Publics." In D. Apter, ed., *Ideology and Discontent*. New York: Free Press, pp. 206–61.

Costa, P. T., Jr., C. M. Busch, A. B. Zonderman, and R. R. McCrae. 1986. "Correlations of MMPI Factor Scales with Measures of the Five-Factor Model of Personality." *Journal of Personality Assessment* 50: 640–50.

Costa, P. T., Jr., J. H. Herbst, R. R. McCrae, and I. C. Siegler. 2000. "Personality at Midlife: Stability, Intrinsic Maturation, and Response to Life Events." *Assessment* 7: 365–78.

Costa, P. T., Jr., and R. R. McCrae. 2006. "Age Changes in Personality and Their Origins: Comment on Roberts, Walton, and Viechtbauer (2006)." *Psychological Bulletin* 132: 26–8.

———. 1994. "Set Like Plaster?: Evidence for the Stability of Adult Personality." In T. Heatherton and J. Weinberger, eds., *Can Personality Change?* Washington, D.C.: American Psychological Association, pp. 21–40.

———. 1992. *Revised NEO Personality Inventory (NEO-PI-R) and NEO Five-Factor Inventory (NEO-FFI) Professional Manual*. Odessa, FL: Psychological Assessment Resources.

———. 1988. "Personality in Adulthood: A Six-Year Longitudinal Study of Self-Reports and Spouse Ratings on the NEO Personality Inventory." *Journal of Personality and Social Psychology* 54: 853–63.

———. 1980. "Influence of Extraversion and Neuroticism on Subjective Well-Being: Happy and Unhappy People." *Journal of Personality and Social Psychology* 38: 668–78.

Courneya, K. S., and L. A. M. Hellsten. 1998. "Personality Correlates of Exercise Behavior, Motives, Barriers and Preferences: An Application of the Five-Factor Model." *Personality and Individual Differences* 24: 625–33.

Cox, B. J., S. C. Borger, G. J. G. Asmundson, and S. Taylor. 2000. "Dimensions of Hypochondriasis and the Five-Factor Model of Personality." *Personality and Individual Differences* 29: 99–108.

Crowson, H. M., S. J. Thoma, and N. Hestevold. 2005. "Is Political Conservatism Synonymous with Authoritarianism?" *Journal of Social Psychology* 145: 571–92.

Cullen, J. M., L. W. Wright, and M. Alessandri. 2002. "The Personality Variable Openness to Experience as it Relates to Homophobia." *Journal of Homosexuality* 42: 119–34.

Dahlen, E. R., and R. P. White. 2006. "The Big Five Factors, Sensation Seeking, and Driving in Anger in the Prediction of Unsafe Driving." *Personality and Individual Differences* 41: 903–15.

David, J. P., P. J. Green, R. Martin, and J. Suls. 1997. "Differential Roles of Neuroticism, Extraversion, and Event Desirability for Mood in Daily Life: An Integrative Model of Top-Down and Bottom-Up Influences." *Journal of Personality and Social Psychology* 73: 149–59.

De Bruijn, G. J., S. P. J. Kremers, W. van Mechelen, and J. Brug. 2005. "Is Personality Related to Fruit and Vegetable Intake and Physical Activity in Adolescents?" *Health Education Research* 20: 635–44.

De Raad, B. 2000. *The Big Five Personality Factors: The Psycholexical Approach to Personality*. Seattle: Hogrefe & Humber Publishers.

# References

Deluga, R. J. 1995. "The Relationship between Attributional Charismatic Leadership and Organizational Citizenship Behavior." *Journal of Applied Psychology* 25: 1652–69.

Denny, K., and O. Doyle. 2008. "Political Interest, Cognitive Ability and Personality: Determinants of Voter Turnout in Britain." *British Journal of Political Science* 38: 291–310.

Di Palma, G., and H. McClosky. 1970. "Personality and Conformity: The Learning of Political Attitudes." *American Political Science Review* 64: 1054–73.

Dickson, D. P., G. R. Barr, L. P. Johnson, and D. A. Wieckert. 1970. "Social Dominance and Temperament of Holstein Cows." *Journal of Dairy Science* 53: 904–7.

Digman, J. M. 1997. "Higher-Order Factors of the Big Five." *Journal of Personality and Social Psychology* 73: 1246–56.

———1996. "The Curious History of the Five-Factor Model." In J. S. Wiggins, ed., *The Five-Factor Model of Personality: Theoretical Perspectives*. New York: The Guilford Press, pp. 1–20.

———1990. "Personality Structure: Emergence of the Five-Factor Model." *Annual Review of Psychology* 41: 417–40.

———1989. "Five Robust Trait Dimensions: Development, Stability and Utility." *Journal of Personality* 57: 195–214.

Downs, A. 1957. *An Economic Theory of Democracy*. New York: Harper.

Dudley, N. M., K. A. Orvis, J. E. Lebiecki, and J. M. Cortina. 2006. "A Meta-Analytic Investigation of Conscientiousness in the Prediction of Job Performance: Examining the Intercorrelations and the Incremental Validity of Narrow Traits." *Journal of Applied Psychology* 91: 40–57.

Duriez, B., and B. Soenens. 2006. "Personality, Identity Styles and Authoritarianism: An Integrative Study among Late Adolescents." *European Journal of Personality* 20: 397–417.

Easton, D., and J. Dennis. 1967. "The Child's Acquisition of Regime Norms: Political Efficacy." *American Political Science Review* 61: 25–38.

Eaves, L. J., H. J. Eysenck, and N G. Martin. 1989. *Genes, Culture and Personality*. London: Academic Press.

Eaves, L. J., and P.K. Hatemi. 2008. "Transmission of Attitudes toward Abortion and Gay Rights: Parental Socialization or Parental Mate Selection?" *Behavior Genetics* 38: 247–56.

Elshaug, C., and J. Metzer. 2001. "Personality Attributes of Volunteers and Paid Workers Engaged in Similar Occupational Tasks." *Journal of Social Psychology* 141: 752–63.

Endler, N. S. 1989. "The Temperamental Nature of Personality." *European Journal of Personality* 3: 151–65.

Eperjesi, F. 2007. "Do Tinted Spectacle Lens Wearers Have a Different Personality?" *Ophthalmic and Physiological Optics* 27: 154–8.

Erdheim, J., M. Wang, and M. J. Zickar. 2006. "Linking the Big Five Personality Constructs to Organizational Commitment." *Personality and Individual Differences* 41: 959–70.

Etheredge, L. S. 1978. "Personality Effects on American Foreign Policy, 1898–1968: A Test of Interpersonal Generalization Theory." *American Political Science Review* 72: 434–51.

Eysenck, H. J. 1992. "Four Ways Five Factors are Not Basic." *Personality and Individual Differences* 13: 667–73.

# References

1991. "Dimensions of Personality: 15, 5, or 3? – Criteria for a Taxonomic Paradigm." *Personality and Individual Differences* 12: 773–90.

1990. "Genetic and Environmental Contributions to Individual Differences: The Three Major Dimensions of Personality." *Journal of Personality* 58: 245–61.

1971. "Relation between Intelligence and Personality." *Perceptual and Motor Skills* 32: 637–8.

1967. *The Biological Basis of Personality*. Springfield, IL: Thomas.

1954. *The Psychology of Politics*. London: Routledge.

1951. "The Organization of Personality." *Journal of Personality* 20: 101–17.

1947. *Dimensions of Personality*. London: Routledge.

Eysenck, H. J., and S. B. G. Eysenck. 1969. *Personality Structure and Measurement*. London: Routledge.

Eysenck, H. J., and G. D. Wilson, eds. 1978. *The Psychological Basis of Ideology*. Baltimore, MD: University Park Press.

Eysenck, M. W., and H. J. Eysenck. 1980. "Mischel and the Concept of Personality." *British Journal of Psychology* 71: 191–204.

Fazio, R. H. 1990. "A Practical Guide to the Use of Response Latency in Social Psychological Research." In C. Hendrick and M. S. Clark, eds., *Research Methods in Personality and Social Psychology*. Newbury Park, CA: Sage, pp. 74–97.

Feldman, S. 2003. "Enforcing Social Conformity: A Theory of Authoritarianism," *Political Psychology* 24: 41–74.

Feldman, S., and K. Stenner. 1997. "Perceived Threat and Authoritarianism." *Political Psychology* 18: 741–70.

Ferguson, E. 2004. "Personality as a Predictor of Hypochondriacal Concerns: Results from Two Longitudinal Studies." *Journal of Psychosomatic Research* 56: 307–12.

2000. "Hypochondriacal Concerns and the Five Factor Model of Personality." *Journal of Personality* 68: 705–24.

Finkel, S. E., and J. G. Geer. 1998. "A Spot Check: Casting Doubt on the Demobilizing Effect of Attack Advertising." *American Journal of Political Science* 42: 573–95.

Fiorina, M. P. 1981. *Retrospective Voting in American National Elections*. New Haven: Yale University Press.

Fiske, D. W. 1949. "Consistency of the Factorial Structures of Personality Ratings from Different Sources." *Journal of Abnormal and Social Psychology* 44: 329–44.

Floderus-Myrhed, B., N. Pedersen, and I. Rasmuson. 1980. "Assessment of Heritability for Personality, Based on a Short Form of the Eysenck Personality Inventory." *Behavior Genetics* 10: 153–62.

Flynn, F. J. 2005. "Having an Open Mind: The Impact of Openness to Experience on Interracial Attitudes and Impression Formation." *Journal of Personality and Social Psychology* 88: 816–26.

Flynn, K. E., M. A. Smith, and J. Freese. 2006. "When Do Older Adults Turn to the Internet for Health Information?: Findings from the Wisconsin Longitudinal Study." *Journal of General Internal Medicine* 21: 1295–301.

Forret, M. L., and T. W. Dougherty. 2001. "Correlates of Networking Behavior for Managerial and Professional Employees." *Group and Organization Management* 26: 283–311.

Fowler, J. H., L. A. Baker, and C. T. Dawes. 2008. "Genetic Variation in Political Participation." *American Political Science Review* 102: 233–48.

# References

Fowler, J. H., and C. T. Dawes. 2008. "Two Genes Predict Voter Turnout." *Journal of Politics* 70: 479–94.

Francis, L. J. 1997. "Personal and Social Correlates of the 'Closed Mind' among 16 Year Old Adolescents in England." *Educational Studies* 23: 429–37.

Francis, L. J., and W. K. Kay. 1995. "The Personality Characteristics of Pentecostal Ministry Candidates." *Personality and Individual Differences* 18: 581–94.

Franklin, C. E. 1984. "Issue Preferences, Socialization, and the Evolution of Party Identification." *American Journal of Political Science* 28: 459–78.

Franklin, C. E., and J. E. Jackson. 1983. "The Dynamics of Party Identification." *American Political Science Review* 77: 957–73.

Friedman, H. S., and S. Booth-Kewley. 1987. "The 'Disease-Prone Personality': A Meta-Analytic View of this Construct." *American Psychologist* 42: 539–55.

Friedman, H. S., J. S. Tucker, C. Tomlinson-Keasey, J. E. Schwartz, D. L. Wingard, and M. H. Criqui. 1993. "Does Childhood Personality Predict Longevity?" *Journal of Personality and Social Psychology* 65: 176–85.

Funder, D. C., D. C. Kolar, and M. C. Blackman. 1995. "Agreement among Judges of Personality: Interpersonal Relations, Similarity, and Acquaintanceship." *Journal of Personality and Social Psychology* 69: 656–72.

Galton, F. 1884. "Measurement of Character." *Fortnightly Review* 36: 179–85.

Geer, J. G. 2006. *In Defense of Negativity.* Chicago: University of Chicago Press.

George, A. L., and J. L. George. 1964. *Woodrow Wilson and Colonel House: A Personality Study.* New York: Dover Publications.

George, J. M., and J. Zhou. 2001. "When Openness to Experience and Conscientiousness are Related to Creative Behavior: An Interactional Approach." *Journal of Applied Psychology* 86: 513–24.

Gerber, A. S., G. A. Huber, D. Doherty, C. M. Dowling, and S. E. Ha. 2010. "Personality and Political Attitudes: Relationships across Issue Domains and Political Contexts." *American Political Science Review* 104: 111–33.

Gerber, A., G. A. Huber, C. Raso, and S. Ha. 2008. "Personality and Political Behavior." Unpublished manuscript.

Gibson, J. L. 2003. "Social Networks, Civil Society, and the Prospects for Consolidating Russia's Democratic Transition." In G. Badescu and E. M. Uslaner, eds., *Social Capital and the Transition to Democracy.* London: Routledge, pp. 61–80.

Gibson, J. L., and A. Gouws. 2003. *Overcoming Intolerance in South Africa: Experiments in Democratic Persuasion.* New York: Cambridge University Press.

Goldberg, L. R. 1995. "What the hell took so long? Donald Fiske and the Big-Five Factor Structure." In P. E. Shrout and S. T. Fiske, eds., *Personality Research, Methods, and Theory: A Festschrift Honoring Donald W. Fiske.* Hillsdale, NJ: Erlbaum, pp 29–43.

1993. "The Structure of Phenotypic Personality Traits." *American Psychologist* 48: 26–34.

1992. "The Development of Markers for the Big-Five Factor Structure." *Psychological Assessment* 4: 26–42.

1990. "An Alternative 'Description of Personality': The Big-Five Factor Structure." *Journal of Personality and Social Psychology* 59: 1216–29.

1981. "Language and Individual Differences: The Search for Universals in Personality Lexicons." In L. Wheeler, ed., *Review of Personality and Social Psychology.* Beverly Hills, CA: Sage, pp. 141–65.

# References

Goldberg, L. R., J. A. Johnson, H. W. Eber, R. Hogan, M. C. Ashton, C. R. Cloninger, and H. C. Gough. 2006. "The International Personality Item Pool and the Future of Public-Domain Personality Measures." *Journal of Research in Personality* 40: 84–96.

Goldberg, L. R., and T. K. Rosolack. 1994. "The Big Five Factor Structure as an Integrative Framework: An Empirical Comparison with Eysenck's P-E N Model." In C. F. Halverson, Jr., G. A. Kohnstamm and R. P. Martin, eds., *The Developing Structure of Temperament and Personality from Infancy to Adulthood.* New York: Erlbaum, pp. 7–35.

Goldberg, L. R., D. Sweeney, P. F. Merenda, and J. E. Hughes, Jr. 1998. "Demographic Variables and Personality: The Effects of Gender, Age, Education, and Ethnic/Racial Status on Self-Descriptions of Personality Attributes." *Personality and Individual Differences* 24: 393–403.

Gomez, R., K. Holmberg, J. Bounds, C. Fullarton, and A. Gomez. 1999. "Neuroticism and Extraversion as Predictors of Coping Styles during Early Adolescence." *Personality and Individual Differences* 27: 3–17.

Gosling, S. D. 2001. "From Mice to Men: What Can We Learn about Personality from Animal Research?" *Psychological Bulletin* 127: 45–86.

Gosling, S. D., and O. P. John. 1999. "Personality Dimensions in Nonhuman Animals: A Cross-species Review." *Current Directions in Psychological Science* 8: 69–75.

Gosling, S. D., V. S. Y. Kwan, and O. P. John. 2003. "A Dog's Got Personality: A Cross-species Comparative Approach to Evaluating Personality Judgments." *Journal of Personality and Social Psychology* 85: 1161–9.

Gosling, S. D., P. J. Rentfrow, and W. B. Swann, Jr. 2003. "A Very Brief Measure of the Big- Five Personality Domains." *Journal of Research in Personality* 37:504–28.

Graziano, W. G., L. A. Jensen-Campbell, and E. C. Hair. 1996. "Perceiving Interpersonal Conflict and Reacting to It: The Case for Agreeableness." *Journal of Personality and Social Psychology* 70: 820–35.

Graziano, W. G., and R. M. Tobin. 2002. "Agreeableness: Dimension of Personality or Social Desirability Artifact?" *Journal of Personality* 70: 695–727.

Greenstein, F. I., ed. 2003. *The George W. Bush Presidency: An Early Assessment.* Baltimore, MD: Johns Hopkins University Press.

Greenstein, F. I. 1992. "Can Personality and Politics be Studied Systematically?" *Political Psychology* 13: 105–28.

Greenstein, F. I. 1969. *Personality and Politics.* Chicago: Markham Publishing.

Guilford, J. P. 1959. *Personality.* New York: McGraw-Hill.

Haggbloom, S. J., R. Warnick, J. E. Warnick, V. K. Jones, G. L. Yarbrough, T. M. Russell, C. M. Borecky, R. McGahhey, J. L. Powell, III, J. Beavers, and E. Monte. 2002. "The 100 Most Eminent Psychologists of the 20th Century." *Review of General Psychology* 6: 139–52.

Hannagan, R. J., and P. K. Hatemi. 2008. "The Threat of Genes: A Comment on Evan Charney's 'Genes and Ideologies.'" *Perspectives on Politics* 6: 329–35.

Hatemi, P. K., K. I. Morley, S. E. Medland, A. C. Heath, and N. G. Martin. 2007. "The Genetics of Voting: An Australian Twin Study." *Behavior Genetics* 37: 435–48.

Heath, A. C., M. C. Neale, R. C. Kessler, L. J. Eaves, and K. S. Kendler. 1992. "Evidence for Genetic Influences on Personality from Self-Reports and Informant Ratings." *Journal of Personality and Social Psychology* 63: 85–96.

# References

Heinstrom, J. 2003. "Five Personality Dimensions and Their Influence on Information Behaviour." *Information Research* 9: paper 165 [available at http://informationR.net/ir/9-1/paper165.html].

Heise, D. R. 1970. "The Semantic Differential and Attitude Research." In G. F. Summers, ed., *Attitude Measurement.* Chicago: Rand McNally.

Hendry, D. J., R. A. Jackson, and J. J. Mondak. 2009. "Abramoff, Email, and the Mistreated Mistress: Scandal and Character in the 2006 Elections." In J. J. Mondak and D. Mitchell, eds., *Fault Lines: Why the Republicans Lost Congress.* New York: Routledge, pp 84–110.

Hibbing, J. R., and E. Theiss-Morse. 2002. *Stealth Democracy: Americans' Beliefs about How Government Should Work.* New York: Cambridge University Press.

——— 1995. *Congress as Public Enemy: Public Attitudes toward American Political Institutions.* New York: Cambridge University Press.

Hibbing, J. R., E. Theiss-Morse, and E. Whitaker. 2009. "Americans' Perceptions of the Nature of Governing." In J. J. Mondak and D. Mitchell, eds., *Fault Lines: Why the Republicans Lost Congress.* New York: Routledge, pp. 148–65.

Hibbing, M. V., A. J. Bloeser, D. Canache, J. J. Mondak, and M. A. Seligson. 2009. "The Impact of Personality on Response Patterns on Public Opinion Surveys: The Big Five and Extreme Response Style." Presented at the International Society of Political Psychology 32nd Annual Scientific Meeting, Dublin.

Hofstede, G. 2001. *Cultures Consequences: Comparing Values, Behaviors, Institutions and Organizations across Nations,* 2nd ed. Thousand Oaks, CA: Sage.

Hofstede G., and R. R. McCrae. 2004. "Personality and Culture Revisited: Linking Traits and Dimensions of Culture." *Cross-Cultural Research* 38: 52–88.

Hofstee, W. K. B. 1990. "The Use of Everyday Personality Language for Scientific Purposes." *European Journal of Personality* 4: 77–88.

Hogan, J. 1989. "Personality Correlates of Physical Fitness." *Journal of Personality and Social Psychology* 56: 284–88.

Hogan, J. C., R. Hogan and S. Gregory. 1992. "Validation of a Sales Representative Selection Inventory." *Journal of Business and Psychology* 7: 161–71.

Hopwood, C. J., L. C. Morey, A. E. Skodol, R. L. Stout, S. Yen, E. B. Ansell, C. M Grilo, and T. H. McGlashan. 2007. "Five-Factor Model Personality Traits Associated with Alcohol-Related Diagnoses in a Clinical Sample." *Journal of Studies on Alcohol* 68: 455–60.

Horn, J., C. E. Nelson, and M. T. Brannick. 2004. "Integrity, Conscientiousness and Honesty." *Psychological Reports* 95: 27–38.

Howarth, E. 1976. "Were Cattell's 'Personality Sphere' Factors Correctly Identified in the First Instance?" *British Journal of Psychology* 67: 213–30.

Huang, T. J., S. C. Chi, and J. J. Lawler. 2005. "The Relationship between Expatriates' Personality Traits and their Adjustment to International Assignments." *International Journal of Human Resource Management* 16: 1656–70.

Huckfeldt, R., E. G. Carmines, J. J. Mondak, and E. Zeemering. 2007. "Information, Activation and Electoral Competition in the 2002 Congressional Elections." *Journal of Politics* 69: 798–812.

Huckfeldt, R., P. E. Johnson, and J. Sprague. 2004. *Political Disagreement: The Survival of Diverse Opinions within Communication Networks.* New York: Cambridge University Press.

Huckfeldt, R., J. Levine, W. Morgan, and J. Sprague. 1999. "Accessibility and the Political Utility of Partisan and Ideological Orientations." *American Journal of Political Science* 43: 888–911.

# References

Huckfeldt, R. R., J. J. Mondak, M. Craw, and J. Morehouse Mendez. 2005. "Making Sense of Candidates: Partisanship, Ideology, and Issues as Guides to Judgment." *Cognitive Brain Research* 23: 11–23.

Huckfeldt, R., and J. Sprague. 1992. "Political Parties and Electoral Mobilization: Political Structure, Social Structure, and the Party Canvass." *American Political Science Review* 86: 70–86.

Iglic, H. 2003. "Trust Networks and Democratic Transition: Yugoslavia in the Mid-1980s." In G. Badescu and E. M. Uslaner, eds., *Social Capital and the Transition to Democracy*. London: Routledge, pp. 10–27.

Inglehart, R. 1989. *Culture Shift in Advanced Industrial Society*. Princeton, NJ: Princeton University Press.

1988. "The Renaissance of Political Culture." *American Political Science Review* 82: 1203–30.

Inglehart, R., and H. Klingemann. 2003. "Genes, Culture, Democracy, and Happiness." In E. Diener and E. M. Suh, eds., *Culture and Subjective Well-Being*. Cambridge, MA: MIT Press, pp. 165–83.

Institute for Personality and Ability Testing, Inc. 2007. Corporate Website. http://www.ipat.com/.

Jackson, R. A. 2002. "Gubernatorial and Senatorial Campaign Mobilization of Voters." *Political Research Quarterly* 55: 825–44.

Jang, K. L., R. R. McCrae, A. Angleitner, R. Riemann, and W. J. Livesley. 1998. "Heritability of Facet-Level Traits in a Cross-Cultural Twin Sample: Support for a Hierarchical Model of Personality." *Journal of Personality and Social Psychology* 74: 1556–65.

Jensen-Campbell, L. A., R. Adams, D. G. Perry, K. A. Workman, J. Q. Furdella, and S. K. Egan. 2002. "Agreeableness, Extraversion, and Peer Relations in Early Adolescence: Winning Friends and Deflecting Aggression." *Journal of Research in Personality* 36: 224–51.

Jensen-Campbell, L. A., J. M. Knack, A. M. Waldrip, and S. D. Campbell. 2007. "Do Big Five Personality Traits Associated with Self-Control influence the Regulation of Anger and Aggression?" *Journal of Research in Personality* 41: 403–24.

Jensen-Campbell, L. A., and K. T. Malcolm. 2007. "The Importance of Conscientiousness in Adolescent Interpersonal Relationships." *Personality and Social Psychology Bulletin* 33: 368–83.

John, O. P., A. Angleitner, and F. Ostendorf. 1988. "The Lexical Approach to Personality: A Historical Review of Trait Taxonomic Research." *European Journal of Personality* 2: 171–203.

John, O. P., L. P. Naumann and C. J. Soto. 2008. "Paradigm Shift to the Integrative Big Five Trait Taxonomy: History, Measurement, and Conceptual Issues." In O. P. John, R. W. Robins and L. A. Pervin, eds. *Handbook of Personality: Theory and Research*. New York: Guilford, pp. 114–58.

John, O. P., and R. W. Robins. 1993. "Gordon Allport: Father and Critic of the Five-Factor Model." In K. H. Craik, R. Hogan and R. N. Wolfe, eds. *Fifty Years of Personality Psychology*. New York: Plenum, pp. 215–36.

John, O. P., and S. Srivastava. 1999. "The Big Five Trait Taxonomy: History, Measurement, and Theoretical Perspectives." In L. A. Pervin and O. P. John, eds. *Handbook of Personality: Theory and Research*, 2nd ed. New York: Guilford Press.

Jost, J. T., C. M. Federico, and J. L. Napier. 2009. "Political Ideology: Its Structure, Functions, and Elective Affinities." *Annual Review of Psychology* 60: 307–37.

# References

Jost, J. T., J. Glaser, A. W. Kruglanski, and F. J. Sulloway. 2003. "Political Conservatism as Motivated Social Cognition." *Psychological Bulletin* 129: 339–75.

Jost, J. T., and O. Hunyady. 2005. "Antecedents and Consequences of System-Justifying Ideologies." *Current Directions in Psychological Sciences* 14: 260–6.

Jost, J. T., B. A. Nosek, and S. D. Gosling. 2008. "Ideology: Its Resurgence in Social, Personality, and Political Psychology." *Perspectives on Psychological Science* 3: 126–36.

Judd, C. M., R. A. Drake, J. W. Downing, and J. A. Krosnick. 1991. "Some Dynamic Properties of Attitude Structures: Context-induced Response Facilitation and Polarization." *Journal of Personality and Social Psychology* 60: 193–202.

Jung, C. G. 1923. *Psychological Types, or The Psychology of Individuation.* New York: Harcourt Brace.

   1917. *On The Psychology of the Unconscious.* Princeton, NJ: Standard Edition.

Kahn, K. F., and P. J. Kenney. 1999. "Do Negative Campaigns Mobilize or Suppress Turnout? Clarifying the Relationship between Negativity and Participation." *American Political Science Review* 93: 877–89.

Kam, C. D. 2005. "Who Toes the Party Line? Cues, Values, and Individual Differences." *Political Behavior* 27: 163–82.

Katigbak, M. S., A. T. Church, and T. X. Akamine. 1996. "Cross-Cultural Generalizability of Personality Dimensions: Relating Indigenous and Imported Dimensions in Two Cultures." *Journal of Personality and Social Psychology* 70: 99–114.

King, G., J. Honaker, A. Joseph, and K. Scheve. 2001. "Analyzing Incomplete Political Science Data: An Alternative Algorithm for Multiple Imputation." *American Political Science Review* 95: 49–69.

Kowert, P. A., and M. G. Hermann. 1997. "Who Takes Risks? Daring and Caution in Foreign Policy Making." *Journal of Conflict Resolution* 41: 611–37.

Kraaykamp, G., and K. van Eijck. 2005. "Personality, Media Preferences, and Cultural Participation." *Personality and Individual Differences* 38: 1675–88.

Kreitler, S., and H. Kreitler. 1990. *The Cognitive Foundations of Personality Traits.* New York: Plenum Press.

Krosnick, J. 1989. "Attitude Importance and Attitude Accessibility." *Personality and Social Psychology Bulletin* 15: 297–308.

Krueger, R. F., and W. Johnson. 2008. "Behavioral Genetics and Personality: A New Look at the Integration of Nature and Nurture." In O. P. John, R. W. Robins, and L. A. Pervin, eds. *Handbook of Personality: Theory and Research.* New York: Guilford, pp. 287–310.

Lasswell, H. D. 1954. "The Selective Effect of Personality on Political Participation." In R. Christie and M. Jahoda, eds., *Studies in the Scope and Method of 'The Authoritarian Personality.'* Glencoe, IL: The Free Press, pp. 197–225.

   1930. *Psychopathology and Politics.* Chicago: University of Chicago Press.

Lau, R. R., L. Sigelman, C. Heldman, and P. Babbitt. 1999. "The Effects of Negative Political Advertisements: A Meta-Analytic Assessment." *American Political Science Review* 93: 851–75.

Laursen, B., L. Pulkkinen, and R. Adams. 2002. "The Antecedents and Correlates of Agreeableness in Adulthood." *Developmental Psychology* 38: 591–603.

# References

Lavine, H., M. Lodge, and K. Freitas. 2005. "Threat, Authoritarianism, and Selective Exposure to Information." *Political Psychology* 26: 219–44.

Lewis, C. J., D. Mitchell, and C. Rugeley. 2005. "Courting Public Opinion: Utilizing Jury Pools in Experimental Research." Poster presented at the 2005 Political Methodology Summer Conference, Tallahassee.

Loehlin, J. C. 1992. *Genes and Environment in Personality Development.* Newbury Park, CA: Sage.

Loehlin, J. C., and R. C. Nichols. 1976. *Heredity, Environment and Personality: A Study of 850 Sets of Twins.* Austin: University of Texas Press.

Loehlin, J. C., L. Willerman, and J. M. Horn. 1985. "Personality Resemblances in Adoptive Families: A 10-Year Follow-Up." *Journal of Personality and Social Psychology* 53: 961–9.

Lounsbury, J. W., J. M. Loveland, and L. W. Gibson. 2003. "An Investigation of Psychological Sense of Community in Relation to Big Five Personality Traits." *Journal of Community Psychology* 31: 531–41.

Mak, A., and C. Tran. 2001. "Big Five Personality and Cultural Relocation Factors in Vietnamese Australian Students' Intercultural Social Self-Efficacy." *International Journal of Intercultural Relations* 25: 181–201.

Malouff, J. M., E. B. Thorsteinsson, and N. S. Schutte. 2006. "The Five-Factor Model of Personality and Smoking: A Meta-Analysis." *Journal of Drug Education* 36: 47–58.

Marcus, B., and A. Schutz. 2005. "Who Are the People Reluctant to Participate in Research? Personality Correlates of Four Different Types of Nonresponse as Inferred from Self- and Observer Ratings." *Journal of Personality* 73: 959–84.

Marcus, G. E. 2000. "Emotions in Politics." *Annual Review of Political Science* 3: 221–50.

Marcus, G. E., J. L. Sullivan, E. Theiss-Morse, and S. L. Wood. 1995. *With Malice Toward Some: How People Make Civil Liberties Judgments.* New York: Cambridge University Press.

Markey, C. N., P. M. Markey, A. J. Ericksen, and B. J. Tinsley. 2006. "Children's Behavioral Patterns, the Five-Factor Model of Personality, and Risk Behaviors." *Personality and Individual Differences* 41: 1503–13.

Markus, H., and S. Kitayama. 1998. "The Cultural Psychology of Personality." *Journal of Cross-Cultural Psychology* 29: 63–87.

Martin, J. L. 2001. "*The Authoritarian Personality,* 50 Years Later What Questions are there for Political Psychology?" Political Psychology 22: 1–26.

Martin, P., G. da Rosa, and I. C. Siegler. 2006. "Personality and Longevity: Findings from the Georgia Centenarian Study." *Age* 28: 343–52.

Masui, Y., Y. Gondo, H. Inagaki, and N. Hirose. 2006. "Do Personality Characteristics Predict Longevity?: Findings from the Tokyo Centenarian Study." *Age* 28: 353–61.

Matthews, G., and I. J. Deary. 1998. *Personality Traits.* New York: Cambridge University Press.

Matthews, G., and K. Oddy. 1993. "Recovery of Major Personality Dimensions from Trait Adjective Data." *Personality and Individual Differences* 15: 419–31.

McAdams, Dan P. 1992. "The Five-Factor Model in Personality: A Critical Appraisal." *Journal of Personality* 60: 329–61.

McClosky, H. 1964. "Consensus and Ideology in American Politics." *American Political Science Review* 58: 361–82.

1958. "Conservatism and Personality." *American Political Science Review* 52: 27–45.

McClosky, H., and A. Brill. 1983. *Dimensions of Tolerance.* New York: Russell Sage Foundation.

McClurg, S. D. 2006. "The Electoral Relevance of Political Talk: Examining the Effect of Disagreement and Expertise in Social Networks on Political Participation." *American Journal of Political Science* 50: 737–54.

McCrae, R. R. 1996. "Social Consequences of Experiential Openness." *Psychological Bulletin* 120: 323–37.

1990. "Traits and Trait Names: How Well is Openness Represented in Natural Languages?" *European Journal of Personality* 4: 119–29.

McCrae, R. R., and P. T. Costa, Jr. 2008. "The Five-Factor Theory of Personality." In O. P. John, R. W. Robins and L. A. Pervin, eds. *Handbook of Personality: Theory and Research.* New York: Guilford, pp. 155–81.

2006. "Cross-Cultural Perspectives on Adult Personality Trait Development." In D. Mroczek and T. Little, eds., *Handbook of Personality Development.* Hillsdale, NJ: Lawrence Erlbaum Associates, pp. 129–45.

2003. *Personality in Adulthood: A Five-Factor Theory Perspective,* 2nd ed. New York: The Guilford Press.

1997. "Personality Trait Structure as a Human Universal." *American Psychologist* 52: 509–16.

1996. "Toward a New Generation of Personality Theories: Theoretical Contexts for the Five-Factor Model." In J. S. Wiggins, ed., *The Five-Factor Model of Personality: Theoretical Perspectives.* New York: The Guilford Press, pp. 51–87.

1989a. "Different Points of View: Self-Reports and Ratings in the Assessment of Personality." In J. P. Forgas and M. J. Innes, eds., *Recent Advances in Social Psychology: An International Perspective.* Amsterdam: Elsevier, pp. 429–39.

1989b. "Reinterpreting the Myers-Briggs Type Indicator from the Perspective of the Five-Factor Model of Personality." *Journal of Personality* 57: 17–40.

1987. "Validation of the Five-Factor Model of Personality across Instruments and Observers." *Journal of Personality and Social Psychology* 52: 81–90.

McCrae, R. R., P. T. Costa, Jr., T. A. Martin, V. E. Oryol, I. G. Senin, and C. O'Cleirigh. 2007. "Personality Correlates of HIV Stigmatization in Russia and the United States." *Journal of Research in Personality* 41: 190–6.

McCrae, R. R., K. L. Jang, W. J. Livesley, R. Riemann, and A. Angleitner. 2001. "Sources of Structure: Genetic, Environmental, and Artifactual Influences on the Covariation of Personality Traits." *Journal of Personality* 69: 511–35.

McCrae, R. R., and O. P. John. 1992. "An Introduction to the Five-Factor Model and Its Applications." *Journal of Personality* 60: 175–215.

McCrae, R. R., M. S. M. Yik, P. D. Trapnell, M. H. Bond, and D. L. Paulhus. 1998. "Interpreting Personality Profiles across Cultures: Bilingual, Acculturation, and Peer Rating Studies of Chinese Undergraduates." *Journal of Personality and Social Psychology* 74: 1041–58.

McCulloch, P., A. Kaul, G. F. Wagstaff, and J. Wheatcroft. 2005. "Tolerance of Uncertainty, Extroversion, Neuroticism and Attitudes to Randomized Controlled Trials among Surgeons and Physicians." *British Journal of Surgery* 92: 1293–7.

McCurley, C., and J. J. Mondak. 1995. "Inspected by #1184063113: The Influence of Incumbents' Competence and Integrity in U.S. House Elections." *American Journal of Political Science* 39: 864–85.

# References

McDonald, M. P. 2003. "On the Over-Report Bias of the National Election Study." *Political Analysis* 11: 180–6.

McNiel, J. M., and W. Fleeson. 2006. "The Causal Effects of Extraversion on Positive Affect and Neuroticism on Negative Affect: Manipulating State Extraversion and State Neuroticism in an Experimental Approach." *Journal of Research in Personality* 40: 529–50.

Medland, S. E., and P. K. Hatemi. 2009. "Political Science, Biometric Theory, and Twin Studies: A Methodological Introduction." *Political Analysis* 17: 191–214.

Milbrath, L. W. 1962. "Latent Origins of Liberalism-Conservatism and Party Identification: A Research Note." *Journal of Politics* 24: 679–88.

Mischel, W. 1979. "On the Interface of Cognition and Personality: Beyond the Person-Situation Debate." *American Psychologist* 34: 740–54.

 1968. *Personality and Assessment*. New York: Wiley.

Mischel, W., and Y. Shoda. 1995. "A Cognitive-Affective System Theory of Personality: Reconceptualizing Situations, Dispositions, Dynamics, and Invariance in Personality Structure." *Psychological Review* 102: 246–68.

Mitchell, D., and J. J. Mondak. 2009. "The Context for Defeat." In J. J. Mondak and D. Mitchell, eds., *Fault Lines: Why the Republicans Lost Congress*. New York: Routledge, pp. 1–21.

Mondak, J. J. 1995a. "Competence, Integrity, and the Electoral Success of Congressional Incumbents." *Journal of Politics* 57: 1043–69.

 1995b. "Media Exposure and Political Discussion in U.S. Elections." *Journal of Politics* 57: 62–85.

 1995c. *Nothing to Read: Newspapers and Elections in a Social Experiment*. Ann Arbor: University of Michigan Press.

Mondak, J. J., D. Canache, M. A. Seligson, and M. V. Hibbing. Forthcoming. "The Participatory Personality: Evidence from Latin America." *British Journal of Political Science*.

Mondak, J. J., and A. F. Gearing. 2003. "Civic Engagement in a Post-Communist State." In G. Badescu and E. M. Uslaner, eds., *Social Capital and the Transition to Democracy*. London: Routledge, pp. 140–64.

Mondak J. J., and K. D. Halperin. 2008. "A Framework for the Study of Personality and Political Behavior." *British Journal of Political Science* 38: 335–62.

Mondak, J. J., M. V. Hibbing, D. Canache, M. A. Seligson, and M. R. Anderson. 2010. "Personality and Civic Engagement: An Integrative Framework for the Study of Trait Effects on Political Behavior." *American Political Science Review* 104: 85–110.

Mondak, and R. Huckfeldt. 2006. "The Accessibility and Utility of Candidate Character in Electoral Decision Making." *Electoral Studies* 25: 20–34.

Mondak, J. J., and D. Mitchell, eds. 2009. *Fault Lines: Why the Republicans Lost Congress*. New York: Routledge.

Moskowitz, D. S., and J. C. Schwarz. 1982. "Validity Comparison of Behavior Counts and Ratings by Knowledgeable Informants." *Journal of Personality and Social Psychology* 42: 518–28.

Moss, S. A., J. McFarland, S. Ngu, and A. Kijowska. 2007. "Maintaining an Open Mind to Closed Individuals: The Effect of Resource Availability and Leadership Style on the Association between Openness to Experience and Organizational Commitment." *Journal of Research in Personality* 41: 259–75.

Moutafi, J., A. Furnham, and J. Crump. 2006. "What Facets of Openness and Conscientiousness Predict Fluid Intelligence Score?" *Learning and Individual Differences* 16: 31–42.

# References

Mueller, G., and E. Plug. 2006. "Estimating the Effect of Personality on Male and Female Earnings." *Industrial and Labor Relations Review* 60: 3–22.

Mulligan, K., J. T. Grant, S. T. Mockabee, and J. Q. Monson. 2003. "Response Latency Methodology for Survey Research: Measurement and Modeling Strategies." *Political Analysis* 11: 289–301.

Mussen, P. H., and A. B. Wyszynski. 1952. "Personality and Political Participation." *Human Relations* 5: 65–82.

Mutz, D. C. 2006. *Hearing the Other Side: Deliberative versus Participatory Democracy.* New York: Cambridge University Press.

Mutz, D. C., and J. J. Mondak. 2006. "The Workplace as a Context for Cross-Cutting Political Discourse." *Journal of Politics* 68: 140–55.

Mutz, D. C., and B. Reeves. 2005. "The New Videomalaise: Effects of Televised Incivility on Political Trust." *American Political Science Review* 99: 1–15.

Nail, P. R., K. E. Bedell, and C. D. Little. 2003. "Should President Clinton be Prosecuted for Perjury?: The Effects of Preference for Consistency, Self-Esteem, and Political Party Affiliation." *Personality and Individual Differences* 35: 1821–31.

Nicholson, N. 2005. "Personality and Domain-Specific Risk Taking." *Journal of Risk Research* 8: 157–76.

Niemi, R. G., S. C. Craig, and F. Mattei. 1991. "Measuring Internal Political Efficacy in the 1988 National Election Study." *American Political Science Review* 85: 1407–13.

Noller, P., H. G. Law, and A. L. Comrey. 1987. "Cattell, Comrey and Eysenck Personality Factors Compared: More Evidence for Five Robust Factors." *Journal of Personality and Social Psychology* 53: 775–82.

Norman, W. T. 1963. "Toward an Adequate Taxonomy of Personality Attributes: Replicated Factor Structure in Peer Nomination Personality Ratings." *Journal of Abnormal and Social Psychology* 66: 574–83.

O'Leary, K. D., and D. A. Smith. 1991. "Marital Interactions." *Annual Review of Psychology* 42: 191–212.

Ones, D. S., C. Viswesvaran, and F. L. Schmidt. 1993. "Comprehensive Meta-Analysis of Integrity Test Validities: Findings and Implications for Personnel Selection and Theories of Job Performance." *Journal of Applied Psychology* 78: 679–703.

Organ, D. W. 1994. "Organizational Citizenship Behavior and the Good Soldier." In M.G. Rumsey, C. B. Walker and J. H. Harris, eds., *Personnel Selection and Classification.* Hillsdale, NJ: Lawrence Erlbaum Associates, pp. 53–67.

Organ, D. W., and J. B. McFall. 2004. "Personality and Citizenship Behavior in Organizations." In D. Schneider and D. B. Smith, eds. *Personality and Organizations.* Hillsdale, NJ: Lawrence Erlbaum Associates, pp. 291–314.

Ormel, J., and T. Wohlfarth. 1991. "How Neuroticism, Long-Term Difficulties, and Life Situation Change Influence Psychological Distress: A Longitudinal Model." *Journal of Personality and Social Psychology* 60: 744–55.

Osgood, C. E., P. H. Tannenbaum, and G. J. Suci. 1957 *The Measurement of Meaning.* Urbana, IL: University of Illinois Press.

Oxley, D. R., K. B. Smith, J. R. Alford, M. V. Hibbing, J. L Miller, M. Scalora, P. K. Hatemi, and J. R. Hibbing. 2008. "Political Attitudes Vary with Physiological Traits." *Science* 321: 1167–70.

Ozer, D. J., and S. P. Reise. 1994. "Personality Assessment." *Annual Review of Psychology* 45: 357–88.

Park, H., and D. Antonioni. 2007. "Personality, Reciprocity, and Strength of Conflict Resolution Strategy." *Journal of Research in Personality* 41: 110–25.

# References

Parkes, K. R., and T. D. B. Razavi. 2004. "Personality and Attitudinal Variables as Predictors of Voluntary Union Membership." *Personality and Individual Differences* 37: 333–47.

Pasek, J., L. Feldman, D. Romer, and K. H. Jamieson. 2008. "Schools as Incubators of Democratic Participation: Building Long-Term Political Efficacy with Civic Education." *Applied Developmental science* 12: 26–37.

Paulhus, D. L., M. N. Bruce, and P. D Trapnell. 1995. "Effects of Self-Presentation Strategies on Personality Profiles and their Structure." *Personality and Social Psychology Bulletin* 21: 100–8.

Peabody, D., and L. R. Goldberg. 1989. "Some Determinants of Factor Structures from Personality-Trait Descriptors." *Journal of Personality and Social Psychology* 57: 552–67.

Pedersen, N. L., R. Plomin, G. E. McClearn, and L. Friberg. 1988. "Neuroticism, Extraversion, and Related Traits in Adult Twins Reared Apart and Reared Together." *Journal of Personality and Social Psychology* 55: 950–7.

Pervin, L. A. 2003. *The Science of Personality*, 2nd ed. New York: Oxford University Press.

Phillips, Julie. 2006. *James Tiptree, Jr.: The Double Life of Alice B. Sheldon*. New York: St. Martin's Press.

Plomin, R., and D. Daniels. 1987. "Why are Children in the Same Family So Different from One Another?" *Behavioral and Brain Sciences* 10:1–16.

Post, J. M. 1991. "Saddam Hussein of Iraq: A Political Personality Profile." *Political Psychology* 12: 279–89.

Pulford, B. D., and H. Sohal. 2006. "The Influence of Personality on HE Students' Confidence in Their Academic Abilities." *Personality and Individual Differences* 41: 1409–19.

Rammstedt, B., and O. P. John. 2007. "Measuring Personality in One Minute or Less: A 10-Item Short Version of the Big Five Inventory in English and German." *Journal of Research in Personality* 41: 203–12.

Renshon, S. A., ed. 1995. *The Clinton Presidency: Campaigning, Governing and the Psychology of Leadership*. Boulder, CO: Westview.

Rhodes, R. E., and N. E. I. Smith. 2006. "Personality Correlates of Physical Activity: A Review and Meta-Analysis." *British Journal of Sports Medicine* 40: 958–65.

Riemann, R., A. Angleitner, and J. Strelau. 1997. "Genetic and Environmental Influences on Personality: A Study of Twins Reared Together Using the Self- and Peer Report NEO- FFI Scales." *Journal of Personality* 65: 449–75.

Riemann, R., C. Grubich, S. Hempel, S. Mergl, and M. Richter. 1993. "Personality and Attitudes towards Current Political Topics." *Personality and Individual Differences* 15: 313–21.

Robbers, M. 2006. "Tough-Mindedness and Fair Play: Personality Traits as Predictors of Attitudes toward the Death Penalty." *Punishment and Society* 8: 203–22.

Roberts, B. W., O. S. Chernyshenko, S. Stark, and L. R. Goldberg. 2005. "The Structure of Conscientiousness: An Empirical Investigation Based on Seven Major Personality Questionnaires." *Personnel Psychology* 58: 103–39.

Roberts, B. W., K. E. Walton, and W. Viechtbauer. 2006a. "Patterns of Mean-Level Change in Personality Traits across the Life Course: A Meta-Analysis of Longitudinal Studies." *Psychological Bulletin* 132: 1–25.

2006b. "Personality Traits Change in Adulthood: Reply to Costa and McCrae (2006)." *Psychological Bulletin* 132: 29–32.

Robinson, M. D., and M. Tamir. 2005. "Neuroticism as Mental Noise: A Relation between Neuroticism and Reaction Time Standard Deviations." *Personality and Individual Differences* 89: 107–14.

Rokeach, M. 1960. *The Open and Closed Mind: Investigations into the Nature of Belief Systems and Personality Systems*. New York: Basic Books.

Rose, R. J., M. Koshenvuo, J. Kaprio, S. Sarna, and H. Langinvainio. 1988. "Shared Genes, Shared Experiences, and Similarity of Personality." *Journal of Personality and Social Psychology* 54: 161–71.

Rubenzer, S. J., T. R. Faschingbauer, and D. S. Ones. 2000. "Assessing the U.S. Presidents Using the Revised NEO Personality Inventory." *Assessment* 7: 403–20.

Rudolph, Thomas J., and Elizabeth Popp. 2007. "An Information Processing Theory of Ambivalence." *Political Psychology* 28:563–85

Rushton, J. P., D. W. Fulker, M. C. Neale, D. K. B. Nias, and H. J. Eysenck. 1986. "Altruism and Aggression: The Heritability of Individual Differences." *Journal of Personality and Social Psychology* 50: 1192–98.

Satterfield, J. M. 1998. "Cognitive-Affective States Predict Military and Political Aggression and Risk Taking: A Content Analysis of Churchill, Hitler, Roosevelt, and Stalin." *Journal of Conflict Resolution* 42: 667–90.

Saucier, G. 1992. "Openness Versus Intellect – Much Ado about Nothing." *European Journal of Personality* 6: 381–6.

Saucier, G., and L. R. Goldberg. 2001. "Lexical Studies of Indigenous Personality Factors: Premises, Products, and Prospects." *Journal of Personality* 69: 847–79.

1998. "What is Beyond the Big Five?" *Journal of Personality* 66: 495–524.

1996. "The Language of Personality: Lexical Perspectives on the Five-Factor Model." In J. S. Wiggins, ed., *The Five-Factor Model of Personality: Theoretical Perspectives*. New York: The Guilford Press.

Scarr, S., P. L. Webber, R. L. Weinberg, and M. A. Wittig. 1981. "Personality Resemblances among Adolescents and their Parents in Biologically Related and Adoptive Families." *Journal of Personality and Social Psychology* 40: 885–98.

Schmitt, D. P., J. Allik, R. R. McCrae, and V. Benet-Martinez. 2007. "The Geographic Distribution of Big Five Personality Traits: Patterns and Profiles of Human Self- Description across 56 Nations." *Journal of Cross-Cultural Psychology* 38: 173–212.

Schoen, H. 2007. "Personality Traits and Foreign Policy Attitudes in German Public Opinion." *Journal of Conflict Resolution* 51: 408–30.

Schoen, H., and S. Schumann. 2007. "Personality Traits, Partisan Attitudes, and Voting Behavior: Evidence from Germany." *Political Psychology* 28: 471–98.

Schroeder, M. L., J. A. Wormworth, and W. J. Livesley. 1992. "Dimensions of Personality Disorder and Their Relationships to the Big Five Dimensions of Personality." *Psychological Assessment* 4: 47–53.

Schwartz, M. D., K. L. Taylor, K. S. Willard, J. E. Siegel, R. M. Lamdan, and K. Moran. 1999. "Distress, Personality, and Mammography Utilization among Women with a Family History of Breast Cancer." *Health Psychology* 18: 327–32.

Seligson, M. A. 2002. "A Renaissance of Political Culture or a Renaissance of the Ecological Fallacy?" *Comparative Politics* 34: 273–92.

Shweder, R. A. 1975. "How Relevant is an Individual Difference Theory of Personality?" *Journal of Personality* 43: 455–84.

Sibley, C. G., and J. Duckitt. 2008. "Personality and Prejudice: A Meta-Analysis and Theoretical Review." *Personality and Social Psychology Review* 12: 248–79.

# References

Silver, B. D., B. A. Anderson, and P. R. Abramson. 1986. "Who Overreports Voting?" *American Political Science Review* 80: 613–24.

Silvestri, T. J., and T. Q. Richardson. 2001. "White Racial Identity Statuses and NEO Personality Constructs: An Exploratory Analysis." *Journal of Counseling and Development* 79: 68–76.

Simonton, D. 1988. "Presidential Style: Personality, Biography, and Performance." *Journal of Personality and Social Psychology* 55: 928–36.

———. 1986. "Presidential Personality: Biographical Use of the Gough Adjective Check List." *Journal of Personality and Social Psychology* 51: 149–60.

Smith, G. M. 1967. "Usefulness of Peer Ratings of Personality in Educational Research." *Educational and Psychological Measurement* 27: 967–84.

Sniderman, P. M. 1975. *Personality and Democratic Politics.* Berkeley: University of California Press.

St. Angelo, D., and J. W. Dyson. 1968. "Personality and Political Orientation." *Midwest Journal of Political Science* 12: 202–23.

Stenner, K. 2005. *The Authoritarian Dynamic.* New York: Cambridge University Press.

Stouffer, S. A. 1992 [1955]. *Communism, Conformity, and Civil Liberties.* New Brunswick, N. J.: Transaction Publishers.

Stough, C., C. Donaldson, B. Scarlata, and J. Ciorciari. 2001. "Psychophysiological Correlates of the NEO PI-R Openness, Agreeableness and Conscientiousness: Preliminary Results." *International Journal of Psychophysiology* 41: 87–91.

Strauss, J. P., M. L. Connerley, and P. A. Ammermann. 2003. "The 'Threat Hypothesis,' Personality, and Attitudes toward Diversity." *Journal of Applied Behavioral Science* 39: 32–52.

Sullivan, J. L., J. Piereson, and G. E. Marcus. 1982. *Political Tolerance and American Democracy.* Chicago: University of Chicago Press.

Suls, J., R. Martin, and J. P. David. 1998. "Person-Environment and Its Limits: Agreeableness, Neuroticism, and Emotional Reactivity to Interpersonal Conflict." *Personality and Social Psychology Bulletin* 24: 88–98.

Tellegen, A. 1991. "Personality Traits: Issues of Definition, Evidence, and Assessment." In W. M. Grove and D. Cicchetti, eds., *Thinking Clearly about Psychology: Essays in Honor of Paul Everett Meehl, Vol. 2.* Minneapolis: University of Minnesota Press, pp. 10–35.

Tellegen, A., D. T. Lykken, T. J. Bouchard, K. J. Wilcox, N. L. Segal, and S. Rich. 1988. "Personality and Similarity in Twins Reared Apart and Together." *Journal of Personality and Social Psychology* 54: 1031–9.

Tett, R. P., D. N. Jackson, and M. Rothstein. 1991. "Personality Measures as Predictors of Job Performance: A Meta-Analytic Review." *Personnel Psychology* 44: 703–42.

Thoemmes, F. J., and L. C. Conway. 2007. "Integrative Complexity of 41 U.S. Presidents." *Political Psychology* 28: 193–226.

Thoms, P., K. S. Moore, and K. S. Scott. 1996. "The Relationship between Self-Efficacy for Participating in Self-Managed Work Groups and the Big Five Personality Dimensions." *Journal of Organizational Behavior* 17: 349–62.

Thorndike, E. L. 1903. *Educational Psychology.* New York: Lemcke & Brechner.

Thurstone, L. L. 1953. *Thurstone Temperament schedule.* Chicago: Science Research Associates.

———. 1934. "The Vectors of Mind." *Psychological Review* 41: 1–32.

# References

Timmerman, T. A. "Predicting Turnover with Broad and Narrow Personality Traits." 2006. *International Journal of Selection and Assessment* 14: 392–9.

Tucker, J. S., N. R. Kressin, A. Spiro, III, and J. Ruscio. 1998. "Intrapersonal Characteristics and the Timing of Divorce: A Prospective Investigation." *Journal of Social and Personal Relationships* 15: 211–25.

Tupes, E. C. 1957. *Relationships between Behavior Trait Ratings by Peers and Later Officer Performance of USAF Officer Candidate School Graduates.* USAF PTRC Technical Note No. 57–125. Lackland Air Force Base. TX: U.S. Air Force.

Tupes, E. C., and R. E. Christal. 1992. "Recurrent Personality Factors Based on Trait ratings." *Journal of Personality* 60: 225–51.

    1961. *Recurrent Personality Factors Based on Trait Ratings* USAF ASD Technical Report No. 61–97. Lackland Air Force Base. TX: U.S. Air Force.

    1958. *Stability of Personality Trait Rating Factors Obtained under Diverse Conditions.* USAF WADC Technical Note No. 58–61. Lackland Air Force Base, TX: U.S. Air Force.

Turkheimer, E., and M. Waldron. 2000. "Nonshared Environment: A Theoretical, Methodological, and Quantitative Review." *Psychological Bulletin* 126: 78–108.

Tyson, N. D. 2009. *The Pluto Files: The Rise and Fall of America's Favorite Planet.* New York: W. W. Norton.

Van Hiel, A., M. Kossowska, and I. Mervielde. 2000. "The Relationship between Openness to Experience and Political Ideology." *Personality and Individual Differences* 28: 741–51.

Van Kenhove, P., I. Vermeir, and S. Verniers. 2001. "An Empirical Investigation of the Relationships Between Ethical Beliefs, Ethical Ideology, Political Preference and Need for Closure." *Journal of Business Ethics* 32: 347–61.

Vecchione, M., and G. V. Caprara. 2009. "Personality Determinants of Political Participation: The Contribution of Traits and Self-Efficacy Beliefs." *Personality and Individual Differences* 46: 487–92.

Verba, S., K. L. Schlozman, and H. E. Brady. 1995. *Voice and Equality: Civic Voluntarism in American Politics.* Cambridge: Harvard University Press.

Wagerman, S. A., and D. C. Funder. 2007. "Acquaintance Reports of Personality and Academic Achievement: A Case for Conscientiousness." *Journal of Research in Personality* 41: 221–9.

Walsh, K. C. 2004. *Talking about Politics: Informal Groups and Social Identity in American Life.* Chicago: University of Chicago Pres.

Watson, D. 1989. "Strangers' Rating of the Five Robust Personality Factors: Evidence of a Surprising Convergence with Self-Reports." *Journal of Personality and Social Psychology* 52: 120–8.

Watson, D., B. Hubbard, and D. Wiese. 2000. "Self-Other Agreement in Personality and Affectivity: The Role of Acquaintanceship, Trait Visibility, and Assumed Similarity." *Journal of Personality and Social Psychology* 78: 546–58.

Wattenberg, M. P., and C. L. Brians. 1999. "Negative Campaign Advertising: Demobilizer or Mobilizer?" *American Political Science Review* 93: 891–99.

Weisberg, H. F. 2005. "The Structure and Effects of Moral Predispositions in Contemporary American Politics." *Journal of Politics* 67: 646–68.

White, J. K., S. S. Hendrick, and C. Hendrick. 2004. "Big Five Personality Variables and Relationship Constructs." *Personality and Individual Differences* 37: 1519–30.

# References

Wiggins, J. S., and A. L. Pincus. 1989. "Conceptions of Personality Disorders and Dimensions of Personality." *Psychological Assessment* 1: 305–16.

Winter, D. G. 2006. "Authoritarianism – With or Without Threat?" *International Studies Review* 8: 524–7.

2003a. "Assessing Leaders' Personalities: A Historical Survey of Academic Research Studies." In J. M. Post, ed., *The Psychological Assessment of Political Leaders*. Ann Arbor: University of Michigan Press, pp. 11–38.

2003b. "Personality and Political Behavior." In D. O Sears, L. Huddy and R. Jervis, eds., *Oxford Handbook of Political Psychology*. New York: Oxford University Press, pp. 110–45.

Wolfinger, R. E., and S. J. Rosenstone. 1980 *Who Votes?* New Haven, CT: Yale University Press.

Woods, S. A., and S. E. Hampson. 2005. "Measuring the Big Five with Single Items Using a Bipolar Response Scale." *European Journal of Personality* 19: 373–90.

Woodworth, R. S. 1919. "Examination of Emotional Fitness for Warfare." *Psychological Bulletin* 16: 59–60.

Wright, C. I., D. Williams, E. Feczko, L. F. Barrett, B. C. Dickerson, C. E. Schwartz, and M. M. Wedig. 2006. "Neuroanatomical Correlates of Extraversion and Neuroticism." *Cerebral Cortex* 16: 1809–19.

Xu, S. 2006. "Population Genetics: Separating Nurture from Nature in Estimating Heritability." *Heredity* 97: 256–7.

Yamagata, S., A. Suzuki, J. Ando, Y. Ono, N. Kijima, K. Yoshimura, F. Ostendorf, A. Angleitner, R. Riemann, F. M. Spinath, W. J. Livesley, and K. L. Jang. 2006. "Is the Genetic Structure of Human Personality Universal?: A Cross-Cultural Twin Study from North America, Europe, and Asia." *Journal of Personality and Social Psychology* 90: 987–98.

Yang, K., and M. H. Bond. 1990. "Exploring Implicit Personality Theories with Indigenous or Important Constructs: The Chinese Case." *Journal of Personality and Social Psychology* 58: 1087–95.

# Index

52831650R00148

Made in the USA
Lexington, KY
13 June 2016